The Sick Rose

SATŌ HARUO

The Sick Rose

A Pastoral Elegy

TRANSLATED BY FRANCIS B. TENNY

University of Hawaii Press
HONOLULU

98 97 96 95 94 93 5 4 3 2 1

Library of Congress Cataloging-in-Publication Data
Satō, Haruo. 1892–1964.
 [Selections. English. 1993]
 The sick rose : a pastoral elegy / Satō Haruo ;
translated by Francis B. Tenny.
  p. cm.
 Translation of: Den'en no yūutsu ; Okinu to sono
kyōdai ; Tokai no yūutsu.
 Contents: The sick rose, a pastoral elegy, or,
Gloom in the country—Okinu and her brother—
Gloom in the city.
 ISBN 0–8248–1534–3 (alk. paper).—
ISBN 0–8248–1539–4 (alk. paper : pbk.)
 1. Satō, Haruo, 1892–1964—Translations into
English. I. Tenny, Francis B. 1920– . II. Title.
PL838.A86A28   1993
895.63'44—dc20   93–27266
                                    CIP

The costs of publishing this book have been defrayed
in part by the 1992 Hiromi Arisawa Memorial Award
from the Books on Japan Fund with respect to *Tales of
Tears and Laughter* and *The Aesthetics of Discontent*
published by the University of Hawaii Press. The Award
is financed by The Japan Foundation from generous dona-
tions contributed by Japanese individuals and companies.

University of Hawaii Press books are printed on acid-free
paper and meet the guidelines for permanence and
durability of the Council on Library Resources

Designed by Kenneth Miyamoto

THE SICK ROSE

O Rose, thou art sick!
  The invisible worm,
That flies in the night
  In the howling storm,

Has found out thy bed
  Of crimson joy,
And his dark secret love
  Does thy life destroy.

Contents

Preface

Retiring from a career in the American foreign service has brought me leisure to browse in Japanese literature of the 1920s. For me, the 1920s were years of a happy childhood in Japan, and, for Japan between the wars and before the big depression, they were a time of relative freedom and experimentation, a period often called Taishō Democracy. I came thus across the magical, sweetly forlorn fairyland of Satō Haruo—novelist, poet, and critic, who lived from 1892 to 1964. No translation can match the original work of art, but I have tried to give an English approximation of some of Satō's early writings—his best.

These are period pieces. Beyond the attempt to be faithful to the meaning and style of Satō's prose, I have sought to find English equivalents natural to the readers of literate English of the 1920s. This has guided me in the choice of English words and idioms and in the romanization of Chinese names and places and some Japanese words and names. Japanese names, however, are given in the normal Japanese order with the surname first. I have kept the use of Japanese words to a minimum except for a few household words, like shoji and tatami, that are well known internationally and for which no English equivalents convey the picture of the Japanese originals. In particular I have hoped to retain Satō's sequence of thought and discovery. Japanese syntax is antithetical to English in many ways, but, where I felt I could do so in good English, I have stayed with Satō. I translate for readers of English, but the fact should not be obscured that these stories are of Japan and of the Japanese.

Readers who enjoy these selections are referred to two more of Satō's best stories, which appeared in excellent English translations thirty years ago. These are *The House of a Spanish Dog*, translated by George Saitō and included in *Modern Japanese Stories*, edited by Ivan Morris (Tuttle, 1962); and *The Tale of the Bridal Fan*, translated by Edward Seidensticker (*Japan Quarterly* 9, no. 3 [1962]).

Many people, both in person and in memory, have made these translations possible, and I thank them all. Errors, misinterpretations, and infelicities in the translations are entirely the responsibility of this translator. My appreciation is deep for all the following:

Tom Rimer for his continuing encouragement and advice and for the introduction on Satō's place in literature—I am no scholar, and Tom has filled that dimension.

Howard Hibbett, Edwin McClellan, Marius Jansen, and Taka Hauge for reading some of these selections and offering advice and encouragement to continue.

The University of Hawaii Press—especially Sharon F. Yamamoto, my editor, and the anonymous readers for the press, whose corrections and suggestions have been invaluable.

My daughter Carol Tenny, a linguist who has published her own translations of Yosano Akiko and other Japanese poets, for assistance in translating the Japanese poetry that Satō quotes in his texts.

All my family—those who soaked in Japan in their childhood: my mother, Betty Pettee Tenny, born in Okayama in 1881; my sister, Ruth Hana Tenny Hall; and my children, Carol, Charles, and Laura; and those who came as adults to the paradoxical charm of Japan: my father, Charles Buckley Tenny, first president of Kantō Gakuin University; and my wife, Robin, whose everlasting patience and mastery of the word processor have been indispensable.

Countless Japanese friends and teachers, despite whose best help my comprehension is still a foreigner's.

Satō Haruo himself, whom I do not recall ever meeting, but whose work this is—his work speaks for itself.

Introduction: SATŌ HARUO

J. THOMAS RIMER

I

On the face of it, there seems to be little reason why literary and historical or political events need be tied together; nevertheless, it is clear that there did indeed exist a Taishō mentality, a shift in attitudes that seemed to move the artistic insights of Japanese writers away from those strenuous concerns of the preceding Meiji period (1868–1911), when the country first faced the need to rejoin the larger world, from which it had been cut off for well over two hundred years. Culturally speaking, the Meiji period had been one involving absorption from Western culture; in Taishō (1912–1926), a new and sophisticated modern sensibility began to assert itself. Foreign ideas and inspirations were increasingly domesticated, and a new and authentically contemporary Japanese sense of self began to emerge. Perhaps the first work to herald this shift was a remarkable collection of modernist verse published in 1917 by the gifted poet Hagiwara Sakutarō (1888–1942), titled *Howling at the Moon* [Tsuki ni hoeru]; yet for many readers, Satō Haruo's *Gloom in the Country* [Den'en no yūutsu], written a year later, in 1918, when the author was twenty-seven, marked the shift most strongly. For that reason, *Gloom in the Country* has remained an icon of the period.

The kind of introspective fantasy revealed in the story drew on the author's literary skills already honed both by a deep interest in classical Japanese and Chinese literature and by a strong interest in the great works of modern Western literature. During the Meiji period, the greatest of Satō's predecessors had attempted to introduce new models derived from Western literature in order to expand the aesthetic canons in late nineteenth-century Japan. Nagai Kafū, for example, who lived in America and France from 1903 to 1907, taught French literature at Keio University for several years after his return and made every attempt, through his elegant translations, to introduce Baudelaire, Verlaine, and other French poets to his contemporaries. Mori Ōgai, who lived in Germany from 1884 to 1888, spent much of his career translating such important European writers as Goethe, Ibsen, and Strindberg. Natsume Sōseki's sojourn in England from 1900 to 1903 turned him from a haiku poet into a novelist and helped him, through his exposure to Meredith and other nineteenth-century British novelists, to create his own model for a style of modern fiction suitable for the literary expression of his own moral convictions.

The next generation, Satō's own, could now begin to assume a knowledge of and sympathy for such Western texts as part of their own literary background and, increasingly, as part of their reader's as well. The style of much of the verse included in Hagiwara's collection *Howling at the Moon* might have been impossible to compose without the example of Baudelaire; yet the poetry stems altogether from the author's own special vision. Satō's lucid yet mysterious inner world glows with a special light refracted from poems of Blake and Goethe with which the author finds a special closeness. Reading the text of *Gloom in the Country* seventy-odd years after its composition, the effect on the reader seems virtually seamless; the author inhabits the whole world of literature, East and West alike, and finds himself drawn, first in one direction and then in another, more by his modern sensibility than through his cultural status as a Japanese. This is not to suggest that Satō's writings have lost the pith of his specific culture—far from it. Rather, this cosmopolitan stance reveals the author's skill at taking advantage of any literary congruence. Nothing seems beyond the reach of his intellectual or literary sympathies. In this regard, if in no other, the critics are justified in speaking of a new Taishō mentality.

Gloom in the Country made Satō's reputation as a writer of prose (he was already highly appreciated as a poet) and came to form the core of a series of works that wove together a number of themes common to all. Some of the events portrayed in these short novels are closely related to Satō's own activities during the period. Indeed he and his first wife, a hopeful young actress, did go to live in the country from May to December in 1916 and then returned to Tokyo, where the young writer found himself increasingly estranged in his marital situation. Nevertheless, the artistic connections, rather than any autobiographical similarities, are what give these works their power.

Elements helping to create the mood of an extended fantasy of the sort visible in *Gloom in the Country* were first adumbrated in Satō's 1914 short story, *The House of a Spanish Dog* [Supein inu no ie], in which the narrator wanders into a Maeterlinck-like woods with his dog Fratty (a constant companion in all these works and an altogether more jolly animal than Hagiwara's poor howling canine in his lonely poem), where he finds a mysterious, deserted Western-style house, a poetic glimpse of a European-inspired haven that would continue to haunt him. *Gloom in the Country*, written four years later, replaces the European cottage with a Japanese traditional house, but Satō's new and increasingly relentless articulation of the interior life continued. In a brilliant turnabout, Satō composed in the same year, 1918, an objective yet highly evocative story about the life of the maid who figures briefly in *Gloom in the Country*; the actual facts of her remarkable life, as recorded in *Okinu and Her Brother* [Okinu to sono kyōdai] are cunningly arranged to suggest a pathos worthy of one of the British novels of society, as well as in the sort of social cruelty found in Trollope's *The Way We Live Now* or in certain pages of Dickens. Finally, in 1922, Satō composed a new variation on the theme, *Gloom in the City* [Tokai no yūutsu], in which the same lyric, melancholy sensibility now plays over the relative poverty and downtrodden mentality that seemed to characterize Satō's vision of modern urban life. Each can be read as independent works of art; read in sequence, as is now possible thanks to Frank Tenny's persuasive translations, the shifts in lyric intensity and mordant irony that made Satō famous are here apparent to English readers for the first time.

Satō had a long career. Born in 1892 in a physician's family in Wakayama, south of Osaka (and in the same prefecture as the distinguished postwar novelist Ariyoshi Sawako), Satō became a student at Keio University in Tokyo and studied French literature under Nagai Kafū himself. His works—poetry, prose, essays, and autobiographical memoirs—fill twelve-odd volumes. His career was a long one, and he himself sustained many vicissitudes, including a burst of wartime patriotism that was later to cause him, by all accounts, both political trouble and, perhaps, a certain spiritual grief before his death in 1964. There are works from every period of his life that are of great potential interest, and it is to be hoped that a similar collection of writings from the later periods of his career can at some point be put beside this one. Nevertheless, the three stories presented here belong together; these are the works that gave Satō his first wide fame in Japan, and they represent a privileged place to begin to seek out the secrets of his art.

II

What was the quality that seemed so fresh to Japanese readers who encountered these works for the first time? Part of the appeal, surely, lay in the worldly sophistication of the narrator. Yet above and beyond this attraction lay Satō's ability, apparent I believe, even in translation, to move with a sinuous linguistic grace, rising to create clusters of powerful insight that probe into the interior world of his narrator. A writer like Natsume Sōseki (whom Satō much admired) had certainly served as a precursor in this desire to make manifest in language the inner movement of the psyche of his characters. Sōseki, however, did not manage to do so directly; in the two of his late works perhaps closest to Satō in aspiration, *The Wayfarer* [Kōjin] (1913) and *Kokoro* (1914), the reader is shown the interior mental state of their respective central characters through the device of letters; in *The Wayfarer,* a friend describes the mental state of Sōseki's protagonist Ichirō; in *Kokoro*, the narrator describes his own feelings in epistolary form. In Satō's work, this formality (by no means a defect in Sōseki's work, to be sure) disappears altogether; the reader is much closer to the ebb and flow of the narrator's own rapidly shifting moods, timidities, passions, hopes, and regrets. *Gloom in the Country* is closer to poetry than to ordinary prose; if *Okinu* describes the outward events, *Gloom in the Country* becomes them on a psychological, even spiritual level. In that regard, a comparison between the two works is revelatory of Satō's great gifts as a writer. He could do with his material what he wished.

The narrative technique employed in *Gloom in the Country* is in no way a naive one. Satō is a master craftsman: a counterpoint of emotionally fraught moments, juxtaposed with poetic symbolism worthy of Bashō and other haiku masters, pushes the narrative along. Indeed, Satō announces his methods early in the text: ". . . This village with its graceful line of hills, its sky, its expanse of mixed forest, its wet and dry fields, its skylarks, was a veritable prose poem in miniature" (16). The narrator learns much during his country sojourn by his observations of nature. Yet, as a modern man, he is estranged from his surroundings and so must often be led to nature through art. Satō's love of French poetry, doubtless encouraged by his contact with his teacher Nagai Kafū and his close friend Horiguchi Daigaku (1892–1981), famous for his translations from the French, as well as Satō's love of Western painting, helps him compose his descriptions of scenery with vivid colors and arresting psychological freight. The narrator's dependence on art as a means to permit the perception of the natural world is described in a striking passage in *Gloom in the Country*:

> A commitment to prevailing artistic tradition was deeply embedded in his personality. In this spirit he had chosen to work in the arts. His artistic disposition, born of this cause, had been awakened early. . . . These things had brought him unconsciously to love the rose so much. Before he knew how to pluck spiritual beauty and joy directly from nature, he came through the artistic conventions of the past to offer his deep love only to this flower. It may have been absurd, but he felt a love even for the word *rose*. (33)

Here, the recourse to language and to literature functions on the level of a specific image. Equally striking, perhaps particularly so to a Western reader, is Satō's skillful use of the long tradition of the diary of withdrawal so familiar from classical Japanese literature. The author pays homage both in *Gloom in the Country* and in *Gloom in the City* to the great traditions of such medieval classics as *An Account of My Hut* [Hōjōki] by Kamo no Chōmei (1153–1216) and *Essays in Idleness* [Tsurezuregusa] by Yoshida Kenkō (1283–1350). In both these classical texts, so influential in the development of Japanese literature, the protagonist-narrator has retired from the world and so observes society, and himself, with a detachment linked on occasion to a kind of lyric melancholy. That melancholy, it might be argued, was closely tied to a sense of Buddhist pessimism over the state of the mundane world; Satō's texts, although partaking of these antecedents, seem to recast certain attributes of that melancholy in terms of modern alienation, both intellectual and personal. In country and city alike, the narrator finds himself alone. "It's not that I don't have affectionate feelings. I'm just ashamed to reveal them. It's the nature I was born with," he blurts out to his wife. (*Country*, 20). This particular kind of rueful self-knowledge marks these works as modern ones.

In the medieval works mentioned above, Chōmei and Kenkō withdrew from the world, on the witness of their writings at least, for what were for them rational reasons concerning the state of society and their place in it. The narrator that inhabits *Gloom in the Country* and *Gloom in the City*, however, places the blame for his withdrawal directly on himself; perhaps the times are out of joint, but, by the same token, he is certainly out of joint with them.

Living in the country, the narrator sums up his situation as follows:

> The only way to live anew in this old, old world was for him to change his state of mind completely. When he could understand that, how could he make his kind of self into something fresh? What did *courage* and *drive* mean in that angry letter his father had sent him? Where could he get them and how could he cultivate them? How could he instill them in his heart? He could never know all that. In the country,

in the city, nowhere was there a paradise that could give him peace on earth. There was nothing. (*Country*, 38)

Later, in the city, faced not with his father but with strangers, the narrator's insights become sharper still.

"If I had been doing the hiring," he thought, "I wouldn't have taken on a man who looked like the me of ten minutes earlier. Two years ago I would have been able to face another person more boldly. Why am I so stupid now? To be smart and to be bold. I don't know whether that's good or bad, but it's essential in order to live in this society. I've lost that powerful weapon." (*City*, 216)

The sense of malaise is palpable, the dislocation with society virtually complete. Such are the links made with contemporary society, with the objectivity of everyday life. They serve as anchors crucial to linking these texts to mundane reality, but such hooks are few and far between. The thrust of both these works is resolutely toward the interior.

III

The nature of Satō's work, when juxtaposed against the work of other writers of his period who are better known in the West through translation, may help to indicate something of his own particular accomplishments and explain some of the reasons for his continuing reputation in Japan. In this regard, however, the early prose works contained in this collection cannot explain the full range of his appeal.

If one examines the decade of the 1920s, for example, a certain congruence of themes and interests with other important writers is apparent. The celebrated novelist Shiga Naoya (1883–1971), many of whose most adroitly composed short lyrical pieces appeared during this period, also found as a central theme the relation between man and nature, notably in his short piece "At Kinosaki" [Kinosaki nite], written in 1917. It was during these years also that Shiga did much of the work on his long novel, *A Dark Night's Passing* [An'ya kōro], which was completed by 1928; the final chapters, in which the protagonist has a mystic vision of nature, took him virtually another decade to write, so that the completed book, usually considered his masterpiece, did not appear until 1937. In some ways, the character and mode of expression of the narrator of *Gloom in the Country* and *Gloom in the City* might be compared to Shiga's protagonist Kensaku in *A Dark Night's Passing;* both seek some balance between the urgent, turbulent demands of their own egos and the example of a calm and transcendent nature that alone can perhaps heal the petty torments of modern man. In this regard, Satō's narrator remains at an early stage of his spiritual enlightenment; in neither of these two short novels does he gain more than a glimpse of a solution to his sense of the weariness of life. Shiga's character, created in final form a decade later, manages to struggle through his veil of ego to achieve harmony, although perhaps at the cost of his life. The comparisons between the first two-thirds of Shiga's novel with these early works of Satō are striking, for they reveal not so much a relation of mutual influence as details of a psychic map of the intellectual and spiritual world of this period, when Japanese intellectuals, now increasingly freed from the moral constraints of the Tokugawa past (a struggle won for them during the Meiji period by such writers as Ōgai and Sōseki), found themselves as awash as any European in what they perceived to constitute the relativity, and the nihilism, of modern life.

A second writer with whom Satō can and should be compared is Tanizaki Junichirō (1886–1965); indeed, Tanizaki, who was older by six years and quickly established as a writer of importance, was one of the first to discover and promote Satō's talents. Tanizaki encouraged his younger colleague and remained fascinated by his literary skill and his elegance of mind. Doubtless they came to know each other too well, for in one of the most celebrated literary scandals of the period, Satō, now divorced himself, was to marry Tanizaki's ex-wife in 1930 after her own divorce. Both men, perhaps not surprisingly, described the emotional complexities of the incident in their own fiction.

Whatever the quality of admiration the two felt for each other's writing, however, the two possessed talents of differing sorts. A comparison between Tanizaki's 1925 novel *Naomi* [Chijin no ai] and Satō's 1922 *Gloom in the City* reveals these differences at once. Both chronicle the amatory confusions of their protagonists who inhabit in modest circumstances the vast, changing city of Tokyo. Tanizaki makes use of the new culture, imported from the West, of the café and dance hall for purposes of mordant satire. Satō, although every bit as gifted in picturing the contemporary scene— the world of the shoddy Asakusa theater, for example, or the gloomy modern hospital—remains, despite the newly clipped quality of his prose, a writer close to, and sympathetic with, the lyrical interior passions of his narrator. Satō can display a talent for irony, but he refuses, unlike Tanizaki, to make light of his protagonist's ailing spiritual condition.

Going beyond the period of the 1920s into the following decades (and so beyond the scope of the author's work as represented by these present translations), Satō's work can be seen to have a congruence as well with that of another writer, Akutagawa Ryūnosuke (1892-1927). Akutagawa, now famous around the world as the author of *Rashōmon*, from which Kurosawa made his famous film, took up the challenge set by Mori Ōgai and continued to write stories based on historical themes. Both Satō and Akutagawa revered this Meiji master, and both found a rich lode of material in historical events in the Japanese and Chinese past, which both writers, each in their own way, attempted to repossess in contemporary terms. Akutagawa's many historical stories often show a mordant reflexivity; they represent the striking accomplishment of a modern intellectual. Satō, true to form, however, continued to reveal his love of poetry and his bent for composing lyrical prose. His interest in classical Chinese verse and in Japanese classical literature allowed him to produce in the 1930s and after a number of striking works that dealt with such diverse historical figures as the great Tokugawa writer of ghost stories Ueda Akinari (1734-1809), the medieval Buddhist recluse mentioned above, Kamo no Chōmei, the Buddhist priest Hōnen Shōnin (1133-1212), the Christian daimyō Arima Harunobu (1567-1612), and the southeast Asian adventurer Yamada Nagamasa (?-1633). Some of these works maintain their reputations even today, but they remain, so far as I know, altogether unexplored by Western scholars and translators. To grasp the thrust and significance of Satō's full career, one must examine these recreations of the past in terms that Satō felt might be meaningful to the present. Like his admired Mori Ōgai, Satō continued to feel an urgent need to take a hold of the past before it slipped away altogether. These enthusiasms, too, might help to explain, although not to explain away, Satō's infatuation with Japan's military adventures during the China war and afterward. His own path through history, as it turned out, was to be a complicated one.

IV

In attempting to locate among Satō's many literary essays some central statement of his predilections and his artistic imperatives, there is perhaps no better example to put forward than his 1924 essay *Fūryū* (an elusive term used in classical Japanese literature sometimes translated "elegance"). This essay has long been considered a central text in modern Japanese writings in aesthetics. The translations cited below are taken from Mr. Tenny's English version of this striking work.[1]

The author's concerns expressed in this essay both reflect back on the earlier works contained in this volume and forward to the historical works and poetry that would increasingly interest Satō in his later years. The essay, certainly as read now in the 1990s, seems driven by an intent to explore the means by which the modern Japanese can repossess their own classical culture and so maintain a sense of wholeness and balance. It should be said at the beginning that Satō was by no means alone in his quest to tie the two together. One thinks in particular of the eminent philosopher and essayist Watsuji Tetsurō (1889–1960), who himself helped articulate the new mentality of the Taishō period and began his career writing on such Western figures as Nietzsche and Kierkegaard; yet when he made a first trip to Kyoto and Nara in 1917, he suddenly came to realize that the hidden past of Japan was every bit as important for him to discover as was the high culture of the West. Finding a sense of the whole became for many writers and intellectuals at this time a crucial project.

Satō's essay itself is fairly lengthy and reveals, to a Western reader at least, a certain meandering quality, as one idea or feeling suggests another, in precisely the elegant fashion that Satō's text sets out to characterize and define. Although a few citations taken at random inevitably misrepresent the suggestiveness and complexity of the work as a whole, they can, I think, help clarify something of the nature of Satō's own aesthetic vision, one that has already been at work in the composition of the three works included in the present volume.

The beginning of any true understanding, for Satō, comes with the realization of the true relation between man and nature.

> Whether we think of humanity as a people or as an individual, humans became aware of the existence of self at an age when one can think about such things, perhaps in one's youth. . . . A person . . . will stare in wonder at the contrast between nature and mankind. That very wonderment will change into a feeling for the total contrast between the eternity and infinity of nature and the momentary and minuscule status of man. After sensing the infinitely vast, a person will see the thing nearby as infinitely small. . . . You may say this is the beginning of wisdom. You may say it is the awakening of the soul.

For Satō, it is precisely at this point in the trajectory of a human life that man's authentic understanding of himself becomes possible.

> I have no doubt . . . about the depths of our human wonder at discovering the contrast between nature and mankind. It may seem too fanciful, but to say that all human civilization stems from this fact is no mistake. All man's religion, his philosophy, his art derive directly from wonder at the contrast between man and nature. The bitter reality of the contrast between the infinity of nature and the minuteness of man is the stimulus for mankind.

Satō also sees in this realization a temporal dimension; for him, the poets of the classic Heian period anthology of court poetry, the

Kokinshū, which set so much of the tonality for the whole range of classical Japanese literature, created their art based on the fact that "once they noticed the eternity of nature and the momentary nature of themselves, they must have looked at themselves with undreamed of terror . . . in their fleeting but deeply rooted grief they first discovered a new world of poetry".

This aesthetic conviction lay at the bottom of Japan's elegant poetic tradition.

> The more our people's artistic style progressed, the simpler it became —isn't that strange? When we consider it minutely, though, that strange phenomenon strikes us as entirely appropriate. Literature close to silence, art close to nothingness make for a stark secrecy, based on a "sense of impermanence," or human activity at its irreducible minimum. There is nothing mysterious about it when we understand it as the sensibility of an instant existing on the border between being and nonbeing.

Satō, then, attempted to define this elegance that seems to provide such an important element in the makeup of the Japanese literary mentality.

> What do I consider true elegance? I can assert it now without the least hesitation. In the spirit of elegance, human will is at the lowest level possible, its irreducible minimum. In the language sense, it is the ancient rather than the present, the poet or poetry rather than the novelist or the novel, solitude rather than company, telepathic understanding rather than eloquent discussion. . . . If you were to show to some artists of elegance a modern novel with all its meaning constructed from the complications in the entanglement of human wills, and you explained that this was a great work of art, they might fall over in an instant swoon. Balzac and Bashō are at the two poles of literature.

Satō's own efforts, perhaps intuitive when he wrote *Gloom in the Country*, then with an ever-increasing self-awareness in the decade that followed, were by no means antiquarian. Like his mentor Ōgai, he wanted to use the past as a means to evaluate the real significance of the present. His essay on elegance betrays no sense of loss; indeed he shows the same sense of excitement at his understanding of the buried principles of classical literature that Watsuji showed struggling through the muddy mountains to reach the remote temple of Jōruriji in the mountains north of Nara. A new sense of the whole seemed for both the prize to be sought.

Satō's quest for aesthetic and spiritual balance, and a wholeness of spirit between past and present, can help contemporary readers, I believe, grasp more clearly the artistic statements represented by the three works that make up this present collection of translations. The narrator's gloom, in both the country and the city, may seem familiar enough; yet in the end it is not altogether of a modern, alienated kind. Indeed, certain aspects of that gloom represent a literary construct that harks back to those great classical works of the past mentioned earlier. After all, Satō was perfectly capable, as *Okinu* shows, of writing a thoroughly artistically objective account of the lives of the characters he portrays. This is a gloom with its own elegance. This melancholy possesses a spiritual dimension, one that reveals a state of being that, despite the fact that certain of its particulars are endemic to modern times, nevertheless reveals roots in long centuries of human understanding particular to the Japanese literary tradition. Thus, for all the Taishō modernism that the texts may reveal, there is about them a suggestiveness, a classical restraint, that provides them with strong ties to the past. Satō's ability to reauthenticate these classical models through the witness of his own personal experience make these early stories effective experiments in cultural amalgamation. It is no wonder that they have continued to fascinate and delight Japanese readers ever since. I hope that the human insights reflected in them can interest those outside Japan as well, for, even if unfamiliar with the traditions on which the author draws in order to create his own elegant variations, readers will find the human states described are familiar —all too familiar. The literary terms of reference provided in the most natural way by Satō, as a modern, cosmopolitan Japanese writer, may be Goethe or William Blake. The image of the soul in disarray portrayed, however, is one that reflects, even if mutedly, modes of understanding developed through long centuries in which the pain of self-understanding was recorded by the great

Buddhist writers on Japan's classical past. It is the measure of Satō's sophistication that the synthesis seems inevitable.

Note

1. Translation as yet unpublished. Original Japanese text can be found in *Satō Haruo Shū*, Vol. 30 of *Gendai Nihon Bungaku Zenshū* (Chikuma Shobō, 1954), pp. 410, 412, 413, 414.

The Sick Rose

A Pastoral Elegy,
or Gloom in the Country
(DEN'EN NO YŪUTSU, 1918)

I dwelt alone
In a world of moan
And my soul was a stagnant tide.
Edgar Allan Poe

*T*HAT house—it floated now before his eyes.

At first the two dogs, raising clouds of dust in their high spirits, had romped about him, now behind and now ahead, until at last, settling into line, they trotted slowly behind their master. The road made a sharp turn under a grove of tall trees.

"Well, here we are," she said.

She was their guide, a fat redheaded woman who pointed ahead with one hand while using the other to wipe the dripping sweat from her sunburned brow with a dirty towel. There, following her pointing finger, as thick as a man's, their eyes fell on a small thatch roof that, although buried in the dark green, glimmered gray and sedately through the summer morning's shimmering, dazzling light.

That was the first time he had seen the house. He and his wife had cast their roving eyes on that roof of thatch and then looked at each other and exchanged words . . .

"My hunch is that's a good house."

"I think so, too."

They walked along looking at the thatch roof. If this was the house, hadn't he seen it somehow once before, he thought, perhaps sometime long ago, or in a dream, or a vision, or even from the window of the speeding train? The view focused on that grass roof was surely a common country silhouette you could see anywhere. Still, it captivated him even now. His present longings stemmed from that moment. For no other reason he chose this place for his dwelling.

Here were hills where the broad Musashino plain changes, runs out at its southern limit and poises to enter mountain country—hills you could say were both an epilogue bearing the dim suggestion left by the mountains and a prologue billowing to the wide and nearby plains. Here, threading through this landscape of trivial rolling hills as far as the eye can see, ran two roads, one level running east to west, the second cutting north to south, roads strung with a cluster of humble thatch-roof homes making a remote country village. A mere fifteen or sixteen miles to the big cities of T, Y, and H, as if in a vacuum created on the margins of three violent whirlwinds, the village lay dejected, left behind by the century, forgotten by the world, washed away from civilization.[1]

The first time he found himself on this road, happy beyond limits and refreshed as never before, was on a late spring day of that same year. He was startled to find here such a remote countryside. Rarely had he encountered a tranquil scene like this. Compared to the dramatic landscapes of his ancestral home on the tip of a far southern peninsula, where a rushing torrent hurtled and jostled toward the stormy sea, buoying and bouncing the little rafts that passed his village, a village where people, pinned between the raging sea and the rugged mountains, eked out with their wits a bare existence—compared to that, this village with its graceful line of hills, its sky, its expanse of mixed forest, its wet and dry fields, its skylarks, was a veritable prose poem in miniature. If nature in that earlier scene recalled his rigid father, in the latter it recalled his loving mother. In the midst of the suffocating city, he who likened himself to the prodigal son had long clung to the hope of melting into the embrace of a nature that was gentle and yielding and for that very reason commonplace. Yes, a classic well-being and joy surely awaited all who came here. "Vanity of vanities. Vanity. All is vanity." But even if that were not true . . . No, his desire was beyond reasoning. In the city he was stifled; he felt crushed by the weight of humanity. He was a machine too acutely sensitive to be held captive there—far too sensitive indeed. What's more, the boisterous mood of spring that surrounded him there had made him feel all the more isolated. "Oh yes," he would tell himself, "on an evening like this how I would like to settle under the dim, red lamplight of a cozy, thatch-roof country home—it matters not where—stretch out my arms and legs, and drift into a deep sleep, oblivious to everything." Such a poignant yearning would often well up in his heart as he trudged like a weary wanderer along stone-paved roads under brilliant incandescent lamps. "Oh, deep sleep," he would murmur, at times to himself and at times out loud, "how many years has it been since I have known you? Deep sleep! You are akin to religious ecstasy. What I most want—the rapture of sound sleep. The rapture of the flesh that is truly alive. That I yearn for most of all. I shall go where it is. I must go quickly!" A nameless feeling like nostalgia drove him irresistibly to go he knew not where. (He was a young man possessed of the intellect of an old man, the passions of a youth, and the will of a child.)

Now that house stood revealed before his eyes.

A small ditch ran along the right side of the road. Where the road turned sharply, the ditch followed the turn. Water flowed now this way, now that, through the ditch. It ran past the foot of the wooded mountains, along the edge of a persimmon orchard, along the side of a stable, under a thicket, past a grove of paulownia trees, and in front of a farmhouse garden where huge hollyhocks and lilies had burst into bloom in a corner. The six-foot ditch carried water to irrigate the fields, but its beauty recalled a mountain torrent, all the more because it flowed directly from its source in the far mountains. Sunlight filtering through green leaves confirmed that impression. The shallow running water bleached the red-clay sludge and stripped it free of mud; the stream, stopped up at times, flickered and flashed improbably or, for all that, gleamed delicately as the creases in crepe, like the onset of a small, twitching convulsion. Tiny sparkles overlapped like scales of a fish. When a cool breeze slid gently across the surface of the water, the stream for a moment was a narrow strip of silver foil. There were ornamental grasses and a thicket mass of wild roses that had early lost their small, white sentimental flowers, as if pleading with a lover. These and other nameless shrubs and grasses, each with its own fruits and flowers, hung luxuriantly from both banks and overlapped a grassy tunnel of running water. Shadows floating dark and cool flickered and flowed away. At times unhurried, the water slackened to a stagnant stop. It was like a traveler lingering to look back from whence he came. The water mirrored the turquoise color of the gemlike morning sky or the color seen sideways through a pane of glass. Flying against the breeze and flow of stream, a lively dragonfly glided lightly above the surface, dipping its tail to lay its eggs in water. Riding the breeze, it briefly trailed a cluster of others, flying at the same speed and direction, and then soared on impulse into the sky. He looked at the water; he looked at the sky. He felt welling in his heart a childlike well-being, a wish to call his blessing on that dragonfly. It made him joyous to think of the cheery river flowing past that house.

As if to express the pain and the pleasure of intense heat, leaf after leaf gleamed like the face of a jewel, while cicadas shrilled from below as if on fire. The burning sun climbed nearly to the zenith. His wife, however, hardly felt the heat. What warded off the heat for her was not the parasol (the poor woman's canopy) embroidered with purple hydrangeas; it was her brooding thoughts. She walked along absorbed in her reflections, so absorbed there was no time to think of heat. If they did it, she was thinking, she could get away to somewhere cool, away from that rented room in the temple where the afternoon sun streamed in so fiercely. Better yet, she could be free of that coarse and vulgar, nagging and greedy woman, the wife of the priest. And so, quietly and in coolness, the two of them would live, two together as they wanted to live, saying only what they wanted to say, saying nothing of what they wanted not to say. In this way his spirit and his mood, oversensitive like the sea, elusive like the wind, would become calm. Although he ached with ardor for the country, he hardly thought of how he would use the fields he had purposely bought. (That's how she thought it would be from the start.) He would not read a line; he would not write a word; it seemed he would do nothing. But if she were to say as much, she would surely be scolded. If not scolded, she would be given up as hopeless—especially since their too-early and unreasonable marriage (and with no concern for his parents, who apparently thought so), he lived idly the dream of each day for that day. He would have called it idle even were it not: to think how many finely detailed house plans he had drawn, with not a scrap of utility, not fit to build, and then to think how he would suddenly run into the garden, act like a dog, play with the dogs, crawling and tumbling in the burning, smelly grass, how this man would suddenly call out, burst out laughing with a broken shout, how lonesome he must really be. Because he never talks to me, he can't expect me to understand. He may be hiding something from me. . . . His wife recalled *Spring,* a novel by Shimazaki Tōson that she had finished reading five or six days ago. In her simple head, without questioning her husband's nature, she saw one of the characters step out of the novel to become her husband in front of her eyes, alive beside her. . . . Did he really want to waste away his life in the country, abandon everything, forget the artistic work that he seemed so much to believe in? What wonderful dream was he seeking? . . . This man who was so kind and gentle to others, why was he so sullen with me? I came into his heart when an earlier love for another woman was not yet faded, but, even though he forgot her for a time, I wonder whether that lingering love hasn't sprouted again without my knowing it, leaving me in the lurch? He treats me harshly. . . . As things are, the man is surely in distress, and he cannot abide the one closest to him. When he doesn't like my answer, he may beat me and hit me hard enough to knock me down, and, if I ask what is wrong, he may not say a word for two or three days. . . . Surely the man regrets he married me. Sometimes he must think of how happy he would be if he were living with that other woman. He didn't only think it. He actually said it to me: "If only I had stayed with that innocent, gentle girl, she would have brought me harmony, and in many ways I would have had a better and more beautiful life." . . . But in fact I know very well that she was more beautiful and more gentle than I. I know how deeply he thought of that woman. No, that's not so. He was so absorbed in other things. . . . That's it. My husband said, "Just leave me alone." And then suddenly:

"It's not that I don't have affectionate feelings. I'm just ashamed to reveal them. It's the nature I was born with."

The woman walked along ruminating on those words her husband had used with her last night in a rare moment when he confided in her. Then she thought of the room arrangement in the home she had not yet seen. She felt more lively than usual, motivated simply by moving her home, even in such heat, even roused early from her bridal dreams. That she could think that way in sadness, in joy, and in solace was the privilege of a young wife who yet knew nothing of the world. That was why she gave only uncivil, inattentive, and empty answers to the guide woman who talked on so endlessly about the history of the house. . . . That woman talked without stopping all the way along the sweltering road. She was one of those simple people who believe that what they themselves are interested in should be of great interest to anyone else.

They walked another couple of miles along the road. Then the house was in front of their eyes.

Sure enough, the ditch ran in front of the house. A small earthen bridge led people in a straight, narrow trodden path across the six-foot ditch and through rampant weeds to the entrance of the house.

A large persimmon tree stood at the left of the entrance. Inside the gate was another. The fat, freely twisting branches told the beholder's upward-gazing eyes, "We have stood here for a long time. We do not bear much fruit any more." Mistletoe grew from the old trunk under the big branches. A narrow gutter, running along to the right of these trees, set off the house from a paulownia grove next to it. What water was this? The water had dried into a narrow trickle. It gasped and gurgled, thinner than a man's belt—a narrow stream through part of a narrow gutter. Spiderwort with sky-blue flowers grew lushly over the sodden ground. Spreading through the spiderwort were pale-pink, candy-shaped flowers that children call bonbons and wildflowers that children call red rice. The grassy area called up nostalgic memories of his youth. At midday from the short grasses that were a likely home for fireflies came the rustling sound of reeds. Their long, wide, fresh leaves, vividly dyed with vertical white stripes, fluttered in the wind where a group of fifteen or sixteen grew together. The water, coming from behind the house and threading through the stalks of grass, washed clean the short nodes of the reeds as it flowed, winding and rolling in a willowy way, gleaming like a clump of silk threads unraveled. The tall, slender leaves of sprouting grass were knocked down by the meager flow of water, momentarily blocked in its flow along the leaves before plunging into the larger ditch beside the road with a plop like water in a water clock. The setting made him guess there might be a fresh spring bubbling up behind the house.

Behind the house a bamboo thicket stretched into the mountains. A splendid tall camellia stood awkwardly like a heretic amid the neat bamboo. The building's garden was enclosed by a high hedge of *sakaki* trees taller than a man. Seen from as far away as you could still point it out or from close at hand, the whole house was buried in branches of trees left to grow dense, set in grass left to grow rank.

The dogs ran down off the bridge to taste in turn the irrigation water.

Without making to cross the bridge he gazed sympathetically for a spell at the house that made him want to recite the old verse about the hermit's home: "Three Paths to the Wild."[2]

"It's nice, isn't it, the feel of the entryway?" he said to his wife, picking among the charms appropriate to a feeling of retreat and seclusion about this house.

"Yes, but it's kind of dilapidated. We'd better go in and see."

A bit warily but wisely, his wife spoke in her usual tone of reproach to her capricious husband. But immediately reconsidering, she added, "Any place is better than the temple we're in now."

The two dogs, quickly refreshed by their drink of water, bounded into the garden a step ahead of their masters. Choosing a shady spot at the base of a pine tree, the dogs flopped down on the ground as if they owned the place. They plunked their heads down side by side in the same manner, thrusting out their muzzles and resting their jaws and throats on the ground. Their bodies curved in just the same way. Their hind legs stretched out in appealing symmetry. As they panted desperately, their red tongues hanging out, they stared up innocently at the faces of their masters entering the garden and flopped their tails gently and happily. Their settled appearance showed that, before their masters, they fully presumed this place to be their home. If his wife had been by his side, he would have said to her:

"Look, Fratty and Leo [the names of the dogs] approve."[3]

But his wife was with the guide woman, who was clattering the keys at the keyhole and trying to open the long-closed porch-way door.

The trees were lushness upon lushness; the greens were layer upon layer. The intricate branches formed nettings and walls and eaves. Sunlight scarcely penetrated the garden. The smell of earth rose chilly from the black ground. He savored the piercing odor arising from the earth he stood upon; that sharpened his senses as does the scent of incense, until the cool clinking noise of keys ceased and the porch-way door was opened.

❋　❋　❋

"Well, now it looks like a house."

Yesterday she had washed the shoji sliding doors clean in front of the gate and then repapered them, a chore to which she was unaccustomed. When the last one was finished, she looked at the back of her husband, who was standing, about to install it in the sill, between the tea room and the middle room; she spoke, gleaming with satisfaction.

"Now it looks like a house." She said it again. "They say they are coming right away to change the tatami floor mats. I really didn't like it, though, when I first saw the house the day before yesterday. I wondered how anyone could live in it."

"It's no witching foxes' lair."

"Well then, it's 'the House in the Reeds.' "[4] Or if not that, it's a cricket house. How about it when the crickets were hopping all over the tatami floor mats? It was horrible."

" 'The House in the Reeds' is it? All right . . . then let's call it our 'Hut of the Rainy Moon.' "

(Both of them, the wife under the husband's influence, admired the works of Ueda Akinari.)

The wife was happy looking at her husband's cheery smile, which she had not seen for a long time. "Then, we'll have to clean out the well. It's terrible. Water hasn't been drawn for a year. It must be really foul."

"If the water is foul for not being drawn up every day, it must be like the rot in my head."

"Not again," his wife thought when she heard these words. Losing her cheerful mood, she stared nervously at her husband's face. But she could see that what he said was no more than words, and the smile had not left his bony face. To that extent he was in good spirits. Reassured, she added sweetly, "Well, you ought to do something about the garden. The gloom is so unpleasant!"

Their pet cat stole limply and lazily into her lap as she sat, tired, leaning against the wall.

"Ao [the pet cat's name], you're suffering from the heat, aren't you?" she said, hugging the cat.

In the household there were dogs. There was a cat. When it came to loving them, the unstinting fondness that was his nature became the habit of the house. Both he and his wife talked normally to the dogs and to the cat as they would to people. . . .

❊   ❊   ❊

Several years before the husband and wife began to live in this house . . .

An old man of the N family, said to be the wealthiest in the village, felt himself very lonely, being old. The most necessary thing for a normal person in this situation is a person of the opposite sex —never mind whether old or young. So the old man brought a young woman from the city. In this elegant gentleman's generation the wealthy family had lost half its rice fields, but the old man thought of himself naturally as a wealthy man. . . . Still, he did not bring home a woman of beauty alone and no ability. Even if she were rather plain, he could put up with that if she were young. He chose a woman for the sake of the village or rather more for the sake of his own economic situation. In a word, he kept a mistress who could carry on a sideline business as a midwife, a service hitherto lacking in the village. He dismantled the annex to his house and rebuilt it in a place just below. There was a twenty-four-foot porch facing south, so the winter sun would strike it from morning to evening. Passing through a three-mat entry hall one came into a six-mat tea room with a fireplace in the floor. The villagers' eyes popped when they saw the black persimmon-wood ornamental post in the alcove and the delicate workmanship on the frame of the shoji sliding doors set in the overhead transom and ornamented with hemp-leaf chains. "That post was chosen among all others and cut from our mountains; there is not a single unsightly knot," the carpenter said as he stroked it. He praised the old timber as if it were his own. The kitchen was changed from the awesomely broad dirt-floor room of a farmhouse with its heavy ridgepole and soot-blackened beams. In this house the kitchen planking was covered, and successions of women in white socks and trailing hemlines seem to have stood and worked there. The old man turned the family headship over to his oldest son, who was in his forties. The old man was happy. The villagers gossiped avidly about the old gentleman whose tea-loving companions were not yet half his age. This did not hurt the old man's happiness.

But all peace and happiness are of the briefest in a brief life span. They are like the shadow of a bird falling by chance on a sunny window screen in autumn. What comes of a sudden goes of a sudden. In the moment of seeing the shadow of a bird there wells up a sense of loneliness. The old man's days of peace were but a fleeting moment.

His young mistress soon lured a young man from the city. The villagers called the young man "clerk" or "clerk to the midwife." Whether the midwife really needed a clerk they did not know. The old man was displeased that his young mistress hired a young clerk without even warning him. He was extremely displeased. In the first place the young couple's life-style was too lavish in the eyes of the country folk. It was too much at odds with the old man's budget. The old man began to think they should be more moderate. He said as much to his young mistress from time to time. He said it first in a reserved and roundabout manner, but gradually he said it more forcefully. One evening their argument grew in vehemence through the night. Very likely the clerk heard this conversation through the wall. The next day, one year after the young woman had come to town, a half year after the young woman had "hired" the young clerk, the couple disappeared suddenly from the village. A wagon driver coming home from the village in the evening saw a round, white face looming up clearly, and the next morning he informed the people of the village that after taking a good look he had concluded it was Mr. N's midwife. Very likely he never really made that sighting, but, when he heard that the pair had disappeared, the lie came into his head. Otherwise, curious and triumphant, he would have reported that fact immediately on his return. Everyone has an artistic bent that makes him want to report the news at such a time. . . . No matter, for some time the story gladdened the country people who were starved for gossip. The prevailing opinion was that a young man of twenty-four or twenty-five was more appropriate for a woman of twenty-eight than a retired man of nearly seventy.

Then, sad to say, the old man who was deserted by his young mistress became absorbed in the pastime of gardening. He collected flower-bearing trees in his garden. Today he transplanted that one here. Yesterday he moved this one from another garden to his own. Tomorrow he must seek out a good one somewhere. Day after day there was no respite from his gardening. In the spring there were peonies; in the summer, morning glories; in the autumn, chrysanthemums; in the winter, narcissi. The old gentleman who loved flowers had a hard time sleeping, with his two granddaughters of ten and seven in the bed next to him in place of the young mistress who had fled. He was devoted to hackneyed poetry.

The old man died only one year later. He had barely enjoyed the flowers of those trees he had collected. The house became the property of the headmaster of the village elementary school along with his youngest daughter. The master had become the old man's adopted son. A shrewd nurseryman promptly cheated the schoolmaster and family head, who was skilled in the rules of arithmetic and the use of the abacus but totally indifferent to beauty of any kind. The nurseryman pulled out all the ornamental plants in the garden: giant magnolia, camellia, black pine, crab apple, black bamboo, weeping cherry, large-flowering pomegranate, plum, oleander, and various kinds of potted orchids. All these unlucky trees and shrubs had to be moved about busily. They had no time to become acclimated. Some among them may have withered from it.

The headmaster lived in part of the newly built schoolhouse. The house that he had inherited he left vacant. He thought he would like to rent it if he could find a tenant. With no one living there the house would only go to ruin. The headmaster thought very clearly that for two yen or even one yen fifty in rent he would suffer no loss. In the country, though, most people owned their own homes. Even if it were a dilapidated house with broken eaves and green moss growing thickly on the rotten thatch roof, an individual's house was passed down from parent to child and from child to grandchild. No matter how splendid the house, the farmer who would have to rent it as a last resort among last resorts would be the very poorest, one who had lost his own home by foreclosure of the mortgage. And so that house, which the old gentleman had built for the woman he loved as well as for his own pleasure in old age, truly became home to the poorest of the poor. In the hearth of the tea room, where the old man had hung his teakettle, smoldering pine chunks lay tossed in a jumble. The smoke, trapped by the useless ceiling of this country house, had no way to escape. The walls that formed the room, the sliding shoji doors, the ceiling, and the floor mats soon became sooty. The unfortunate farm family did not worry about the enveloping smoke. They felt grateful instead for its warmth, for, braiding ropes and making straw sandals, they had to work late into the long autumn and winter nights. Rent payments fell behind after four or five months. The floor mats were worn threadbare. Traces of carving from various occasions were cut in various shapes into the pillar. Even though the headmaster thought, "The night soil must be piled up," the privy was always empty when his farmhand came to clean it out in the morning.

That was because the poor farmer-tenant had already carted it off to his own rented fields. The headmaster began to think very poorly of his tenant. He complained to everyone he met, railing at the poor farmer's guile. The headmaster concluded simply, "A poor man is a crafty fellow who knows nothing of duty." Other townspeople soon showed that they agreed with the headmaster's opinion. The headmaster felt this confirmed the truth of his own logic. He wondered whether it wouldn't be better to let the house fall into ruin rather than continue to rent to this man. To rent to this man was to leave the house to positive ruin. To leave it vacant would be the passive way. So the tenant was kicked out. The villagers thought the headmaster's attitude was reasonable.

During the period after the old gentleman's death no one gave a thought to the grass or trees in the garden. House and garden fell into ruin. Only one person, the poor farmer's daughter, plucked the flowers she found every autumn morning and used them as ornaments in her curly hair—the small, yellow and white chrysanthemums planted when the old man was alive but now lost in a wild tangle of grasses, their leaves pitiful and their stems twisted by the years. . . .

*   *   *

. . . While he stood on the porch staring at the garden, the fat guide woman continued her roadside chatter. Sunk in his own peculiar fantasies, he pondered without knowing he pondered blankly, thought without thinking he thought.

"Fratty, Fratty." From the back veranda came the voice of his wife and the barking of the dogs. "Oh, all right. Hasn't Leo come, too? Sweet ones. I haven't given you anything. Fratty, that grass is no place for you to play. There are snakes there. Don't you think I worry about seeing the tip of your nose bitten, your throat swollen and your face puffed up, looking haughty like the chief priest of the temple? All right. Fratty understood because he learned by experience. Leo, you be careful. You're the gentle one, so you'll be all right. . . ." His wife spoke to the two dogs as if they were adopted sons, her voice and feeling suggesting a girl singing a pastoral song.

The wind off the cool thicket of bamboo blew by him where he stood.

     *   *   *

The abandoned garden was lush with midsummer.

Trees stretched their roots as deep as they could to suck up the power of the soil. They put out leaves on every side to soak in their fill of light from the sun. . . . The pines lived as pines, the cherries as cherries, the yews as yews. To bathe freely in the sun's light and so to grow bigger, each tree thrust out its branches. To achieve its will, branch piled on branch, layer on layer, colliding, intertwining, jostling with one another. To gain the favor of the sun no branch could consider another. Branches untouched by the sun grew thinner by the day. One small pine stood withered and red beneath a cedar. The *sakaki* hedge was uneven in height, its top line undulating awkwardly. The sunny parts grew luxuriantly taller; other parts shaded by the big trees were sunken hollows. Some could grow no leaves at all; they were like gaping peephole windows in a castle wall. Elsewhere the leaves grew thickly, one upon another, forming lush, round clumps. In places there were complete breaks in the hedge. Just there, under the cover of the tall pines growing alongside, a wild wisteria burst abruptly from the middle of the hedge. Fatter than a man's thumb, the vine split the hedge and climbed, coiling the trunk of the old pine like a rope that had captured a prisoner, until the twining vine reached the highest visible tip of the tree and there, seeming still dissatisfied, it grasped impatiently for the nothing beyond, like the desperate finger of a writhing body. One of the twining vines crawled across to a neighboring cherry, markedly taller than the pine, where it stretched higher into the sky than any of its companions. In another corner of the garden the young branch of a plum stood erect and tall like a spear trying to pierce the heavens. The soft earth that was once the chrysanthemum bed was now matted with strong-rooted weeds—weeds so tough they were like bamboo. The tough stems and blades crept out, weaving a net over the ground, and each, to secure its own territory, put out roots from the nodes and spread in every direction. If you tried to pull up a piece, countless thin, tufty roots would bring along handfuls of soil mixed with sand. It is their will to life. It is the burning form that summer commands in all things. The whole garden, the lush leaves and branches of the varied trees and grasses, wore the gloom of tangled hair hanging from a madman's leaden brow. The invisible weight of the foliage pressed on the narrow garden from above and made one feel the house in the center was encircled and compressed within its perimeter.

Still, the thing that frightened him was not the will to violence in nature. It was the thread of man-made refinement lingering faintly in all this disorder. It was the ghost of a will. That shrewd nurseryman had robbed this abandoned garden of almost everything, but in all that was left there lay unconcealed the old man's delight in flower culture. Nature in all its power could not yet obscure that presence. The white-spotted cedar, for example, made one think it must formerly have been pruned in the dense shape of a Chinese date tree. It stood between the garden gate and the entryway to the house. There was a camellia that hid the privy from the living room. In the shade underneath was daphne. There were several Kirishima azaleas shaped like covered pots. There were old hydrangeas; their large leaves wilted from the heat, and their large flowers withered and dried in the shade. These plants were cluttered about the garden as if they had been tossed out by a giant in a rage—the magnolia, the daphne, the Japanese camellia, the begonias, the plums, the rose of Sharon, the old umbrella pine, the fall-blossoming camellia, the bush clover, the pots of orchids, the large natural rocks, the shaggy green mosses, the weeping cherries, the black bamboo, the China pinks, the large-flowering pomegranate trees, the irises by the water. The old dreams of that time when these things were well arranged and cherished by the hands of a man were left to the ravages of a nature more violent than any northern barbarians; yet today, with no one to notice, the dreams seem not forsaken. Now even in a corner of the garden where there was not one of those trees remaining, or even at the entryway where the overgrown pine was today rampantly, tightly covered with long, fat, stiff needles—even there one could easily recognize that once the hand of a man had cared for those branches, pruned those needles, stroked those trunks. Indeed, the headmaster-owner was thinking of selling that pine tree next. He thought he would have the roots pruned and the old needles removed on this tree when the tenant next called for the nurseryman.

Look how the old man's last will and testament have been steadily destroyed by the power of fate and of a nature sometimes savage because it is so grand. The remaining trees, the garden, are neither nature's vigorous, barbaric power nor man-made artificial formality. Here is an artless, incoherent mixture of both. Rather than the ugly, it has within it the ghastly without reason. The new master of the house loitered in the shade of the trees and stared at summer in the abandoned garden. He felt something menacing. A momentary sense of terror passed through him. What it was he did not know. The minute he tried to catch it, the feeling was gone in a flash. It was mysteriously, he thought, more a physical than a spiritual fear, like an animal's kind of fear.

That day he walked around and looked, for a bit, under the shade trees amid that appalling and pathetic garden of his new home.

A long black line of ants was marching along under a white-oak tree next to the house. The ants were carrying large morsels of food as if they were family treasures. One largish ant running here and there appeared to be issuing orders to the others. When they met, they would pause head to head as if exchanging greetings or gossip, or conveying messages. Moving must be a common thing for ants. He crouched down and stared at the tiny caravan. For a time he drew a childish pleasure from these ants. He realized he had seen nothing like this for many years, or if he had, he was not prepared to notice. As a child he used to enjoy such things more than other children, but he had forgotten now even such memories. . . . Since his childhood he no longer sat quietly looking at the moon or watching birds. To realize this made him strangely sad and then happy. Feeling that way, he stood up and started to walk about, when he noticed the cast-off shell of a cicada, its forelegs shaped like fangs, biting comically into the trunk of the white-oak tree. It was a small suit of armor gleaming red, its back split open. Looking closely at the tree, he found a cicada fixed to the trunk about three or four inches above the old shell. It was not unnatural that the insect was unmoved by the presence of man. He understood at a glance that the cicada had just emerged. Its very soft body had not yet hardened. Clinging there without moving, the insect was quietly feeling the mystery of air. Its soft, not-yet-perfectly-formed wings were milky white overall but a bit shriveled, pitiful, and pathetic. The green veins stood out sharply. It was a refreshing cheerful green that suggested a bean sprout that was splitting and sprouting from a cracked white seed. Not only its color but also its wings as a whole resembled the shoots of a plant. He saw revealed in this birth how insects and grasses differ yet share a common form. Maybe there was no law in nature. Still, a man could find the laws he wanted. On further scrutiny he saw that something minute, more brilliant than a ruby, was exquisitely inlaid there precisely in the middle of that insect's flat head. What the jewel-like thing was, scientifically, he had no way of knowing (even whether it were a single eye). Yet he thought he understood its beauty better than anyone else. That beauty made him feel the birth of this tiny, trivial insect was a sacred act worthy of worship. It was truly powerful.

He wondered in his mind—hadn't he heard from somebody, somewhere, sometime, perhaps a student of agriculture, that cicadas matured into adult insects only after twenty years? These tiny insects have a life, seen to be without meaning by people who dismiss them with the caterwauling of frogs and cicadas, yet nearly as long a life as his own age! And they would live scarcely a few days, two or three, or a week! For what purpose did nature ever create such a life? But no, not only these insects—couldn't you say that about people, too? About himself? The nature that the gods created, wasn't it haphazard? The more you tried to solve the haphazard without noting it haphazard, the more you couldn't see the mystery. No, he did not understand a thing. All he understood was cicadas were short-lived. Who would say the life of a loquacious human member of parliament was not that of a cicada? As he watched, he could see the shriveled wings extending. As they did, the translucent milky-white color cleared moment by moment, slowly but surely, into a colorless transparency. The green color, weak but fresh as a new sprout, gradually turned black, until like the green of young grass turning the color of an evergreen tree, it displayed a certain real strength. He gazed over twenty minutes at these things; no, it was more a morbid examination of them. He felt the rigor of his breath being compressed.

Suddenly he came to himself. "Look. The torment of birth. What perseverance this little thing has in trying to be born!"

Then he added, "This little bug is I! Fly away quickly please, bug!"

He made this his strange prayer. Not just for now, but for always, he made it.

*   *   *

There were several roses in a corner of the garden.

They were growing like a hedge along the water runoff from the well. If they had been fully flourishing, they would have made a beautiful flowering hedge for five or six yards with blossoms on every branch. But these were a most unlucky crew. The morning sun was blocked by a grove of cedar. At evening the big shadow of the house lay heavy upon them. Around noon the persimmon trees and plum branches robbed the roses of their sunlight. Above the roses the luxuriant branches of cedar, plum, and persimmon had the sunlight to themselves; they made a roof. The stems of the roses were miserably tapering vines that struggled up, faltering amidst the foot-high grasses.

Although it was late August, there was not a single green leaf on the roses, let alone any flowers—literally not one. To see whether these stems were still alive, he snapped one off. The light and warmth of the sun was skimmed off by all the other plants. The nutriments stored in the earth were stolen from their roots by the spreading nameless grasses. The roses appeared to get none of the benefits of nature. The place was favored by spiders as the perfect scaffold for their webs. That was the roses' only value and that was why they had to continue to live.

Roses were one thing that he loved most dearly. Sometimes he spoke of them as "my own flower." Wasn't that because Goethe had left for him a line of poetry, unforgettable and full of solace, about this flower? ("If it's a rose, the flower will bloom.")[5] There was not only a logical reason for that, he thought. He loved that flower with all his heart. Its rich beauty, overabundant like an overflowing wine cup, especially in the red flowers, captivated him. Its dizzying heavy fragrance recalled the sweetness of a first kiss. If he felt this way about it, so many poets since ancient times have written so many beautiful poems to this flower. Western writing has crowned the rose in poetry since the time of the ancients. Chinese poets, too, have not failed to sing the splendor of this flower in their pictorial writing. They prized the attar of rose from ancient Arabia, and they lamented that it could not be extracted in China. The poetic words have a thread of tradition that has today become a firm convention, like a vein of precious metal in a poetic domain reserved for this flower. Anyone who once enters the world of poetry hears of roses everywhere. If we take in as fertilizer the numberless excellent poetic words for the color, the scent, even the leaves and thorns of this flower, it will light for us a vision of beautiful writing, so that we think it like a tree overburdened with fruit. The thought inspired him all the more with the beauty of this flower. Was it fortunate, or rather wasn't it much more unfortunate? A commitment to prevailing artistic tradition was deeply embedded in his personality. In this spirit he had chosen to work in the arts. His artistic disposition, born of this cause, had been awakened early. . . . These things had brought him unconsciously to love the rose so much. Before he knew how to pluck spiritual beauty and joy directly from nature, he came through the artistic conventions of the past to offer his deep love only to this flower. It may have been absurd, but he felt a love even for the word *rose*.

Nonetheless, these were shabby shrubs of roses he saw before him now! In the garden at his childhood home he used to see the roses that budded in the depths of the cold, thanks to the very warm sunshine. They had large pink flowers. He had seen them bud out, induced by the unnaturally warm sun, but, when there was no morning and evening sunlight, the winter in the south was too cold for roses. He had seen the buds close up tightly; they had experienced the sun in vain. Mysteriously every day the outermost pale-pink petal among the white would develop thin green lines like the character of a leaf, stiffened into something you might say was midway between a petal and a leaf. The roses he saw before him now were incomparably more pathetic than those onetime buds. Looking at these vines he was struck by an impulse: somehow he wanted to pour the benefits of sunshine onto these shaded vines, these long-suffering roses. He wanted them to make flowers. That was his sudden wish. The wish was filled in great part with a sporting and poetic attitude that it was right for him to do just that, deliberately—so much so that he could not miss it. (In any case the feeling seemed somehow to belie his sincerity.) Well, anyway, he felt that he wanted his fortune divined by the rose. ("If it's a rose, the flower will bloom.")

He went around by himself to the neighboring farmhouse. The two sharp-eyed dogs recognized the figure of their swift-footed master, and they chased after him. He carried a rusty saw and mulberry clippers, and, accompanied by his two dogs, he was back in his garden exultant within five minutes. He stood smiling next to the roses. Thinking the sun would shine best here, he picked his spot, looked up and around, and bared his shoulder. First he began to saw on the most intrusive of the thick persimmon branches. White powder dropped crumbling from the branch. When the saw teeth had cut in more than half way, the uncut part of the weakened branch could no longer support its own weight. It snapped off with a crack. The heavy limb fell to the ground bringing twigs with it. Sunlight streamed instantly through the hole as if flung down, pushing and spreading until it drenched the near-dead roses. The sunlight embracing the roses spread gradually wider. That was because the overhanging branches and leaves of the plums, cedar, and persimmon were gradually trimmed away. With the mulberry clippers he cut out the spider webs from the tops of the roses. Various kinds of spiders were lurking there. The short, small-footed, fly-catching spiders had built nests like paper bags in the crotches of the branches. The large, glossy, long-legged, tortoise-shell silk spiders had stretched big structures of web works. When the clippers disturbed the nest, the spiders escaped, spinning a thread with the skill of an acrobat. The big clippers chased after them. Spitting thread, the spiders dangled in front of the clippers, scuttled, and dropped onto the ground, into the grass, and onto the pool of water. There they were chopped apart by the clippers.

The activity soaked his body in sweat. It excited his mind. His wife, hearing the largest branch drop to the ground, came to see what strange thing he was doing. She seemed to call out something to her husband, but he made no answer. When the two dogs knew that their master would have nothing to do with them today, they started chasing each other around and making an uproar in the garden. There was something ecstatic in his pleasure. He felt that he wanted recklessly to lop off everything he could reach.

With one heave at the clippers he cut the base of the fat wisteria vine that was twined around the pine. He was surprised that he had so much strength. He felt that the pine tree seemed to breathe a deep sigh of relief as he pulled the coiling vine away from the trunk. He grabbed the cut end of the vine with both hands and yanked with all his might. It was useless. He jerked on that vine that wrapped both the pine from its twigs to its top and the neighboring cherry, but, although the pine and cherry branches bent and shook heavily, needles and leaves were torn off and dropped to the ground, and the caterpillars clinging to the cherry branches fell onto his straw hat, the vine itself merely stretched like a bowstring. "Aren't you surprised that I'm as strong as you? Go ahead. Try harder if you want!" the vine boasted, taunting him impudently. Well, he had burned his fingers on this vine. There was nothing for it but to quit. He turned and began to prune the hedge.

He pursued this diversion from a little after noon until evening, when the top of the hedge had become a strikingly straight line and the sides became flat like a wall. Just then the evening sunlight, shining parallel to the hedge, lit up the hard, black *sakaki* leaves and made them sparkle beautifully. Staring at the leaves, he noticed that the big open space was all the more unsightly.

"Say, that's a neat job I've done."

He spoke, praising himself, when a farmer passing on his way home stared at the house through the hole in the hedge. Next he trimmed up the stems of the pussy willow that hung over the ditch. That evening he ate an unusually large supper. That night he fell eagerly into a sound and pleasant night's sleep. When he awoke in the morning, he had to admit wryly that his joints hurt and his body was as stiff as a tree.

A few days later when the real nurseryman—well, he was half farmer—came into the garden, the leaves, like centipede feet on the wisteria vine that clung so tenaciously to the pine and the cherry, had wilted and in some places the green was totally gone. The coiling vine with its frantic, pointing finger had collapsed, limp and weary. Feeling the joy of watching a villain's last appearance on stage, he squatted under the eaves and looked at the vine, which the nurseryman up in the tree had brutally hacked into pieces.

"When this dries for four or five days, it'll make good kindling," the nurseryman shouted down suddenly from the tree above.

"That's a thick one, for sure," he answered. "Yep, it is that," he thought to himself. The wisteria reminded him of the old saying, "The stubborn vine wilts so quickly into ugliness from the same power of the sun that made it grow so lush." My will, human will, he thought, controls the power of nature. Or rather he was proud to have accomplished as a man the will of nature. For nature, there was nothing wrong with a wisteria growing there; yet somehow in a garden made at first by the hand of man the hand of man was necessary to the end. So he thought to himself at random.

Then how will the roses change? Will they blossom? He stood up and walked around in anticipation. To look at the roses. The sun was shining on them brightly and hopefully, but, other than that, there was no change yet. He should have known as much from looking at them this morning.

The days slipped by. He forgot the roses. More days passed.

*　　*　　*

The seasons changed quietly from summer into fall. He could see it clearly. Nights came on strong and it was autumn. The katydids, the crickets—all the insects that are harbingers of autumn began their chirping in the grass or in front of his desk or under his bed. Premonitions of a pleasing, pastoral early autumn gladdened the hearts of the villagers. The young men of the village walked with sturdy strides six or eight miles through the cool night breeze to seek out the girls. Some people practiced on the drums for the village festival. The eager boom of their simple music echoed across the fields and into his window until late at night.

The girl student who had returned to the village—she attended normal school in Y city and was the only girl in the village to go away to school—had become a friend of his wife. At the end of the summer, happily returning to school in the city, she left his wife behind.

His feelings of frenzied impatience seemed to leave him at last after his move to this house. Now on the eve of autumn he was spontaneously serene. He felt a kind of happy pride to know that he was as susceptible to the influence of nature as were the grasses, the trees, the winds, and the clouds. The lights of evening were a glow of nostalgia. To a person like him, tired in mind and body, the lamp cast a sweet and gentle radiance. He had bought the lamp for some twenty sen from a peddler who came by. The paper shade cost another sen. The glass jar of the lamp base was beautiful with an amber glob of translucent kerosene. Sometimes it became a pale purple, reminding him of an amethyst. He thought at first he would like to read by the lamp the life of Saint Francis, but soon he tired of reading. When it came to perseverance, he had now not a whit. Whatever book he tried to read, he found them all, this one or that one, uniformly dull. What's more, it was really strange to think that all those boring books were immensely satisfying to the world at large. It seemed that something was dragging mankind, himself, into another world made of everything completely different from this world or that this old, old world spreading untidily before his eyes appeared as something totally apart—or that it was lying in utter shambles, toppled off its base. Any of these, or even something much grander, might somehow, somewhere be probable. He often mused aimlessly like this. Is it true that "there is nothing new under the sun?" If so, what use can people in general ever have for living? Wasn't it only a matter of their living boldly without even noticing that all one's dreams were nothing, empty dreams each built proudly on that person's own stupidities? . . . Wasn't that so for a wise man or a fool, a philosopher or a merchant? What was human life after all but the value simply of being alive? Death, too—what was death but the value simply of dying? He thought about these things every night. The oppressive, exhausting boredom hung in the depths of his heart. All things in

the world that the owner of that heart could see, everything, anywhere, anytime, were tedious, and properly so. The only way to
live anew in this old, old world was for him to change his state of
mind completely. When he could understand that, how could he
make his kind of self into something fresh? What did *courage* and
drive mean in that angry letter his father had sent him? Where
could he get them and how could he cultivate them? How could he
instill them in his heart? He could never know all that. In the
country, in the city, nowhere was there a paradise that could give
him peace on earth. There was nothing.

"Thou, God that maketh all things, Thy will be done."

Should he try to say that? But his heart wasn't breaking. It was
only downcast. . . . He listened to the sound of the drums and pictured in envy the spirited people clustered around the sources of
the sound.

On his desk the pages of the books he was not reading, could not
read, lay exposed to his eyes. He found the writing without meaning. Sometimes he would take out his big dictionary. He would
look up the most unusual words. With his tired mind and body he
could not read a sentence as an organic whole formed from a group
of words. Instead he could call up idle fancies for each word. He
thought he could see their spirit vividly, the spirit of language. He
thought then that words were something indescribably wondrous.
There was a deeply divine character to words, he felt. Words, one
by one of themselves, were already fragments of human life. Didn't
the meeting of words in itself make a world? Don't the feelings of
anyone who first invented and used a word still linger on nostalgi-
cally and miraculously in the word? Whenever a single new word is
created, a word that all people can use in everyday life forever,
doesn't that person live on eternally, universally in the word he
created? Yes, that's right! You've got to be clearly aware of it. . . .
He felt rather vague about that. He groped to conceive the miraculous, inscrutable actions and desires of people who tried to convey
a single sentiment clearly to another person. When he grew tired of
words, he took pleasure in learning from the minute pictures in his
dictionary about things he had never seen nor imagined before: a
fish, an animal, grass, a tree, an insect, a species of marine life, vari-

ous household utensils, weapons, various implements used since ancient times to punish criminals, boats and various devices for their rigging, and building sections. There were varied hints in the trivial shapes of these instruments and in the animals and plants. He felt that these man-made devices were, like the power of words, brimming with the thoughts, the life, the dreams of mankind—but only in fragments. Just then the life of his mind had only the strength appropriate for thinking about these fragments.

Sometimes late at night at the end of these fancies he wrote something like poetry. That night he would convince himself that it was very superior verse. When he awoke the next morning and first looked at the paper, though, it was nothing more than a line of meaningless letters. That was rather surprising—he had after all chanced on a good idea. When he tried to grasp it, there was nothing there. When he thought he had it, there was only space—just like embracing a lover in a dream. Each time he experienced impatiently the anxiety you get when you turn around, thinking your name has been called, but find no speaker there.

He began again to draw house plans. He imagined the structure of a very complicated labyrinth. He then considered a house that had nothing but one big room for parlor and for kitchen, such as a Corsican house was said to have. Almost every night he drew in his notebook the design details for exteriors, room arrangements, and window parts in vertical and horizontal sections. Finally, without a single white page remaining he hunted out that most precious thing, a blank square inch. He filled that tightly with an assortment of many lines. For each of the meaningless lines he saw endless fancies. His feelings were like those of a mad artist absorbed in painting arabesque designs, innocently and intently, in solitary confinement.

And so at length the lifeless tedium came again. It continued for days.

*　*　*

One night something flew with a whirring noise into the paper shade of his lamp.

He looked, and it was a katydid. The neat green insect settled on the red-tinged rim of the lamp shade. The contrast of red and green first drew his eyes; then slowly the form and motion claimed his interest. The insect crawled greenly around on the red section of the lamp's round shade, gently waving in the air its long antennae, almost half the length of its body. It was, he thought, like the gait of a man assuming airs as he strolled around the outer edge of his round garden. The slender, green, graceful insect had a reddish-brown tip to its delicate back. When he had first noted the red spot on the nape of a firefly's neck, he had been able to feel the sentiments put into verse by the haiku poet Bashō.[6] The insect walked around the rounded shade in circles. Abruptly now and again it would fly nimbly and noisily across to a horizontal beam in the wall, to a crosspiece in the shoji sliding paper doors, to his cluttered bookshelves, or to some place atop the mosquito net where his wife lay asleep, as she left her husband to his own devices late into the night, undecided when to sleep. "Just to be born human need not to be happy," some poet wrote of the cricket. "Next time I am reborn, I'd like to be this bug." Thinking that and watching the insect, he chanced to imagine the small world of an ant lion he had once seen sitting on a silk hat. That small insect with large transparent wings on its back and the fluttering breath of a pallid young girl had landed shakily but precisely on the sharp corner of a rather strange-shaped shiny black hat and had crawled sluggishly along the line of the edge. . . . The bright electric light had shone silently down on it from above. . . . He looked up suddenly at the light. It was not electric; it was a kerosene lamp. He had confused the light of the lamp in his idle thoughts because he thought he was back there under the electric light.

What suddenly called to his mind the contrast between the silk hat and the ant lion? Himself, he did not know. Yet the world of such queer, delicate, uselessly minute forms of beauty was most congenial to his own state of nerves.

The katydid visited his lamp every night. He didn't know at first the meaning of the insect's yearning for the lamplight and its circling of the shade. Then as he watched he suddenly understood. Surely it came not for pleasure nor for play. It came leaping there to eat the other smaller insects swarming on the shade. Those were greenish bugs so minute you would say they were the dust left by nature at the end of summer. The katydid, grabbing with its little feet, raked in the insects and crammed them into its mouth. That mouth, devised like an exquisite steel machine, would snap open, and then quickly clamp shut all around. The smaller, squirming insects were to be eaten by the strong. Those being eaten, even as one watched the eating, were too small to invite any special emotions or affection. When he pressed them lightly with his fingertip, the tiny insects vanished, leaving a spot the color of green tea.

The katydid arrived one night missing one of its long jumping legs. How and where did that happen? One of its long feelers, too, was broken off short.

Finally, on the bookcase one night, the cat, who paid no heed to his restraints, captured the unfortunate insect that had become its master's nightly friend. After toying with it mercilessly, the cat gobbled the katydid. When he recalled how good, he thought, to be reborn as that insect, he considered that the life of the little bug was perhaps not so carefree after all.

While he was absorbed in, drunk with, playing with these fairy-tale fantasies, his wife was absorbed in a different fairy tale as she listened to the shrill sound of a cricket under the bed. . . . The cricket's song led her to think about preparing the winter clothes and to reflect on her empty bureau, where the cat leapt and made it shake, and on her finest clothing that she no longer had at hand. The stripes, patterns, and colors of those clothes flashed clearly in minute detail through her mind. She reviewed the history of each box of clothes. A sigh mixed with each memory to become a tear. With her special self-centered woman's subjectivity, she found life's bitterest sufferings in those very anxieties about her woman's playthings. There was no appeal from that grief. If she were at long last to tell him about it, he would say there was nothing to it and would quote the Bible: "Having nothing, we yet possess all things."[7] The wife surely had to believe that she could not turn to him, her husband who lived for himself as he willed, and who lived his dreams in an ivory tower, looking out on mankind without pretense. Sometimes she ran through her mind like a dream her thoughts on coming to this mountain village, her brief past, and her fate. Even now in contrast to her own existence she longed for the brilliance of her rivals in the arts, who lived the life of the stage (for she had been an actress). . . . Five miles to the small mountain station N, three and a half miles to where you got the carriage—either way from there one hour by the electric railway car. If you went straight from the village, some fifteen miles or more. To Tokyo it took half a day. . . . She had to blame her husband more for saying let's live in the country, for whatever high ideals, than herself for carelessly consenting. Far off Tokyo . . . nearby Tokyo . . . nearby Tokyo . . . far off Tokyo . . . The streets of Tokyo, the arc lights, the show windows, the corridors of the theaters in season, the dressing rooms. All these passed leisurely before the eyes of his wife as she was about to sleep.

*   *   *

Sunsets followed day after day. Not the flaming red sky of two or three weeks earlier—only the upper surface was red, overshadowing a pleasant, cheery yellow below. The sunset bore no threat of tomorrow's heat; the evening glow promised a clear, bright day. In the southwest sky the pure-white peak of Mt. Fuji, showing in the hollow between the nearer hills, glistened boldly in the evening glow. Because only a small part of this vulgar but famous mountain could be seen, the mountain could preserve its intrinsic beauty. When one looked at the gray-black line stretching along the western horizon and wondered whether it was part of the clouds, or whether it was mountains in the shadow of those newly layered clouds, one knew for sure there was a range of mountains far off somewhere there. Each day when he looked at the evening glow, he felt momentarily welling within him that usual regret that today was another day wasted. The emotions induced by color may have stimulated his heart in this morbid way. When he looked down at the earth under his feet, the water flowing in the ditch below the earthen bridge where he stood was gleaming with a broad, red line reflecting the sky's evening glow.

On the surface of the rice fields the wind carved its shape in wavy lines like those on a beach when a gentle breeze goes wriggling by. That was the cool evening breeze. The fields had not yet turned yellow, but the flowers had gone to seed. Locusts were hatching here and there among the lightly drooping spikes of grain. Now and then locusts hopped out from under his feet as he walked the rice-paddy dikes, overgrown with fruitful round, red grasses known as Indian strawberry. His companions on these walks, the two dogs, seeing the locusts quickly or not, tried to stamp on them with their front paws, and they ate them hungrily as the insects lay on the ground, half dead, half alive. One dog was quicker than the other in finding locusts. The second was more agile in catching them with its paws. One dog gave up quickly on those that got away. The other persisted in chasing them down into the paddy mud. He was intrigued to see how different were the dogs' natures; that made him love them more. As the spikes of rice drooped gradually downward, the locusts multiplied. Running ahead each day, the dogs enticed and led him to the rice fields. As he watched the locusts he sometimes wanted to catch and feed them to the dogs. He grabbed at the insects with his outstretched hand. Seeing their master's stance, the dogs seemed to understand his intentions. They stopped their hunting in mid-course, and, their eyes following the master's hand, they waited for him to give them what he had caught. But not in more than one try in five could he catch a locust. He was left holding nothing but a broken-off leg. At catching locusts he was clumsier than the unskilled dogs. Still, the dogs believed in the superiority of the master's skill. They seemed to trust in him. When he opened his empty hand to show them the insect had escaped, the dogs looked suspiciously back and forth between the master's palm and the master's face. They tilted their heads alike, curled their lips a bit, and looked up at his face with sweetly shining eyes. Although disappointed and surprised at the master's failure, they fawned on him for no reason. For dogs they surely had a rich expression! No matter how often they experienced the loss of hope they never lost faith that the master was better at catching insects than they. Every time they saw his stance and his gesture for catching locusts they would let go the locust they had successfully caught, and, staring at the master's hand, they would wait at length for his bounty. With his extended empty hand he would pat the heads of the disappointed dogs. Satisfied, the dogs wagged their tails. The unthinking trust of the dogs and the fact that he could not reward them were strangely distressing. He felt much more inexcusable toward these genuine devotees than he did for the many breaches of faith to his human colleagues. Troubled by the special clear-eyed way they looked up at him, he was as careful as he could be to avoid the reflex snatch at the insect he saw before him.

About a week after he had trimmed the overhanging branches from the trees above the shaded roses, to let the sunlight stream onto them, pale-red buds first appeared here and there on the twigs of the roses no longer shaded. In two or three more days the astonishing power of the sun had turned the buds into young leaves. He came to the well each morning to wash his face, but, before he knew it and without so intending, he had completely forgotten the roses.

Unexpectedly one morning—it was less than twenty days after he had trimmed those branches—he chanced to discover a flower blooming on a new, vivid-green stem. Red, tall, and only one. "At last, after a long, long year as if in jail, is it May again?" So the out-of-season flower on the half-withered shrub seemed to say as it let out a deep sigh of joy and looked about. The light of a near-autumn day poured over it. Oh, rose flower. His own flower. "If it's a rose, the flower will bloom." Without thinking he recalled keenly his own feelings on the day he trimmed those trees. He raised his hand and seized the twig. There were soft thorns there, clear pink like a baby's fingernails. The hand that lightly grasped the branch they pricked lightly. It reminded him of the itching when his pet cat, fawning on him, would gently nibble on his finger. He bent the branch and pulled it closer to him. The single flower, oh, it was just the size of an anemone. The double petals were smaller than those of a wild cherry. Rather than a garden flower, this was a roadside blossom. The small, pitiful, deformed flower was redder than the lips of a child, with the lovely elegance and grace characteristic of a rose. When he pulled it to his nose and realized how fragrant it was, he was struck with an inexpressible admiration. Whether it was sadness or joy, he was seized by a painful feeling that it was hard to tell which it was. It resembled his feeling when those inno-

cent dogs that trusted their master looked up with clear and stead-
fast eyes, but this was much more intense. It was like the feeling at
a chance meeting with a girl for whom he had once done some
kindness on an impulse of casual curiosity and then had completely forgotten, and she said to him, "I have thought of nothing
but you since that time." Trembling with a mysterious emotion, he
blinked unexpectedly and the small red rose blurred suddenly
before him. Tears oozed involuntarily from his eyes.

As the tears came, the feeling soon passed. He stood rooted
there, dumbfounded, with the flowering branch in his hand. The
drying tears stiffened on his cheeks. He stared into his heart. How
many companions he could hear conversing there in his heart as if
it were none of his business.

"You fool. I'm crying like a poet for good feelings. Over the
flower? Or over my idle thoughts?"

"Is it my youthful retirement in the country, where I hunger for
humanity?"

"I'm a terrible hypochondriac."

✻   ✻   ✻

One night there was a buzzing noise in the garden. He
looked. A dim-white mist of quiet rain covered the fields, the hills,
the trees, and drenched them. Under the straw-thatch roof you
could not hear the patter and drip of early autumn's soft soaking
rain. It shed a quiet gloom in the atmosphere of the house and a
tender glow in the light of the lamp. Enveloped in this aura as he
sat there erect, he was seized with a vague feeling for the loneliness
of a journey. The autumn rain itself was passing over this village
like a lonely traveler on a distant trip. Sliding out the nighttime
shutters, he gazed at the retreating white rain.

The rain passed two or three times over the village. The cat, feeling the cold of the evening breeze, snuggled next to its master. He
shivered in the unlined summer kimono that was all he wore.

The rain that started one night continued until dawn. Through
a second day and a third day it never stopped. At first he had a certain feeling of enjoyment for the rain, but then the dreary weather
wearied him. And still the rain would not stop.

The dogs' bodies were infested with fleas. Those pitiful dogs hunted the fleas on each other's back and tip of the tail. He watched their actions with a feeling of affection. Before he knew it, the dogs' fleas had moved over onto the man. Every night he was tormented with fleas. They crawled slowly in countless thin lines over his body.

For lack of exercise his chronic but long-forgotten stomach trouble made him melancholy, first about his body. Melancholy then spread to his spirit. Day after day the same menu dulled his appetite. He could not but think the unchanging diet was fouling his blood. The dogs, too, grew tired of their food. Barely shoving the tips of their noses into the dish, they turned away with no further notice. He should say nothing about it to his wife, though; that was all the food to be had in this village.

His thin summer kimono clung shriveled and twisted around him. The soles of his feet were sticky with greasy sweat. As he sat squatting, the sweat from his feet and a strange warmth spread into his buttocks; the fleas liked this and gathered there. He felt fleas in the hair of his head as well. When he tried to comb them out, his hair, grown chilly and wet, snagged on the comb and broke it. He thought he would like to take a bath in order to wash and cleanse himself of that fleas'-nest feeling, but his house had no tub. At the farm homes in the neighborhood they would heat the bathwater on every day of good weather, but in this rainy weather with no fieldwork to be done there was no need to trouble oneself to draw the water for a bath, they said. There were families in the farm homes who did nothing and ate nothing from morning to night but who only slept.

The cat went out each day and returned to stalk around the house with muddy feet and drippy body. Not only that—one day the cat brought a frog back in its mouth, and then day after day the cat brought more frogs that had grown sluggish with the cold. His wife would scream and flee. No matter how much she scolded, the cat would not stop bringing frogs. The wife did not stop screaming. The frogs died on the parlor floor and exposed their pale-white underbellies. The cat thought of the house as a wilderness. And so the house became like a wilderness.

One day the farmhand at the house next door saw the two dogs catch and eat one of their chickens. The man beat the dogs roundly, and they slunk home. When the wife went to apologize to the neighbors, she found the wealthy old farmer's wife, who had never learned smooth talk, in an unexpectedly ill mood. She would like to have the dogs tied up all the time from now on. If the dogs had to be exercised, because they were idle people anyway, they could very well walk the dogs themselves. "The dogs come into the garden and scatter their droppings about. They ravage the fields and paddies. At night they are noisy with barking. It wakes the children. What's more, it's unbearable to have them eat a fine chicken that began to lay eggs only last week. They're just like wolves. If they come into my garden again, I'll beat them for sure because there are lots of chickens in the garden and out." Exasperated for other reasons as well, she raged on at the dogs in a harsh, hysterical voice. The voice reached his ears where he sat in his home. The elderly woman had found it very unpleasant that the owner of those dogs did not pay her the respect that the other village people did. Oddly enough, her simple woman's interpretation of the fact that neither husband nor wife did any fieldwork led her to infer that her new neighbors lived a life of luxury. The two young, growing dogs should therefore be chained up every day. The next few days he took the dogs out himself for their exercise. It was hard for one man to lead two dogs. Then he had to carry an umbrella. The road was very muddy. When he thought of that statement, "You're a man of leisure; if they need exercise, you walk them," he smiled sadly as he strode. Those big, young dogs were not at all satisfied with five or six blocks of walk. They wearied of the regular road. Spirits overflowing, they tugged mightily at their leashes and dragged him staggering toward the rice-paddy dike paths, soaking their legs in dew as they plunged into the fields. One of the dogs in particular had great strength and the spirit of a fighting dog. He thought the old lady next door should have seen how it was from her house. Once she really did. One night, chained up and hot tempered for lack of exercise, the dogs gulped their food at one bite without a sidelong glance, and then, startled by something, they began to yelp their complaints in long lonesome howls.

The sound traveled through space misty and dimly white from the rain. When it reached the hills opposite the house, it reverberated back in an oppressive, echoing howl. Not recognizing their own yelps, the dogs howled back more furiously. The baying resounded again from the mountains. The dogs would not stop howling. Trying to calm them, he called their names, but the terrified dogs shrank back, frightened even of their master. Helpless, he could only leave them to their howling. The piercing, inconsolable sound permeated and shook the depths of his heart, constricting his chest with a flutter of apprehension. For a time each evening the dogs howled frightfully like this. One time on hearing the dogs, a child shouted out from that rich neighbor's house, "What awful dogs!" The old lady had her daughter say that, he perceived with exasperation at the incorrigible woman. A cat is a cat. It will catch frogs, and it will prowl languidly on muddy feet through the parlor at dusk. Sometimes he would kick it and send it flying. Day after day the smoke from the smoldering firewood, damp from the prolonged rains, was carried by the wind to creep perversely into the parlor, where it overspread the ceiling.

In the daytime when the dogs were docile, hordes of hens who had laid eggs at the rich man's house next door would cackle, "Cut, cut, cut, cut, kadaw," in voices to drive a man frantic. More than an hour they would carry on. One day one of the chickens strayed into his yard. Seeing the dogs were tied up, others followed, clutch after clutch trooping triumphantly into his garden. There unperturbed, they began to pick the grains of rice left scattered by the dogs when they ate. The angry dogs gave chase. The hens withdrew a bit. The irate dogs began to bark, but one flock of hens was not alarmed. The dogs darted at the group of intruders but were brought up fast by the chains on their collars. The more they struggled, the tighter were the chains around their necks. The chains became so tangled that finally neither dog could move. They howled in appeal. He went out in the rain and tried to untangle the impenetrable snarl. The dogs pawed happily at his chest with their muddy feet. Because they would not stand still, the chains became more tangled yet. No matter how annoyed he became, he could not get them loose. The dogs set to yelping. The chickens that had once been chased came calmly back and hopped onto the veranda, where they deposited their filthy watery droppings. When he spread his arms and chased them, the chickens squawked loudly. That malicious woman had put them up to it only to tease him, he thought. She pretended not to notice while she watched the whole scene from beyond the hedge. His wife, looking on, was about to shout some spiteful abuse at the chickens, but he stopped her. Not that he thought it wrong for her to do that, but he was too cowardly and obsequious to do such a thing. At heart he was more indignant than his wife. Two slovenly little girls from another neighboring house, carrying a baby at that and having no place to play out of the rain, pushed their way into his house with feet and clothing muddier than the cat. The piggyback baby cried. All three wanted everything they saw. The oldest one, aged thirteen and named Okuwa, already exhibited the special characteristics of a woman. She took to his wife as companion and filled her ears with sharp-tongued gossip, including slander about the rich family next door. These were children of the family at whose house they some-times bathed, and so it was hard to drive them away, his wife said. In truth his wife wanted these children as conversational compan-ions. Still there seemed to be times when his wife found them trou-blesome, too. When she said "Time to go home," the children cried out together, "No way. Everybody's asleep at home. The door's shut. It's all dark. They just tell us to go play at the house down there." *The house down there* meant his house. Surely the children had even more fleas than the cat and the dogs, he thought. Although he was annoyed, the children were still little and he hadn't the heart to scold them as he might have strangers. His wife, apathetic and indifferent to these things, would often send the children out on errands in the rain, saying, "Go buy me some bean curd," or, "The sugar's all gone." If the errands seemed too frequent, he would get nervous and scold her roundly.

When he went next door to the children's home for a bath, the old woman of about seventy, blind and hard of hearing, would ask to hear the news of Tokyo while she was lighting the fire for the bath. It wasn't news of Tokyo; it was news of Edo.[8] She talked dis-connectedly about the time of her girlhood in the "smoky vanished past" (as she herself called it, in the style of Turgenev), about working as a servant in an Edo family mansion, about how in the turmoil of the Meiji Restoration her lord became a municipal official in Kōfu, to no avail, or about how that year was so bad they could not properly perform the Sannō religious festival. She asked him about the old Edo she had seen and could still see before her eyes. She said she had returned to the country at the time of the Restoration, but she had no idea what kind of thing that Restoration really was. "I thought then the whole world was changing, but nothing has changed at all from olden times. If that's so, what was all the uproar about?" she muttered. She hadn't a single notion about the Tokyo that had streetcars running and parks developed. She plied him tirelessly with questions about Edo that he had no way to answer. When she noticed his unfamiliarity with matters of Edo, she rambled on at length with banalities about the golden age of her family at the time of her youth, about her stupid son who was now head of the household, about how as a penny-pincher without property it was impossible to keep up decent relations with the neighbors, and then, remembering that the children often went over there to play, she asked whether they were a nuisance, and what business was he in anyway. She demanded equally lengthy replies to these questions. He was such a poor talker that he did not know how to respond. She was so hard of hearing anyhow, she probably could not hear whatever he did answer. He wanted to yell, "That doesn't interest me. What do other people's affairs matter to me?" He did not understand what this old woman's tedious conversation was all about, but it was more than enough to make him gloomy. She looked at him with an expression of supplication for companionship (an expression that was half dead and the other half insufficient for a dog). She had lost her sight completely at the age of fifty-six, but she stared up at him, stared through him, with two eyes that bespoke her present misfortune. The fire for the bath flickered a while and flared up. It lit up this old stooped-over woman who held a long stick of firewood in one hand and looked like a witch muttering some curse as she floated clearly against the darkness in the big storeroom of the spacious farmhouse.

When he stepped out of the tub, the night breeze caressed his skin, newly freshened by the bath. But when he returned home, he saw that under the light of the hanging lamp with its sooty chimney his wife was reading a letter that seemed to be from her mother at the old family home. Apparently she did not want to show it to him, and she quickly rolled it up lengthwise and put it away. Frowning excessively, she stared right at him and made as if to sigh, her eyes glistening with tears as she gazed. She seemed to be either threatening or imploring. He knew he would not get to read that letter. It was unpleasant for him, but it must be something important to his women. Maybe they were complaining of the bitter poverty his women shared. . . . There was another woman who came to weep in his house. She was nearly forty and named Okinu. She was the woman who had led them to this house and helped them with the move into the home when they first came. As a result, she was a woman who subsequently came and went quite often in their home. She cried a good deal as she set forth her life history. Okinu had wandered into this village after a variety of life experiences. Because people listened with curiosity the first time this woman told her life story, Okinu would forever keep repeating one of those tales. In the end, he became irritated whenever he saw Okinu's face. More mysteriously, looking at her face began to give him a dull stomachache. . . .

Under the floor the dogs were attacked incessantly by fleas. Chasing fleas, the dogs shook their bodies, rattling their chains with a clattering noise he could hear. He sympathized more with the dogs who were tormented by fleas than he did with the story of Okinu's life. He felt countless numbers of fleas wriggling on his own back, on his sides, on his neck, and in the hair of his head. . . .

Every day he looked at the sky and wondered whether it wouldn't clear off even though it was all rain early on. Why did he stare at the sky in the evening? Would the stars come out as he looked across the heavens? Far from stars, there was nothing but white mist on the fields, and the sky was utterly heavy.

The combination or permutation of trivial, monotonous events repeated itself with daily monotony. Once linked to the state of his body and mind, the combination became something altogether melancholy and pessimistic. The rain never stopped. As of today, how many days had it been? Was it five days, ten days, two weeks, or just one week? He did not know. No matter how many days. However many it may have been, how many indistinguishable, monotonous, oppressive, tedious days it was. Would a man in prison pass so many days like this? Oh, that's it! In the shade, whether in May or in the middle of August, there's not a single green leaf, and only the stalks stagger out aimlessly like vines. That's the life of those rose bushes alongside the well for this house. He thought about the roses again. Not only about the roses: sitting habitually in front of his desk, he thought of the anguish of those shaded roses as life itself.

For roses, how pathetic they were as roses. . . . In fact, since one of those deformed flowers blossomed and brought tears to his eyes, nice flowers had blossomed daily, blossomed proudly, but now in this long-continuing rain the petals were all wrinkled like pieces of paper. Soaking wet, they crumbled—crumbled as they bloomed.

*   *   *

For some time now, but only in the dead of night, he had been granted solace and serenity. Only at night when there were no chickens, the dogs were loosed from their chains, and he could imagine them romping spiritedly on the rice-paddy dikes—only then did he feel a sense of relief as he lay in his bed.

But one night it happened: someone called to his house from outside. Sitting at his desk oppressed by his thoughts, he opened a door on the veranda and peered out. A swarthy man was standing in the road beyond the hedge and ditch. Whoever it was, he was calling him arrogantly. Maybe it was a policeman, he thought.

"Is that your dog?"

"Yes. Why?"

"I'm scared of him. I can't get by."

A village like this, a village that fears dogs—there are few like it in the world, he thought. Someone in the village had explained that it was because there were so many mad dogs around here. One of his dogs was a pure Japanese dog.[9]

"It's all right. He looks frightening, but he's gentle."

"What's all right? I'm afraid, and I can't get past."

"He's not a mad dog. He's not even barking, is he?"

"That may be so for the dog's owner. If you're not the owner, he's frightening. How about coming out and tying him up?"

Whoever he was, that fellow had such an arrogant tone just because he felt masked by darkness. The thought made him indignant. Suddenly grabbing a cane there at hand but without opening his umbrella, he dashed into the road. The rain was no more than a drizzle. The unknown man grumbled on about something. "If that dog is not tied up somehow, I won't be able to get past," he insisted. Strange how he feared that dog, and strange how haughty he was. "That's a gentle dog. He's only a puppy, so he's friendly, and he runs along with anyone passing by," he said in defense of his dog. For him dogs were innocent creatures. This guy was a tyrant. He was himself a righteous man. What this man said was entirely unreasonable, he thought, and he called out loudly in abuse at the man. His wife came out to the porch to see what was happening. Observing the state of things, she apologized repeatedly to the passerby in the dark. That made her husband even angrier.

"Shut up. He's a mean one. There's nothing to apologize for. The dog hasn't been bad. This guy is a coward. If he's not a child or a robber, though . . ."

"What, you say he's a robber?"

"Don't you call him a robber! All I said was that a guy this much afraid of a dog who is wagging his tail meekly and not making a sound looks like a robber."

He intended in the end to beat up the guy. They were ten or twelve yards apart and quarreling. Behind the stranger a lantern appeared. Someone spoke to the fellow as the lantern was approaching. They're partners, he decided at once. What if they come close and say something? he wondered, readying his cane for defense.

"Excuse us, please. My dad has had too much to drink."

On the contrary, the man with the lantern was apologizing to him. As soon as he knew the other fellow was drunk, he got foolish himself. He could not laugh. With a feeling that was hard to explain, he swung the cane that he was holding ready, and he brought it down hard on his dog, who was wagging his tail innocently in front of him. Surprised by the beating, the dog howled and ran into the house. The dog that wasn't beaten followed in flight. He stood there amazed, clicked his tongue, threw his cane down into the ditch, and went hastily into the house. The two dogs were hiding far back under the floor. When they saw that their master had come in through the garden, they set up a thin, mournful wail, a howl of appeal. Although he had thrown away the cane, his hands, still clenched, were sticky and wet with sweat.

"You'll just see. I'll get the villagers, and we'll kill those dogs," the drunk was saying as he was led away by the young man with the lantern.

From that night on, the drunkard's parting shot was a source of great worry to him. When he wondered whether the villagers really would kill his dogs, he remembered the words that the fat woman who cried over her life story had once told him. "In this village, when it's winter, they kill and eat dogs. Be careful. Your dogs are young and fat and just right. Maybe it's a joke, but that's what they were saying."

The more he thought about the cane he had just thrown away, the more he regretted it. It was carved with flowers like arabesques and had a silver knob. Although it was not anything special to merit such regret, he deeply regretted the loss. The next day, ostensibly to exercise his dogs, he walked in search of his cane more than ten blocks down the road that followed the ditch. The water in the ditch had become so muddy from the daily rains that it was hopeless: the cane was nowhere to be seen. He had kept secret from his wife the fact that he had lost his cane that way. It was truly something to be ashamed of.

There were times when he worried that the events of the cane and the drunkard's parting words were simply strange. It would have been better if he had beaten up the man—sometimes in his bed, though, he had no regrets about it. . . . Weren't the dogs being abused? To leave them out at night made him worry. Irritated, he would prick up his ears: the dogs were howling. Hastily he would open the door, go out on the porch, and whistle. The dogs would come back from somewhere. So it was some other dog howling. There were times, though, when he whistled and called their names, but they were in no hurry to come back. The barking continued more furiously. He could not stand it. His wife would say, "Those aren't our dogs, are they? Aren't there dogs howling everywhere?" She took no notice of him at first, but he fretted so much that his wild fancies all too soon infected his wife. Both were caught in fear and trembling like people under a spell. What's more, for some reason the flame of the lamp began to flicker and flutter ceaselessly every evening. No matter how they tried to fix it, it would not be fixed. It annoyed him to stare at the lamp wick flickering in the same way that he saw the anxiety in his heart. One night the dog's barking was no ordinary thing, and, when he went into the garden to see, Leo was barking at him as if to raise an alarm. In the distance he could hear Fratty (perhaps) howling in distress. Chasing after Leo, he called, "Fratty, Fratty," and searched for the dog from the sound of the howls. Shortly he saw the dog running toward him, and he noted that its body and half its face were covered with mud. Fratty must have been thrashed and shoved into the mud. From somewhere he heard the sound of a man laughing as if in triumph. . . . After that he let the dogs out for only an hour or two at night and then tied them up again. He also moved the place to fasten their chains to the earthen floor of the entry hall. . . . To tie them in a corner of the garden open to passersby would not be safe. However, when the dogs knew that they were being called home to be tied up, they would not come at his call. If they did come, they would run dodging around the garden, watching their owners' faces. They were very hard to catch. If he tried to attract them by offering food, they would not go near their chains. As offspring of a fighting dog, Fratty had sturdy feet and big fangs. One night he gnawed through the middle of his chain and dug a big hole in the ground under the floor to escape from the four-walled enclosure. He squeezed his big body through the hole and ran around in the night, playing happily in the mud and dragging half a chain dangling from his neck. To inform the master of this, and because he, too, wanted to be freed, Leo set to barking furiously.

In the daytime he thought better of his nighttime worries about the dogs. He had to admit this was a kind of obsession. The dogs probably thought they could protect themselves by their own power. . . . It was shameful and heartless of him to think such nonsense about the dogs. But yet at night: "My dogs are being stolen. They're being killed! For sure!" The dogs were no longer just dogs to him—they had become symbols of something. To say that you love is surely to say that you suffer. He could not forget the cane, either. When he was not worrying about the dogs, he would often lie in his bed and imagine that cane with its silver-fitted knob, now floating, now sinking, at the mercy of the water flowing through the muddy ditch, its top end submerged slightly from the weight of the metal fitting, being carried to some far shoreless place.

*   *   *

When he thought the rain was letting up one day, the next day it would pour all the harder. The day after that it would revert to a drizzle. Then again the day after that it would pour. . . . This on-again, off-again rain, was it going to rain forever? . . . How many days, day after day without end, it rained. . . . It rained as if to rot his soul and body. . . . It rained as if to rot the very world.

> Anything and everything . . .
>   If rot it will, rotted it is . . .
> Rotten as it wills to be . . .
>   Rotting, rotting . . .
> Yours the head it is that will . . .
>   Be the first to be rotten . . .
>   . . . .
>   . . . .
>   . . . .
>   . . . .
>   . . . .
>   . . . .

A voiceless chorus from outside his house, from all directions, it came floating dim and chilling, filling the house. When he looked to see, it was the rhythmic patter of the falling rain. Whether he gazed out the north window, or whether he gazed out the south, the languid rhythm of the rain repeated and repeated endlessly. . . . It rained without hope that it would ever stop.

*   *   *

There was a hill there.

When you looked up from his porch, the branches of the pines and the branches of the cherries in his garden poked out from the sides and mingled to create a vaulted space. The curving lines of the branches and leaves arched down until they were met and held at the bottom by the straight line of the hedge top. You could say they formed a green framework. A picture frame it was: the hill could be seen in the distance by looking through the bottom of the hole framed as for a picture.

When did he first notice the hill? No matter, it drew his attention. He grew intensely fond of that hill. Now, on these long dreary days, rainy day after rainy day, every time he turned his eyes, the windows of his sunken heart, outward and away from the anguish of life, the thing reflected in those eyes was the hill.

Even more when he looked through the dome-shaped frame made by the branches and leaves of his garden trees, the hill itself suggested a different world. He felt it was just far enough away, more dreamy than real, more real than a dream, yet depending on the shading of the rain, sometimes rather nearer to him, other times retreating into the distance. Then at times it would become blurry as if you were looking through frosted glass.

The hill somehow resembled the profile of a woman's body. Countless curving lines ran each at its own fancy with undulating elegance and carefree feeling to form a three-dimensional shape thrust up in arches. The figure took its place precisely within the green frame. That is to say that, spread out boldly, the scene was beautiful with no trace of excess, like a story finely balanced between beginning and ending, in harmony unconstrained. It smiled serenely with a quiet yet lively beauty that somehow recalled the sculpture of ancient Greece. It was like a woman's lips in a noble, winsome smile. On the summit stood a mixed forest. The trees spread their branches as if opening their fingers to the sky, and from where he stood they looked to be about an inch to about five inches tall—sometimes he felt it was one, sometimes five. The trees, standing uniformly like a short haircut, seemed to grow in a beautiful hairline on the bare hill's brow. Tiny ups and downs in the line where trees met sky set a rhythm of endless delight. In one place where the trees seemed a little thinner the monotone was broken by a thatch roof of the lone house that belonged to the forest owner. On the flank of the hill that rose lushly like green velvet were the vertical lines of several hundred trees spaced at regular intervals, drawing conspicuous vertical stripes that slid down the face of the slope in arcs parallel from top to bottom. They were cut faces of moss-green agate. Maybe they were seedling plots of cedar or cypress or something—whatever it was, it was nice. What made the hill so pictorial, so ornamental, was that remarkable effect of the trivial man-made quality unexpectedly present in the midst of nature, like the roof of a house in the middle of a forest. In this case how much was untouched nature and what was man-made could not be distinguished. Human labor at work on nature had melted happily into nature. How beautiful it was! Looking at it, he felt a gentle longing. There is the world of art where I want to live, he thought. . . .

"What are you staring at like that?" his wife asked.

"Oh, that hill. Just that hill over there."

"What are you doing that for?"

"No special reason . . . It's pretty, isn't it? It's beyond description. . . ."

"Yes. It's like a kimono."

His wife thought the hill was wearing a tastefully sober kimono of striped crepe.

It was a picture drawn in green monochrome. But within the monochrome were virtually all colors in equal excellence. The more he looked, the more its abundance overflowed. At first glance it was only a mass of green, but section by section there was infinite variety in the greens. It was woven of a single color tone that was not easily denied. As an emerald, for example, had its own key shade of green; yet each face when polished revealed a different color and effect.

His eyes habitually rested in pleasure on the hill.

"Oh, for clarity of spirit! Clarity of spirit!" The hill confronting his eyes accosted him with these words.

One day after the rain had stopped suddenly the night before, morning dawned through thin clouds. Shortly before noon the shape of the sun, blurred by clouds, showed dimly yellow in the depths of the sky.

On the pretext of preparing the kimono robes for autumn his wife announced that she was going to Tokyo. Rather than considering the weather in the sky, she thought to go before a change in the weather of her husband, so she finished an early lunch and took off hurriedly for the Tokyo that she longed for every night. It would not be wrong to say that her spirits arrived in Tokyo three hours before her body.

He stood vacantly alone on his porch and stared unwittingly at the hill that was his habitual focus. He noticed that the hill was somehow different overall from its customary appearance. It was not only light and weather. He did not at all understand why. Looking at it from all angles, he remembered at last. He rummaged for his glasses in the desk drawer. Although he was severely nearsighted, he had recently been forgetting to wear his glasses. For no reason whatever, his glasses had become almost useless to him. He never noticed that it made him more depressed without his glasses. When he put them on, heaven and earth were entirely different. Today he could see something delightful between heaven and earth. That was because the sky was so bright. He could see the hill clearly. Yes, it did look different from usual—there were flocks of birds over the forest. The hillside, washed in pallid sunlight from above, shone in a glossy greenish gold that gave a polish to the rounded ups and downs. The vertical stripes made by hundreds of seedling trees in plots—yes, that's where the difference lay. When you looked at the space between the vertical stripes, one section on the left became the pivot of a fan-shaped triangle opening upward, where the all-green ground changed for some reason to a dark purple. What, so changed without my noticing? Why has it changed? He had to think it was mysterious. He stared at the hilltop for a while as if some great thing, rare to the world, had come to pass. It made him think the hill was a fairyland. Beautiful and minute, wasn't it even more miraculous today?

After watching for a time, it seemed as though the boundary between the purple and the green on the hillside was swelling upward on its own, and the purple area was spontaneously inching outward. Staring so hard that the space between his eyebrows ached, he saw there a tiny, tiny midget who, stooping and squirming, was hard at work harvesting those green areas. Between the rows of seedling trees the farmer was growing some crop. To his eyes, though, it appeared not that crops were being reaped but rather that the purple areas were swelling.

He gazed into the mysterious depths revealed by his distance glasses; it was like watching a fairy at work in fairyland. Inspired with a feeling of transcendence for this little hill, he stared unblinking with a sense of yearning, like a child looking through a kaleidoscope. At length he took his ashtray and his cushion to the porch where he stared untiringly at the purple earth climbing of its own accord. The purple was flowing upward. Step by step it rose. The purple area was encroaching quickly and continuously onto the edge of the green. The pale sun grew slowly brighter. Through thin cracks that were clearing slowly in the western clouds, the light of the setting sun broke out abruptly in a flowing mass to strike the summit. The hill glowed suddenly in a beam of dancing light. Wasn't it like colored footlights playing on the hilltop? On the summit the fairy and the forest drew long, deep shadows on the ground. The fairyland scene floated more clearly. The newly risen purple earth looked to be calling out in concert, sounding forth like the lowest tones of an organ. The thatch roof amid the trees on the summit became glassy, and from its midst a straight line of thick, white smoke ascended endlessly like smoke from a censer. Now in ecstasy, he was king of fairyland.

The glory of heaven and earth, the rapture of nature herself vanished like a momentary dream when the setting sun disappeared into the clouds. From those clouds the sun dropped further into darker clouds and the range of mountains on the distant horizon. Bright, gleaming light lingered as a memory in a narrow crack in the clouds.

When he perceived it, the hill had become entirely purple. . . . The fairy's work was done. . . . He watched in fascination as the vista slipped away in total darkness. Yet he thought his eyes could still see that fairyland hill there in the darkness as clearly as before.

Soon the hill that he thought he could see forever faded from his sight. . . .

* * *

When he came to himself and was no longer king of fairy-land, the darkness had closed in from the distant fields and the mountains. Darkness crammed tightly into every corner of every room. All about him was dark. Now he had to light the lamp. He lit a match from his ashtray. Then he went through the house striking matches everywhere in search of the lamp. Wherever it had been put, he did not find it there.

Recently he often misplaced things like that. Even things not as large as the lamp, things rather that he had just been holding in his hand, had just been using—his pen, his pipe, his chopsticks—those kinds of things disappeared somewhere without warning. Things that vanished for a time would later reappear suddenly, emerging unforeseen from places that might well be considered habitual for them or from silly places that he ought to have thought to search carefully. When he searched, perversely they were nowhere to be seen. That kind of thing happens to everybody. Surely it does not happen so often to others, though, as it had been happening recently to him. It must be at least two or three times a day now. The unexpected, how important did he view it every time that it occurred? He felt it was something to call inexplicable, even myste-rious, or rather, fateful. He could conceive of someone invisible there, just then hiding those things. His personal belongings, two or three of them a day, were vanishing from him abruptly, he felt. "Not again?" he thought when it came to the lamp. He abandoned the idea of looking for it for the present. Oddly enough the sooner he abandoned the search the sooner it would turn up. He groped for a candlestick that he had noticed on the bureau. Taking it down, he lit it, a dark reddish, flickering flame.

On nights like this in the country and alone with all the shutters on all sides not yet closed, he was apprehensive. . . . In his fancy something strange and unknowable, a different sort of intruder not of known identity like a burglar, an unnatural intruder, had leave to come and go freely. The storage compartments for the sliding-door shutters were perforce at the corners of the house. For him—a natural coward and now so much more so that no ordinary person other than a nervous child could ever understand how cowardly let alone sympathize—for him it was enough to make him think that every corner of the house was a seat of anxiety. When he went to stand and slide the shutter doors one by one, the grating sound crept heavily over the fields and echoed through the void. Were they frightened by the noise? His two dogs, quiet and seemingly asleep, emerged dimly white from under the floor and promptly resumed their perpetual evening baying. . . . He closed the ten or so storm doors on the porch. When he went to shut those on the shorter porch at the other side of the house, he stepped through the six-mat parlor on his way. There in the alcove standing prim and quiet it was: the lamp! Shouldn't he surely have looked there in his earlier search? Was this another case of those usual little things, this big one? . . . Wondering, he felt close to terror. . . . Stupefied, he could not lay a hand on the lamp. The instant he reached for it unsuspecting, he imagined, what if it vanished abruptly again in front of his eyes. . . . Repressing this ludicrous idea, he stuck out his hand decisively for the lamp. Luckily, the lamp was real.

When he had lit the lamp, finished closing the shutters, and returned to the charcoal brazier, wanting some tea, he noticed there was no hot water. The charcoal had burned to a white ash. The teakettle that had been boiling and humming through the day, and the water in it, were dead cold. Naturally so. He had added no charcoal to the fire burning when his wife left the house about eleven o'clock. For him foolishly there had been nothing, no charcoal, nothing in the world, not even himself, other than fairyland on the hill. . . . The dogs by good chance had ended their howling unexpectedly soon this evening, he thought, but they began sniffing around vigorously. They were pressing for their supper. The pangs of hunger troubled not only the dogs and the cat: his own uneasy feelings of cowardice, the chilly feeling, too; one cause for these feelings was hunger, he knew for sure. But tonight to eat supper he would first have to boil rice. . . . His wife announcing her sudden departure for Tokyo had apologized at length that she could not prepare things because of the expedience of the train schedules. On the way to the station she would stop by and ask Okinu to do it, she said. But only last night he had borne grimly through the hearing of Okinu's life story for the tenth time, so he left it that he would cook the rice himself if his wife would wash and prepare it in water for boiling. Sitting now in front of the fireless brazier, he thought it would be all right to skip eating rice for one night. But importuned by his dogs, he pictured the hunger that forever plagued them, and he knew he would have to cook. He had carelessly let night fall, and he would have to start the preparations at once. . . . Recalling his wife's parting words, he took off for the kitchen.

He freed the dogs from their chains and called them to the kitchen. The kitchen with its many dark corners was too lonesome for him alone. As if they understood their master's feelings, the two dogs, Fratty and Leo, snuggled up and sat by their master, who was squatting on the earthen floor. The cat came catlike to the front of the raised wooden floor and crouched near his face. His strange family formed a mute and forlorn circle in front of the high clay oven built in the shape of a horse's hoof, but there at last he could feel secure. He lit the fire. The kindling alone burned well. The blazing fire warmed his heart. The flame soon died, though, and the two or three sticks of firewood he threw on would not catch fire. In vain he burned the kindling. The long rains had soaked the firewood. The kindling, he should have prepared far more than this! With the little bit remaining he fed the fire five or six times until there were no scraps left. He thought of the can of kerosene and fetched it. Gingerly he sloshed some on the firewood. The kerosene erupted and burned in a big ball of feathery flame floating three or four inches above the hearth. It blazed like wild-fire. It burned nervously. It burned much like his own sense of agitation, that of a man with absolutely no power of concentration. It burned at one gasp, without prudence, ignoring reason, and yet without power. Soon it tired and collapsed into embers. The kerosene burned as long as it lasted, and, when it had burned up, the big ball of flame split into many small dots trailing one by one over the surface of the firewood. As he wondered whether those flickering little green flames had ignited the wood, they went out. The smoke with its special dusky smell and dusky color, smoke that left one with the heavy feeling that follows some stupid outburst of emotion, rose listlessly in one sudden clump. Surprised, the cat stood up. The two dogs gravely turned their heads aside in unison. After he had tried the same thing again, he discovered that it burned longest if you poured the kerosene onto the hearth rather than dousing it on the firewood. (In fact he had discovered the burning properties of kerosene through the same kind of diligent research into morbid details as he had used on the particulars that embodied his own irritable feelings.) He took out from the stove the blackened, smoldering pieces of firewood that showed surface traces of the burning oil. Resolutely pouring the remaining kerosene over the ashes in the bottom of the fire pit, he then stacked the firewood on top of the hearth. He tossed in a burning match. A little black smoke and a large flame spurted freely under the iron pot. Bit by bit the wood caught fire.

"Well done! Well done!" Without thinking he said the words to himself. Hearing the low voice, Fratty lifted his narrow, pointed muzzle and looked up at his master's face as if to ask the meaning. The firewood ignited at last, piece by piece, into a promising flame like the vigorous emotions of a man moved to the depths of his heart. Oh, how happy a thing it was, the burning flame! He and his dogs alike stared at the fire with shining eyes as if they were barbarians worshipping a god therein. His eyes riveted on the fire, he felt with no connection that he could see the retreating figure of his wife, very small, as small as the fairy, there somehow amid a massive crowd within the burning flames. . . . Not mere imagination, this was like to a vision flickering before his eyes. . . . He wondered whether this was what a vision was, when a fancy struck him unexpectedly: Oh, she's gone to the movies, he thought intuitively. Then, half on his own accord, his fancy turned toward those busiest places in Tokyo. In the next moment—supposing, wasn't he himself walking among those crowds even now? That impossibility struck him as the most commonplace of ideas. . . . He? Here? Squatting dejectedly in front of the hearth in a corner of his dim, cold kitchen, and gazing intently at the fire that would not burn as he wanted? He, crouching surrounded by his dogs and cat, staring like an ascetic doing continuous penance into the fire that was burning his very mood? If this were not the true he, and the real he were somewhere else, wasn't this he here merely a shadow he? His feelings teemed and seethed. When they had permeated him, a cold sensation ran like a flash down his spine. All his things, himself, the fire on the hearth, the two dogs, the cat, or, if he looked up, also the rice tub, the bucket, the lamp, the drain board and everything else—wouldn't they all just vanish? he feared. He looked around, and it was frightful. On the walls above, three shadows of himself and the two dogs were spread out on three sides of him—projections of large, black images that flickered, now small, now large, at the mercy of the flames. The shadows moved incessantly, looking little by little to be nearing the live body each reflected, to be about to swallow up that body. Suddenly on his left Leo rose and slipped outside through the door that was left open a crack to let out the smoke. The dog began barking at once in short, shrill yelps. Pricking up his ears at his brother's barks, Fratty ran out after him. Their barking voices mingled. . . . As if they were telling him someone unseen was approaching. Fear brought him to his feet. But the dogs stopped quickly and, looking disgusted, returned soberly. They dropped down in their original places next to him.

He did not question the dogs' behavior. Composing himself, he stood on tiptoe and peeked tentatively out through a knothole in the door. Peering through the indistinct darkness, he saw approaching, curiously with no sound of footsteps, the small, black shadow of a person emerging from behind the shadowy trunk of the persimmon tree! What a relief that the figure was small. No doubt about it, though, it was someone who made no sound of footsteps! When the figure approached into the lamplight streaming out through the crack in the door, there was nothing queer to it at all. It was surely Okuwa, the thirteen-year-old girl from the house next-door who often came to play. But then? That girl, who always came chattering, dashing, and calling in a loud voice from far away, or shouting the dog's names, or whistling, but who never came at night to play, she shouldn't be coming tonight like this, he thought. That Okuwa, coming so airily, that was strange. To confirm it, he called to her.

"Okuwa?"

"Oh! You startled me! Are you there, Uncle?"

The one who answered was Okuwa sure enough. Responding to his curiously calm outcry, Okuwa's answer was really exaggerated. The voice was enough to make him jump, he who had been suffering from loneliness. Reassured by her voice, he opened the door. There stood Okuwa with a strange expression looming brightly.

"What happened, Okuwa? . . . Did they scold you at home?"

Okuwa didn't answer right away. Then after a bit the child began chattering on as usual. Is Uncle making rice? When is Auntie coming home? Then, as if she chanced to remember, Okuwa said, "Yeah, I forgot. We're heating the bath at home now. . . . Because of the good weather everybody went out to the fields. They're heating it now. You can come in a little while. . . . You're a funny one, Uncle. You want to take a bath only when there isn't one. When there is one, you don't want it, do you?" As she spoke, she ran off restlessly toward home. He thought that tonight for a change he would like to have Okuwa go on chattering. When the girl had gone ten or twelve yards, she called back, "Uncle, it's raining again."

It was the same old Okuwa as always. . . . She had given him a breath of relief, he thought. . . . When he heard about the bath, the reason for Okuwa's silent footsteps came to him by chance. He recalled his wife's warning to watch out for Okuwa's family. Too much firewood stacked outside had been missing recently. Sometimes in the morning two or three sticks, dropped from bundles, were found by the well.

He understood. It was nothing to him, though. Still, Okuwa's words: "Uncle, it's raining again." Okuwa's shadowy figure popping out by chance just then from behind the trunk of the persimmon tree. They lingered in his heart. Yet, too, in the rice he was taking such pains to prepare, the odor of kerosene permeated, either on the utensils or on his hands. (He poured a cup of tea and peered into it under the lamplight. Nothing was floating there.) No matter what, he could drink only a cup. That night it was not only the rice. The collar of his bedclothes, his pillow, his shoulders, the inside of his mouth, the air itself, his cat sleeping next to him trembling against his arms, its tiny heart throbbing, everything stank of kerosene. Whether it was there or not, even very faintly clinging to the bowls of rice and the tea he had drunk so amply, the odor agitated him intensely. . . . When he thought the stink was there, it was there. When he thought the stink was absent, it was absent. . . . When he thought of striking a match to hunt for the lamp that evening, or of fooling around with kerosene to light the fire, when he said it was interesting to see the little glittering line of sparks on the bottom of the kettle as he took it off the hearth, or he remarked that the room reeked of kerosene, or when it came to him even that Okuwa had come for firewood, all these things gave him a premonition that the house might catch fire that night. . . . The makings were already there in the air; the smell of kerosene offended his senses, for example. That's what he thought. "Well— let it burn. Fire is exhilarating. No, no." If he thought so, the house really would burn, he felt. . . . If there were a fire, the dogs would die, he thought, unless he let them off their chains right at first. It wouldn't do to panic in that situation. Shouldn't he let them off now as a precaution? he wondered. . . . "It's all right. There won't be a fire," he thought, too. Anyway, he wanted the night to end quickly. He had other concerns beyond the thought of fire; he wondered whether his wife really did go to the movies. He pictured again the figure of that fairy at work through the day. He thought of the setting sun suddenly lighting up the hill, and the color again made him think of fire. . . . He felt as if he were thinking it before he fell asleep; yet he thought of it, too, as if it were a dream in his sleep. Whichever it was, he could not, when he later tried, make it out.

*   *   *

It was one evening after the rain had lifted. It may have been many days after, or maybe it was a normal time interval in our story. Which it was we do not know. At least it was a night after the rain had cleared. The big, round moon had risen quietly over the hill as if emerging from the trapdoor of a stage setting.

That night the two dogs barked more sadly and fiercely than ever.

He went out into the garden to let the two dogs romp. From there he continued out from the garden. The moon in the sky delighted him. Almost overhead it was. The eastern sky had cleared. As you turned west, the sky became cloudy, and at the horizon it was jet black. The broad sky had been shaded with a paintbrush. He looked up intently at the moon. He walked. The sound of a distant water wheel, "Katon, katon, katon," echoed across the fields. The moonlight streamed delicately over the woman's profile made by fairyland hill and bathed it in radiance. Again and again he walked back and forth along the road in front of his house. With the moon behind him he gazed at his shortened shadow. Then he walked not seeing his shadow but staring at the center of the immeasurable moon. The two dogs followed after, romping together and frolicking joyfully. When he stopped, they ran round him again and again. He gave ear to the gurgling of the water. Below his feet at the roadside where he stood, the flowing water in the narrow ditch splintered the moonlight. The water— black, shining, and quivering noisily—was like a big sheet of isinglass. Beyond the southern hills the ten-something last train from K to H went by, rocking and resounding through a corner of the moonlit world.[10] The sound lingered. Sounds made him nostalgic. He turned his eyes to the hills in the south beyond the fields made bright as day by the moon—no, a rainy day was darker than this. . . . There where you could hear noises beyond the hills were big, bustling, glorious cities. . . . There from the windows of the houses the lights sparkled in glittering clusters. . . . Abruptly and from no direct connection but only from the echo of the distant train, a fancy struck him: that is to say, for a moment, a mere moment, the whole sky behind the hills flared red with the after-glow of countless lights, or something. . . . So he thought, but directly it faded. It was truly a mystical moment.

"Am I being nostalgic about the city?"

As he wondered, he looked away from the hills. Then he saw the dark shadow of someone walking toward him on the straight road where he stood. The figure was about two blocks away. He stared as the person passed through a stretch exposed to the moonlight, and he thought it rather ominous. A moonlit night was more dreadful than a dark night, he thought.

Then from the figure, "Wheet!"

One, just one, shrill whistle resounded. With the force of a sud-den gale the two dogs rushed off together toward the shadowy fig-ure. "How disagreeable," was his first thought. The dogs had never before responded to the call of anyone other than their master. Now only tonight they rushed off at the call of this one whistle. In dismay he gave the same kind of shrill whistle.

"Wheet!"

It was to get the dogs to return, and, when they heard his whis-tle, they turned back in confusion as if to heed it.

"Fratty!" The shadowy figure called the dog's name.

"Fratty!" Startled, he called the dog's name, too. Strangely his calling voice was identical to that of the shadowy figure. His own voice instantly carried back the same word, sounding the very echo of the shadow's voice. He felt that the two voices were exactly the same in the expression of that difficult sound. The dogs heard them as identical, too, without a doubt. Once they had run longingly toward the shadow's voice, the dogs failed to re-turn.

He stood in amazement there in the road and stared to verify the shadow. The figure turned off the road by a stone Buddha statue as if to walk a dike path through the rice fields. Then . . .

How curious! The shadowy form vanished suddenly from the bright moonlit fields unobstructed in his view.

"Goodness gracious." Swallowing the words, he raced home through the gate and into the house at top speed.

". . . Nobody in the village should know my dogs' names. That name is hard to pronounce. No, the children know it. But in their local accent they would say, 'Kratty,' for 'Fratty.' Even if they did call, my dogs shouldn't run to anyone else's call than mine. Even if they ran, they should surely come back when I call. This has never happened before." He thought that way to himself. ". . . What was that shadow that vanished from sight so suddenly? . . . Do you suppose I split into two identical selves? Is there really such a thing as sleepwalking sickness? If so, don't I have it? Dogs must have very acute powers to distinguish sounds. They're supposed to have that special ability for perfect recognition of their master's voice. . . ."

The furious beating of his heart continued for more than twenty minutes. For some reason he watched the hands on his watch move and thought of various literary allusions to sleepwalking, or of the dogs, while he waited for his heartbeat to slow down. When it was calm at last, he asked his wife to see whether the dogs were in their customary place under the floor. He could believe they had not come back at all from chasing after that shadow. The dogs were not there. But when his wife called them, they returned, luckily (he thought). He asked whether the moon were still out. The moon was out, was his wife's answer.

The next morning he told his wife for the first time about last night's happening. He had been too frightened to speak of it to anyone during the night. When his wife heard the story, she laughed in ridicule, annoying him. The sudden disappearance of the shadowy figure happened no doubt when whoever it was stooped to pat the heads of the dogs, who had run up affectionately to his feet. Then as it walked along the dike path, the figure was hidden by the stalks of rice. That was his wife's explanation. It did seem like a reasonable explanation, he thought. But the strange fear he had felt at that moment would not go away.

* * *

This happened:

A moth was attracted to his lamp late one night. In this silk cultivating area a lot of these insects had been flying around lately. He just hated them. Once before, when one lit on his lamp, he hit it with a homemade flyswatter. Lying there squashed, the insect delicately quivered its thick antennae, shaped like eyebrows or like the teeth of a comb, and then with a final effort it rolled over, exposing its ghastly soft belly and gingerly moving its six little legs all together as if trying to grasp something. Now and then it raised its belly on the strength of its wings. Again and again the moth methodically repeated the little movements of its antennae, feet, wings, and belly to display for him the agony of its death. A small thing it was, but for him who watched, it was enough to terrify. Ever since, he had been especially disgusted and terrified by this insect.

The moth was covered with gray satiny hairs. It had an oddly small head and tiny eyes of subdued reddish luster projecting gruesomely from the gray blackness. Clumsy it looked, clinging fast, its wings pinned against the top of the shade. The sight of it, wildly waving those heavy wings as in a sudden fit of insanity. The sight of it, playfully flying around the lamp, cool, audacious, tenacious, no matter how many times he drove it away. Writhing for joy in its dance of death near to the lamp, the moth cast a grotesque shadow that darkened more than half the drab, whitish walls. Without making a sound, it fluttered about furiously, turbulently, anxiously, like the clamoring of a noisy crowd. Clumsily evading his attempts to drive it off, the moth escaped finally to the top of the shoji sliding door, where the fluttering of its thick wings resounded against the shoji paper like the steps of a boisterous dance.

When he saw that the moth was quiet, he caught it in a sheet of newspaper. Sliding the door open, he tossed the gruesome insect out. He had learned better than to kill them.

In less than ten minutes that moth (or another) stole back to the lamp from somewhere. The boisterous dance of the wings—dreadful, dark, cumbrous, clamorous—began again. Taking a piece of paper, again he caught it. Again he opened the sliding door and heaved it out.

In less than another ten minutes the moth was back from somewhere for the third time. Whether or not this was the same insect that had threatened him twice before he did not know. He had clutched the other so firmly in the paper that it would hardly be so foolish as to come back, to say nothing of even being expected to survive. This must be a completely different one. Two, three, four times his lamp was attacked. . . . What kind of evil spirit was there in this small flying insect? He had to think there was an evil spirit in it. At that thought it became too frightening for him to catch it again by himself. He deliberately called his wife and had her seize it. Taking from his wife's hand the large sheet of newspaper that held the moth, he folded the paper over again and again to pin the small insect. Then he added another sheet of newspaper and folded it in turn. This time, instead of throwing it out the door, he set it on his desk and laid a heavy old magazine on it.

Relieved at last, he went to bed.

After a bit, unable to sleep, he lit the candle. Just then something fluttered tauntingly past the light. It was the moth!

*　*　*

He could no longer sleep.

First the clocks were too noisy for his ears. He stopped the alarm clock and the wall clock. In his present life a clock was utterly useless and nothing but noisy. When his wife arose every morning, she set the clocks going to the proper time. If she did not hear the sound of a clock in the house, she was uneasy and too lonely. He felt the same way. He often experienced that moment of sharp cessation for whatever reason in the voices of the neighbors, the voices of the dogs, the voices of the chickens, the sound of the wind, the voice of his wife, his own voice or anyone's, or other sounds. That moment for him was lonesome, oppressive, or rather fearsome. He felt then that it would be good, indeed that he was waiting impatiently, for someone or something to raise a voice or make a noise. When there was no sound at all, he would turn to his wife and talk of anything without meaning. Failing that, "Uh, yeah," he would say meaninglessly to himself.

But the sound of the clocks at night struck his ears as too noisy, and he could not sleep. Stirred by the clocks' every momentary noise, his feeling of agitation rose step by step. When he went to bed, he had to stop the clocks. Every morning his wife started the clocks that her husband had stopped. The husband stopped the clocks that his wife had started. Starting clocks and stopping clocks had become their daily morning and evening routine.

When he stopped the sound of the clocks, he began to notice the gurgling from the ditch that ran by his garden. That, he felt, was now preventing him from sleeping. The sound of the water was more intense than normal because of the daily rains. One day he peered into the ditch. How long ago was it? When he moved into this house and took on the care of this abandoned garden, he had cut and dropped a thick branch from the pussy willow that stood by the ditch. The branch, still there in the ditch, blocked the current of water and, like a weir, checked the flow of things like leaves and scraps of paper. The water boiled and seethed noisily over the weir. There was the reason for the sound of turbulent water every night. Jumping to that conclusion and drenched with rain, he plunged into the ditch and pulled the branch from the bottom of the water. Slimy green waterweeds twined around the branch's many little twigs. He pulled the branch up onto the roadside. Peering again into the water, his eyes lit by chance on a long object bobbing up and down as it was borne downstream ten or twelve yards in the flux of leaves, paper scraps, straw litter, and women's hair that had been tangled on the pussy-willow dam.

He looked and saw it was the silver-knobbed cane that he had thrown into the water that night after he clubbed the dog and argued with the drunken fellow.

He was intensely happy to have the cane in hand again by some mysterious chance. Feeling foolish and awkward, he had concealed the loss of the cane from his wife, but in the end he carelessly talked of it. When he thought about it—the sound of that turbulent water must surely have been the voice of the cane. It was the cane telling him its hiding place, so he could go and seek it there.

Holding the cane in one hand, he gazed at the surface of the unhindered water, now flowing steadily. Tonight will be quiet and peaceful, he thought. He was mistaken. Was it noisier than last night? The far-from-quiet gurgling sound, although fainter than before, was still strident in his ears. Like the night before it kept him from sleep.

Still, there was nothing more he could do about the sound of the water.

Another, a different noise reached his ears. He could hear it rather late at night, the sound of the last train running beyond the hills to the south. Because it was quite late—although it was not clear what time it was, as the clocks were stopped—it really was too late for the last train, scheduled to leave T station at 10:06 (was it?) and shortly afterward to pass behind the hills two or three miles from his house. It wasn't only once a night, either. Within an hour after he heard the first night train there was the sound of another train passing. If it really was the time for the train, it was all wrong. . . . Even if it was an all-dark freight train, for example, a country rail line like this should not be running freight trains so often late at night. The sounds of the train that he could hear so clearly his wife said she could not hear at all. Listening to the echoing rumble of the distant train, he had to think there might be a friend aboard on his way to an unexpected visit with him here in the country. Supposing there really were such a person, though, who would it be? Would it be O? . . . Would it be E? . . . or T? . . . or A? . . . or K? . . . He tried to recall those friends he could remember. It was unlikely to be any one of them. Yet he could clearly picture the image of a person, someone he knew, leaning alone at a train window. The strange thing was that some nights he could believe it was himself. The image sitting there suggested to him, absorbed as he was in these strange fantasies, the start of a frightening yet fascinating story by Poe.

The ticking of the clocks, the gurgling of the water, the echo of the moving train—he seemed to hear them in that order, and other various noises, every night. A notable one, a noise he often heard late at night in the city, was the distant shrill screech of a streetcar rounding a curve. Now and again it pierced his ears. Some nights as he dozed lightly and chanced to waken, he could hear the cheerful sound of an organ coming from the village grade school about a block up the road. Was it already late morning and they had begun classroom singing? He looked around; his wife was still asleep. No morning light leaked from the crack around the door. There wasn't a sound—except for that organ. It was dead of night. Wondering whether he were half asleep, he verified his ears. Wasn't it the sound of an organ floating toward him on the mercy of the breeze, some very familiar march tune with exactly those special organ tones, refreshing, sweet, with feeling and just the mood of a late spring evening? He listened enraptured, in ecstasy, to the sound of the music. On some nights band melodies that you would hear at the movies came seeping from somewhere. . . . weren't they marches, too? Conscious of the music, he no longer heard the murmuring water. Giving up the effort to sleep, he found it not bad to be unable to sleep. Other than the screeching streetcar, the noises all carried a cheerful and melodious feeling or a pleasant sense of remote profundity. Instead of suspicion at these phenomena, he felt, on listening attentively, an ineffable comfort. The sound of the organ was best. Next was the booming of the band. Then there was the faint recurring peal of a temple gong when struck by a winter pilgrim. He heard the organ music two or three times only, but the band he could hear almost every night without fail. As he listened, he mimicked the sounds with his mouth and, beating time with his whole body, gave himself a slight feeling of floating where he lay. It was a form of pleasure, simultaneously sensual and spiritual, that you could call sexual. If it happened in a monastery, people might call it religious ecstasy.

Auditory hallucinations brought visual illusions. Or the illusions came alone, with no auditory heralding.

One of these was a minute but clear city scene, a section of a city. A tiny built-up street loomed vividly in miniature size and detail just above his nose as he lay on his back. A splendid but unreal scene it was. Although he had never seen the place before, he could imagine and believe that something exactly like this existed somewhere in Tokyo. It was a night scene with lights. A five-story Western mansion was scarcely five inches tall. In it, and in the smaller houses not half or one-third its height, in all of them were doors and windows glittering with light. The houses were generally all white. Even to the green of the window curtains, and of course in its human scale, everything was improbably minute for ordinary human imagination; yet there they were: houses lined up clearly before his eyes. No, that was not all. A star, a single star, sparkled brightly beside the lightning rods on the rooftop towers of the buildings, like a distinct spot of silver thread set in black velvet. . . . Strangely, although it was a perfect night, there was not a vehicle of any kind nor any passing person. . . . The street was lined with willowlike trees. . . . It was quiet and yet full of noise coming from he could not say where but he thought from the lighted windows. . . . That house, why could he sense that it was a Chinese restaurant? . . . As he stared closely, the whole street receded from his nose and became even tinier, seeming about to disappear, but then the scene grew rapidly larger. Unchanged but now very large, almost life-size, the street kept growing relentlessly to become gigantic, as big as the whole world. . . . He watched vacantly and the scene shrank quietly back to its former miniature scale and returned to its former place above his nose. In a few minutes—or was it seconds—it had gone in one flight, he felt, from the fabled Lilliput to the country of giants and then back to miniature Lilliput. When the street scene became gigantic, he felt the space between his eyes widen out like a giant. At one clip his range of vision had expanded. Then by some chance the illusory street scene had stopped dead at life-size. Suddenly feeling he was himself really there on that street, he groped, flustered, for a match, struck it, and looked around in the darkness at the sooty ceiling of his home.

These scenes often reappeared before his eyes. Each time they were unchanged from before. That was one of the mysteries of the apparitions.

Sometimes, but rarely, it was his own head that appeared in place of that scene. He felt it was about the size of a bean. . . . In a twinkling it grew larger . . . filled the house . . . became big as the world . . . limitless. . . . How could such a huge head fit into the universe? Then quickly it shrank back to the size of a bean. Worried, he rubbed his head with his hand without thinking. At last he felt relief. It was a joke, he thought, wanting to laugh. At that moment the "key-y-y-y" screeching sound of a streetcar rounding a curve pierced him between his eyebrows.

There did not seem to be any necessarily close connection between the visual illusions and imaginings on the one hand and the noise hallucinations on the other. Although the noise hallucinations were generally pleasing to him, the visual illusions of expansion and contraction at one leap from infinitely large to infinitely small he found ominous and tormenting.

Those mysterious, morbid apparitions became more intense each night, he felt. He began to think they were coming from his wife: the echo of the train, the screech of the streetcar, the music from the movies, that Tokyo street that he did not know. He began to suppose that his wife's brooding nostalgia for the city, through some magical action but perhaps unconsciously for her, might be giving shape and voice to these illusions in his sleepless eyes and ears. At first it was mere supposition. But without knowing when, he came to feel it was fact. That made him suddenly recall the night when he cooked his rice alone in the kitchen that was forever frequented by his wife and was filled with her idle dreams of Tokyo. That was it, he thought. He had to admit that with the weakening of his own willpower, which could be called almost nonexistent, the stronger will of other persons or the will of those invisible souls teeming in space—much stronger wills than his own—must be at work. This thing called life was a force that subjugated everything around, moment by moment, consumed it, absorbed its inner power into itself, dominated it to the full. That was clear for the body. And so for sure it was for the spirit and the soul. Even now that mystical power that acts to absorb and unify other things was gradually ebbing from him. Rather, that very self he had been until now was just evaporating.

It was now he noticed how the darkness was so heavy with teeming crowds of spirits that no space was left empty.

Thus his joys, his angers, his griefs, his fears had come to have little in common with those of others who lived in this world. Isolation and idleness, what strange powers those twins have. . . . Supposing he was in a monastery now, he sometimes thought—supposing he wasn't living this life with his wife, but, if in his habitual state of body and soul he had worshipped daily at the portrait of the ever-pure maiden, the beautiful Mary, wouldn't those nightly illusions have been mostly of heaven, the unpleasant ones of hell? From that portrait the noble tender lips, alive, wouldn't they have spoken to him? Then all the painful things revealed to him with the ugliness, the odiousness, the terror of the devil as depicted by the painter Spinello Spinelli, all would have haunted his eyes and tormented him. On those nights without a wink of sleep, when light came faintly through the cracks around the door, those lonesome, heartrending, but refreshing feelings that provoked him to tears at the sound of repeated birdcalls would surely have led to a penitent heart. In a monastery the mode of life and hints of thoughts would all call forth, would easily call forth, would have to call forth such visions. They had various tricks to do that. . . .

He thought those things. But his thoughts took shape not so much now as later.

      ✻   ✻   ✻

Shapes of human feet rose before his eyes. Feet alone, they looked to be suspended as if between lives, awaiting reincarnation. He did not know how large they were, but, seeing that the matter of size did not call for any particular attention, they were probably about normal human size. Beautiful white, bare feet they were. As he watched, fingers on white hands suddenly appeared. They were shaped like hands in El Greco paintings with some small thing held, pinched between thumb and forefinger. . . . The hands soon disappeared; only the feet remained, moving as if they were treading lightly on something. With each movement the tips of the toes went up and down, strength flowed in them, and the toes curled and straightened each time like an inchworm. . . . "What a really strange dream," he thought to himself as he dreamt. Yes! Yes! When they went on that outing to Ōzenji Temple and lost their way and stopped at the house of the silk-spinning girl—they were her feet. Her hands. She was pumping the silk-spinning treadle. Her fingers held the spinning threads. . . . As he thought about it, the fingers of the hands reappeared. Such white hands and feet were rare in the country. When she glanced up at him, she smiled. On their way there had been a sudden shower. . . . A rainbow came out. . . . They looked at it amid the mountains. . . . The girl was about sixteen. . . . It would have been nice to see her whole figure more clearly, not just her hands and feet. . . . Full of memories, he continued to gaze at that dream of restless white feet, when the surroundings suddenly brightened. . . . He looked and the glare of a candle shone in his eyes. He awoke. His wife had opened the shoji door and come in from the porch. She must have been coming from the toilet.

"Can't you be more careful, like I always say? Don't I wake up right away whenever a little light shines in my eyes? I just got to sleep after much difficulty." He looked up at his wife, blinked his blinded eyes, and scolded her snappishly.

"I was trying to be careful . . . but you sleep with your eyes open, don't you?" She spoke, and, flustered, she belatedly blew out the candle. "What about Ōzenji? You were just now talking about it in your sleep."

"When?"

"Just now. When I struck a match to light the candle."

He felt foolish. The beautiful feet he thought he saw in his dream were his wife's feet, without a doubt. While sleeping he must have pushed the pillow aside, rolled onto his side on the tatami matting, and in his dream seen his wife's feet walking. The thought struck him. But the girl spinning thread in the house near Ōzenji—he thought it was interesting that the beautiful girl was there, looking lonesome, modestly spinning thread. It was curious that the girl he had completely forgotten was now recalled to his subconscious mind.

That was one instance. It wasn't only then. On those days, no matter how much he wanted to sleep, that was the kind of sleep he often slept.

*   *   *

"You're certainly not feverish. On the contrary, you're rather cool." Putting her hand on his forehead, his wife spoke and then withdrew her hand to her own brow.

"But I'm quite hot."

That was most unsettling to him. Wanting to check their temperatures, he had her get out the thermometer, but it was broken from their frequent long-distance moves.

If it weren't because of a fever, it was because of this weather. Because of the terrible wind, he thought. Truly there was a harsh wind that day. Clouds and wind flew by, driving tiny droplets of sparse rain horizontally. It was steamy hot. Of old, days like this made him terrified of an earthquake, but today, because of the violent wind, he was at ease on that score. Still, a windy day was a windy day. An irritated feeling of unease brought on by the extraordinary weather filled him with nervous apprehension.

> Kitty cat, kitty cat, follow me!
> Kitty cat, kitty cat, go back in!

The chorus of a children's song blew in scraps from the depths of the fiercely raging winds. The shreds of music, borne intermittently on clumps of wind, seemed to penetrate his ears. It must have been hallucination because it was a long-forgotten ditty from his childhood home. On violent, windy days (yes, just like today) the children, especially the girls, while running around would each grab hold of the belt sash on the back of the child in front or would shove their heads under the coattails of the one ahead. As they did, they would sing over and over a melody like that, and frolicking in the wind they would whirl around in circles in the open space in front of the gates of his hometown houses. . . . It was a song with a monotonous but nostalgic and rhythmical refrain and a game that fit the feel of that song to a tee. Enchanted, he saw himself clearly as the child he used to be, standing in a storm of dust. It was an opening to memory. In those days in the dark cedar forest behind the castle ruins—just under the highest stone wall on the castle hill—ran a narrow path. There was a grove of big cedars, and a stream could be seen through a few cracks between tree trunks in the dense wall of cedars. Sails of a boat were visible. Great ferns grew luxuriantly underfoot. The path was forever gloomy. An especially strong, heavy, damp odor clung to the cedar forest. As a child he liked that road best. . . . When he grew larger, it was the same. Then when he was injured on the gymnastic apparatus and was twice given anesthesia, he saw himself in his drugged dream playing on that wooded road. Twice . . . One evening in the woods he found some large black lilies. As he went near and studied them carefully, about to pick one, he was suddenly struck by an eerie dread of the legendary. He ran tumbling down the mountain road. The next day, taking a servant, he searched all over the area, but there was nothing there. That was his first awareness of natural phenomena that could be thought weird. Even when he recalled it now, he knew not whether it was his own childish hallucination or whether it was in reality a queer flower that could be called a hallucination of nature. But the beauty of that flower swaying in the wind lingered long in his heart. He was such a lonely child from that time on; the rare flower was a symbol of the blue flower for him.[11] He had often walked alone on the hill behind his house where the castle ruins were or through the woods along the river beyond. He liked above all the chasm that people called the "pot breaker." There was a hut there where they burned limestone to make lime. The crystals of limestone and calcite taught the little boy the mystery of nature. By that deep pool he would often stare as if in a dream at the many big, swirling eddies, greenish lapis lazuli in color and as large as a small room. He would gaze as in a trance. He may have been around eight or nine at the time. . . . He would lie awake those nights until midnight as if he had told some lie. Worrying like that, he could not get back to sleep. He would shake his mother awake and confess painfully to her, beg her forgiveness, and at last go back to sleep. . . . Then, late every night he would hear the sound of reeds on a working loom. "I must have been about five or six then. I wonder whether I haven't been neurotic for a long time, from back then." The habit of hallucination appeared from that time, he recalled in dismay. He could remember trivial events from his childhood more vividly than recent happenings. (Yesterday's events were vague for him these days.) One strange thing: in a house on the mountain that he had seen around the end of summer, three or four months earlier—lilies and crepe myrtle had bloomed there—there were an old mother and her two young daughters in that large, desolate house. One was the girl with the beautiful white fingers and toes that he had seen in a dream. They had the ambience of a children's story sunk in the depths of his memory. They were like fairies in those remembered woods, fairies mistakenly and forcibly interwoven at times into the recollections of his childhood years. He scolded himself whenever he noticed that he was tending to think that way. No, wasn't that something recent? He reproached and corrected himself. . . . He continued to be absorbed in these childhood reflections. But they were things altogether forgotten, leaving hardly a trace to this day. Becoming the child of his recollections, he thought of, he loved, and longed for his mother, his brothers and sisters, and his father. For someone who scarcely thought of anyone other than himself, in these recent distressing days he had not until now recalled them to mind. He had sent no word to his father, his mother, or his brothers and sisters for more than half a year. He felt especially sad about his hard-of-hearing older sister who had returned home from a divorce. He tried first to recall his mother's face. He had seen her only a half year earlier, but he could not call back the impression. When he could force his disarranged impressions into a collected view, it was unexpectedly, oddly, the strange face of his mother seventeen or eighteen years ago. . . . His mother had caught Saint Anthony's fire. . . . Her face, daubed all over with black medicine like a black mask with only her sunken eyes gleaming, was the face of a monster, waving a hand listlessly when he failed to approach the sick bed. As a child he had fled sobbing to the garden, where he cried some more. The blurry shape of the camellia that he saw through his crying eyes, the blurry clustered flowers one by one— strangely they floated more clearly before his eyes than did his mother's face. . . . These forgotten events came back to him in a line of recollections extending back in time. The feeling made him think of death. It was surely the feeling of an invalid facing death. For all that, wasn't he himself going to die before long? . . . In this mountain village where he knew no one, was he about to die like this? . . . What if he did die? His fancies ran on endlessly. Until now he had not once thought directly about death. For the first time he pictured in a rather curious and fanciful way how his friends would one by one learn of his death. There in the awful wind he strained his ears for the voice of a cricket calling insistently to entice the souls of men from this turbulent world into solitary silence.

He stretched out his hand and was about to pull out a book from the shelf directly over his pillow. The moment his hand touched the bookshelf—crash—there was the sound of something breaking. Startled as if he had dropped something, he looked around. It was the sound of his wife breaking something in the kitchen, a sound carried by the wind to his ears.

His bookshelf was in a wretched state nowadays. A few old books propped each other up in the dust, toppling sideways as they stood. Only a few of not much value remained of their own accord; he had tired of them all in the last two or three years. The one he pulled out now was a translation of *Faust*. To escape from the futile and overly curious fancies of his own death, he would read even a book that aroused no interest. The sound of the wind ceaselessly raked his ears. The single pane of glass set in the kitchen sink, shaking and clattering, kept irritating his ears and his spirits.

Lying on his stomach, he cast his eyes over the opened page.

> The pleasure of the supernatural world
> Lies deep in mountains, mid dark and dew,
> Embracing heaven and earth blissfully to heart,
> Rooting the marrow from nature with all one's might,
> Experiencing in one's breast the six days of God's work,
> Feeling prideful power, tasting what I know not,
> With love at any moment overflowing all,
> The son of earth wholly disappears.

By chance these were the words of Mephistopheles in the scene "Forest and Cavern." He understood the meaning of the words clearly. Weren't those exactly his feelings when he first came here to the country?

He staggered out of bed to get a pen and red ink from his desk. Turning back from the part he had read, he started reading from Faust's monologue in the cavern. Filling the pen with red ink, he underscored line by line as he read. To avoid touching the print even barely or letting his line waver at all, he drew a thin, nervous line. It required great strain on his trembling fingers.

· ·

To put it briefly, I have not grudged your tasting of these self-
deluding pleasures.
But you cannot long endure them.
Already you are overtired.
And if it continues, it will end either merrily in madness or
drearily in cowardice.
Enough of that. . . .[12]

Engrossed in his underlining, he reread the lines for their
meaning. With a start he understood for the first time. Mephistopheles was speaking to him now in this book. What a bad fore-
cast! Drearily it will end in cowardice. Was that true? Even if you
looked diligently through every line of such a vast book, you would
surely not find any words more appropriate to him now than those
in this revelation. The words were an apt critique of his present
life. When he looked at those too-pertinent printed words, the
printed letters struck him as a bit fearful.

"My, what a terrible wind. Look at the trees in the grove out
back. They're such tall, slender things, they're reeling in the wind.
It's frightening the way they're swaying. I wonder whether they
won't break." His wife's voice, sounding far away and half lost in
the roar of the wind, reached his ears as if bearing some important
event or hidden meaning.

When he noticed, his wife was standing at his bedside. She had
been standing there for some time. She was asking him about food.
He made no effort to answer and tried wearily to go back to sleep.
He turned his head away crossly from his wife.

Then at once he turned toward her again. "Hey, something
broke just now."

"Oh, it was a Western-style plate I bought for ten sen."

"So, a Western plate you bought for ten sen? You don't think it's
all right to break just because it's a ten-sen Western plate, do you?
Whether it was ten sen or ten yen, it's a price someone set for their
own reasons. It's more useful to me than ten sen. A plate is a valuable thing. You can say it's like something alive. Sit down there.
You're breaking about five things a month these days. When you
have a plate in your hand, you don't think about the plate. You're

thinking absentmindedly about other things. That's why the plate is offended, and it jumps out of your hand. It just slips out. It's no good at all that you think only of Tokyo. You don't know the key to an abundant life here in the lonely country. Look at how lively it is here: the kitchen utensils that you think are each so trifling, if you would listen to them, how many interesting things they could tell you. To live life, truly to live happily, can there be any other way than to enjoy fully in one's heart all those little things that make up daily life? . . ."

He continued to scold her deliriously. It was an unusually long lecture for him, who these days was prone entirely to silence. He talked on, adding words one after another. As he did so, the words he intended to say to his wife some way changed direction into words pointed at himself. He noticed this as he chattered on, although it was only a fragment of thoughts unexpected, thoughts that did not figure in his normal thinking. When he realized these were new thoughts, and he came to the point of speaking them, the words would not come. Only the surface of the thought slipped out in awkward words. "The sanctity of daily life. The mystery of daily life." He thought to himself how he would like to say these things that were inexpressible in human words. So at last he shut up.

The two listened silently to the noise of the raging storm. After a bit his wife said resolutely, "You. Of that three hundred yen you got from your father in March, there's scarcely ten yen left."

Making no effort to reply, he muttered suddenly these words only: "If I've got no talent, I've got no confidence."

    ❋   ❋   ❋

Blackness pressed about him. A consummately oppressive darkness, it was aggregated of red, green, and purple stacked without a crack between. He groped for a match in the dark, lit the candle by his bed, and got up. Holding the candlestick, he shone the light directly on his wife's sleeping face next to him. She had fallen into a deep sleep and did not stir. For some while he stared at her stolid face in the flickering candlelight. He watched intently and curiously as if he were seeing his wife's face for the first time.

The light of the candle divided the shapes sharply between the two worlds of the light and of the shadow. The human face he saw in that light was bathed in brightness from one side only, and the effect of the strong light and shadow created by the reddish light evoked an altogether different feeling for a face. He wondered whether human faces, not only his wife's, were generally as ugly as this. His eyes saw a strange, ugly lump—dismal and weird. Her loose, Western-style ratted hair lay like a black ball on the pillow. It was strange that he should first realize when he saw that false hair that the woman sleeping here was his own wife.

He stared at her for a long time in various ways as he playfully experimented at altering the effect of the light by raising the candle a bit or holding it right next to her ear. She slept without noticing a thing. She did not move in the bed. Wouldn't this woman sleep serenely even if a sword were plunged into her throat? No, in that case, of course, even this so-stolid woman would instinctively open her eyes. She would have to. He thought so. He wondered whether she were not even now dreaming of being killed. . . . A person could call to mind all kinds of things through the enchantment of light. Haven't there been men since olden times with the determination to kill a person really for just that reason? . . .

"Of course I'm not about to kill the woman now," he whispered without thinking. Flustered, he excused himself for his surprisingly wild idea. "What did I ever do that for?"

Suddenly coming to his senses, he shook his wife awake.

It was the middle of the night.

His wife barely opened her eyes and looked aside to avoid the fluttering glare of the candle. She moved her lips like someone not yet fully awake, holding the words half in her mouth.

"You're locking the doors? It's all right." She spoke and rolled over.

"No, I'm going to the toilet. Come with me, please."

Coming back from the privy and about to wash his hands, he slid the door half open. Moonlight streamed abruptly through the opening. Striking full on the porch, the light shone on the boards in a slanted oblong. Strangely, he had seen the moonlight streaming onto the porch in the same way, exactly the same way, in the dream he was having just now when he awoke. What an odd coincidence. But then it lost its mystery for him. Both of them standing here like this now, wasn't this a continuation of the dream? he wondered.

"Hey, this is no dream, is it?"

"What? You're half asleep."

The candle in his wife's hand, drenched in moonlight, lost its faintly pinkish glow. The flame fluttered in the wind as if about to go out. Shielded from the breeze by his wife's sleeve held over it, the flame flickered wildly. The wind dropped unnoticed, but the clouds raced toward the south with appalling power. From large phantasmal rifts in the gaping jet-black clouds that scattered fine rain as they passed, the moon shone coldly on them.

Forgetting to wash his hands, he gazed at that extraordinary moon. A queer moon, it was. What phase was it, round but the lower half pale and blurry, seeming about to disappear? The upper half floated boldly, fresh and well burnished, set in the depths of the sky between the black clouds. The clear roundness of the upper half resembled something intensely, he thought. Yes, it was like the roundness of the top of a skull. That is to say, the whole shape of the moon resembled a skull—a silver skull, a silver skull well polished or just taken from the smelter. By association it reminded him of a pirate ship. *The sacred pirate ship.* Why did those words come to mind? He stared insatiably at that blue moon. Yeah, it was the same, exactly the same, that time, too. I stood here like this. The shapes of the clouds, the shape of the moon, they were exactly like this. Not a bit of difference anywhere. He was thinking like this that other time. He was thinking the same thoughts then as now. Long ago in the depths of a dim distant hole that was the past it had happened, exactly the same way as now, without the slightest layer of difference. . . . Vacantly, momentarily, he thought so. . . . When was it? . . . Where was it?

Scattered clouds racing across the sky seemed ready to swallow the silver skull that was the moon.

"Can't you close it?" his wife said, feeling the cold.

Coming to his senses at these words, he leaned over to wash his hands. It was at that moment:

"Oh, terrible!"

"What?"

"It's a dog!"

"A dog?"

Quickly he grabbed the bamboo pole used to secure the door and hurled it with all his might toward the garden entrance. He could see a white dog nimbly dodge the tumbling bamboo and then suddenly aim and leap to grab the stick in its mouth and run off at full tilt. With its tail between its legs, ears back, white fangs protruding, and slaver dribbling from the mouth that had clenched the bamboo, the dog ran without stopping down the road in front of his house. He saw in a blur a large, bushy-haired, silver-colored, shaggy dog, bathed in moonlight and running at high speed. It was the dog from the Ōzenji Mountain temple. He perceived that at once, clearly and precisely.

"It's a mad dog!"

Hastily he called his own dogs by name. He kept on calling. Weren't they there? The dogs did not respond to his voice. His wife understood nothing of what had happened. She added her voice to calling the dogs, though, just as her husband was doing. Her high-pitched voice echoed from the hills. After seven or eight calls there was the sound of heavy chains, and two dogs came sluggishly out together. Quivering as they clattered their chains, they seemed dubious of their master's unexpected call, although they sniffed their noses and wagged their tails as if to snap them off.

The moon was swallowed by the cloud.

No sooner had he taken the candle from his wife's hand and thrust it out toward the dogs than it was blown out by a passing gust of wind. Lighting the lamp at once in its place, he looked and saw nothing unusual about his dogs.

"What a surprise. I thought our dogs might have been bitten by that mad dog."

He went back to bed, turned toward his wife, and explained in detail what he had just seen. She disputed it from the first. He couldn't have seen anything as clearly as that by moonlight, no matter how bright. The Ōzenji dog was mad, sure enough, but it had been killed for that very reason a week or ten days ago. Okinu had said at the time, "So, take care of your dogs."

She had said it then, and he must have heard it from that woman herself. . . . His wife, reasoning with him, sought to soothe him with her explanation. Still, he doubted that he really had heard the news that the Ōzenji dog was mad.

"The dog's ghost is running around the fields like that, and I'm the only one that can see spirits. . . ." . . . A gloomy world, a groaning world, a world where spirits wander. Were my eyes made for such a world? . . . A gloomy window in a gloomy room looked out on a gloomy, abandoned garden. That's what he thought. The place where I now live is not in the world of the living, nor so to speak is it the land of the dead. Isn't it a netherworld between the two? Am I wandering alive through the world of the dead? If they say that Dante wandered in flesh and blood through heaven and hell . . . at least, at the very least, the place where I'm standing now is a slope slanting steeply toward the depths of destruction. . . .

*   *   *

The next day, the day after the rainy moonlit night, the weather cleared at last. Sky and earth seemed to revive this morning. Sometime during the long rain all things had changed to late autumn. The sunlight streaming on the heads of rice, the soft breeze, the sky, the clouds floating in a line—all had changed themselves from summer. He saw it all as made of transparent varicolored glass. He felt it all through his body. He took a deep breath. The cool, clear air penetrated straight into his chest; it was sweeter than any drink. His wife was justified this morning in letting the dogs off the chains that held them daily. That was a good move. In the distant fields his dogs Fratty and Leo could be seen romping. A young farmer was patting Leo on the head. Gentle, quiet Leo submitted happily. . . . He gazed enraptured for some time at the fields blessed by the sun, at the dogs, at the farmers stooped over their work, at other such sights. The sun was high. Why didn't he wake up earlier to watch this scene? he wondered. When he stepped down from the veranda to go wash his face, he passed through the garden. There dropped at the base of the bush clover was the bamboo stick the white dog must have held in its teeth last night. He smiled sourly without thinking; no, it was rather a happy smile.

Sparrows flew down by the well to pick up rice that had been dropped—perhaps his wife scattered too much there on purpose, he thought. There was a flock of thirty or forty birds, more than he had ever seen around here before. Frightened at his footsteps, they flew up in a bunch to the branches above, even though there was no need to flee. In the persimmon tree were other little white-faced birds with names he did not know. He recalled Saint Francis, who preached to the birds. The morning smoke ascending from the eaves of his house wreathed the persimmon branches in transparent purple gauze. The roses, beaten down by the rain and unable to bloom, had this morning flowered here and there. The spider webs glowed with ornamental lights from the dew reflecting the sunshine. He could see with fresh feeling the everyday beauty of the dewdrops scattered on the rose leaves and shining as they tumbled onto the spider webs and shook the webs with the weight of momentary jewels the hand could never pluck. The dew ran down the threads, gleaming in flashes and dropping onto the grass below.

When he hauled up the rope and bucket to draw water and he looked down into the bottom of the well, he could see the limitless blue sky marked off in a round circle three feet in diameter of fathomless lapis lazuli lying unruffled—the well water gleaming with its own deep transparence. He had to hesitate before letting the bucket drop from his hand. As he peered down the well, his mood calmed like the water below. The water he had drawn was, on the contrary, muddied by the prolonged rains, but his tranquil mood made up for this.

When he came to the table for the meal his wife had prepared, his heart was peaceful. On the table was a different menu of food that his wife had brought back from her recent trip to Tokyo. The iron teakettle was boiling on the brazier. So, his gloomy feelings came from the miserable weather, just as his wife had said, he thought. As he was about to pick up his chopsticks, he chanced to recall the bud on the rose that he had just seen by the well.

"Hey, you didn't notice? A beautiful flower blossomed this

morning. It's my flower. It's a half-sized blossom. The red is a deep calm color."

"Yes, I saw it. That tall one blossoming in the middle?"

"That one.

> A simple stem
> Alone surpassing,
> Hits the mark
> For the garden's heart.[13]

"That guy," he said to himself. " 'The new flower faces broad daylight.'[14] No, broad daylight is strange. They're out of season."

"At last in September they bloomed."

"How about it? Can you pick it and bring it here?"

"Yes. I will."

"Put it here then." He spoke as he drummed his fingers on the middle of the round table. His wife got up at once and brought out a white tablecloth.

"Well, I'll lay this cloth."

"O.K. Hey, you washed it."

"If it got dirty, I thought I couldn't wash it in all that rain, so I put it away."

"This is great. We'll have a flower banquet."

Listening to his happy laugh, his wife went out to pick the flower.

She came back promptly carrying a glass filled with flowers. In she came cheerily and presented them in an unnatural, slightly melodramatic manner. This was oddly displeasing to him. He felt he had been mocked and shamed. He spoke coldly: "Oh, you took a lot of them."

"Yes, all there were. All of them."

She answered in triumph. It vexed him. The meaning of his words hadn't gotten through.

"Why? One was enough for me."

"But you didn't say so."

"Look—did I say lots of them? One was enough for me."

"Shall I throw the others away?"

"It's all right. You brought them on purpose. O.K. Put them

there. . . . What's the matter with you? You didn't bring me what I told you to, did you?"

"My goodness. Whether you said it or you didn't, that's all there is to it! Over there."

"Maybe so. I was thinking there was a red bud tinged in the center with sky-blue color. I only wanted the one."

"Oh, that? You say it's tinged with sky blue in the center but that's not so difficult. Surely it's just the reflection of the sky."

"Oh, really now? . . ."

"Come on. It's nothing to make such a frightful face over. If I did something wrong, forgive me. Why, I thought the more the better. . . ."

"Don't be so quick to apologize. I'd rather you understood what I said. . . . One of them. I wanted to watch one of them set in front of me, set in the sun, one bud until it became a flower. One, right? The others could have been left on the branch."

"So, you don't like abundance."

"Rather than so many trivial things, only one of something good. That's true abundance." He spoke with feeling as if he were savoring the words himself.

"Well, please get your good temper back. Especially on such a beautiful morning . . ."

"Yes, just because it is such a beautiful morning, this business is unpleasant to me."

As he was saying these things, his wife was gradually growing miserable. He noticed this of his own volition. On his wife's forefinger blood was oozing where it must have been pricked by the thorn of a rose. The sight struck him. Because of his nature, the words to express his feelings to his wife would not come from his mouth. Instead, he concealed those feelings, so they would not be known, could not be known. He did not know how to cut off those unpleasant words. That irritated him the more. He clenched his mouth shut. He picked up the glassful of flowers. First holding it even with his eyes, he peered through the glass. The green leaves soaked in water were even greener. Here and there the undersides gleamed silver. Pinkish thorns could be seen in the shadows. The thick bottom of the glass glistened like crystal, icily. The small world in the small glass was a beautiful clear autumn of green and silver.

He put down the glass in front of him. One by one he scrutinized the flowers minutely. All of them, petals and flowers, had unfortunately been eaten by insects. There was not a single perfect one. That upset his spirits, which had become rather calm.

"How about that? These flowers! You should have checked them more carefully before you picked them. Huh, they're all eaten by bugs."

He spit out the words without thinking, but his wife looked pitiful again. Suddenly he pulled out the most beautiful bud from the bunch and softened his words.

"Oh, this one. The bud I spoke of. It's here! It's here!"

With these words he felt he was moderating himself and trying to restore his wife's good humor. She made no effort to reply; silently she heaped rice into her bowl. He stole a sidelong glance at her face. What if he were to throw the glass over there, at the top of her head? No, that wouldn't do. Basically he was the selfish one. Helplessly, with lonesome and painful heart, he held the plucked bud up to his eyes and stared at it. . . . In the still firm bud, there in its swollen side, was a needlelike hole. Small, white, deep, it pierced through how many layers, how many folds of red petals to the stamens. Needless to say, it was the work of insects. He frowned in disgust and looked again at the bud.

With a start he let it drop.

With the same hand he lifted the boiling teakettle quickly from the brazier. Again he picked up the bud. He threw it directly into the fire. . . . The petals sizzled as they scorched. . . . As he watched the flaming red coals—

"Oh!" he cried out involuntarily. He started to rise and then managed to stifle the impulse. . . . If I get up now, I'll go mad, he thought. Again quickly, but with all possible composure, he picked up the burning bud from the brazier with the tips of the tongs and tossed it into the nearby charcoal basket. That done, he peered fearfully into the fire. There was nothing there: nothing of what there just had been; nothing to shout about in surprise. He stirred the charcoal and looked. Nothing came up from below. More quickly than oil spreads as it drips into water, a deep blue-green flared across the surface of the charcoal! What he saw: it must have been an illusion of a mere moment's duration.

He retrieved the bud from the bottom of the basket. Pinched by the tongs, the bud was faded by the fire and smeared with black charcoal dust. Again he examined the stem. There as he had seen the first time, the stem that trembled with his fingers, from the calyx of the flower through to the underside of two worm-eaten leaves—what insects were these? . . . The very same green as the stem and so very, very fine, these insects were piled closely on each other like the stone walls in his phantom miniature street scene. Countless insects mantled the entire surface of the stem, leaving no open space the size of a needlepoint. The sheet of blue-green that he had seen spreading on the surface of the charcoal was an illusion, but this mass of insects enveloping the stem, that was no illusion. . . . all over the surface, deep blue-green, countless, countless . . .

"Oh, Rose, thou art sick!"[15]

By chance he heard it. It came from his own mouth. But to his ears it sounded like the voice of another. He could think only that someone else was putting words in his mouth. It was a line from a poem by somebody. He recalled that someone had quoted it on a title page or somewhere.

As a way to compose himself as much as possible he picked up the covered rice bowl in front of him and quietly passed it to his wife. The moment he stretched out his hand:

"Oh, Rose, thou art sick!"

The words came again from his mouth, without meaning.

He managed to finish one bowl of morning rice.

His wife was crying. "Oh, is it beginning again?" she muttered to herself about her husband. As she was clearing up the breakfast table, she picked up the glass of flowers, but she could not decide what to do with them. The burned, bug-eaten bud—he must have torn and crushed it unconsciously. . . . Shredded red bits lay scattered on the shelf of the brazier where the cat napped. Pretending not to notice, he stepped down with one foot from the veranda to go into the garden. At that moment:

"Oh, Rose, thou art sick!"

On fairyland hill the line that formed a woman's profile was embossed even more boldly on the deep-blue sky. Beautiful clouds floated lightly over the trees, whose luxuriantly spreading tops towered above the higher slopes. The yellowish red-brown color was so beautiful it made him want to cry. The color of the earth that had changed to purple the other day enhanced the vertical green stripes. Threads of black shadow were interwoven with the stripes today. It was doubly attractive to his eyes.

"Am I going to end up hanging myself over there? Something there is calling me to it.

"You fool. Don't make such a stupid suggestion on a whim.

"It will be all right if the end is not dreary."

His fantasy led him unexpectedly to raise his hand. Now, wasn't that like throwing an invisible obi sash around the invisible branches on the hilltop? . . .

"Oh, Rose, thou art sick!"

The water in the well was brimming round and still as it does in the morning. His face was reflected there. A blighted leaf from the persimmon tree fluttered, dropped, and floated, solitary. Round ripples spread silently across the surface from its gentle touch. The water quivered and then returned to its former stillness: stillness that was stillness—limitless stillness.

"Oh, Rose, thou art sick!"

In the clump of roses not a single flower was left. There were only leaves. They were eaten by insects, every one. Then he happened to notice without so intending that the glass his wife had filled with flowers this morning stood as if in hiding, small, quiet, lonesome, red, there on one side of a shelf in the dark corner of the kitchen. The sight struck his eyes.

"Why do you get angry at trifling things? You toy with life. It's a terrible thing. . . . You know no patience."

"Oh, Rose, thou art sick!"

Kudzu leaves were twined around a bamboo shoot in the thicket behind the house, and, although there was little breeze, one of the leaves was fluttering with surprising vigor. With every flutter the underside flashed white. . . . He stared transfixed. . . . The dogs, finding him, came flying back from the fields and jumped on him from both sides: even as he dodged to avoid them. . . . even as a shrike on some branch of a tree somewhere warbled its piercing, whirling song . . . even as he watched the flight of a flock of migrating birds disheveling the dazzling sunset sky by their swooping and scattering . . . even as he gazed at the brilliant ultramarine blue of the evening sky . . . even as he watched the slim trail of smoke from the evening meal ascending in silence, without a flicker, from the house at the foot of the opposite hill . . .

"Oh, Rose, thou art sick!"

The words kept chasing him forever. They came from his mouth but they were not his voice. His ears heard them as another's voice. If not another's voice, his mouth was copying impromptu the voice of another that his ears had heard. . . . He could not have said anything himself all day.

The dogs were baying in concert. Frightened by their own echo, they howled the more fiercely. The echo grew ever fiercer. The dogs howled more fiercely yet. . . . His feelings became the barking of the dogs; the dog's howl became his mood. In the dark kitchen his wife kindled the fire in the oven. His wife's desire to move to Tokyo was surely fostered there at a time like this. The cat that had come back from somewhere wailed incessantly for its supper. When the fire flared up, his wife's face loomed ugly, silhouetted in red. In a corner of the kitchen the glass of roses loomed alone in the darkness. Those roses, the roses eaten by insects—they were suffering from smoke!

When he went to light the lamp, he struck a match. The moment the light flared in his hand:

"Oh, Rose, thou art sick!"

As he bent his ears to the voice, he forgot he was holding a match to the lamp wick. When the thin stick of the match had burned, it became for a moment a streak of red and then promptly, wearily went out. The blackened head of the match dropped to the tatami floor. "The air in the house has gone gloomy, dank, and stale; perhaps the lamp won't light," he wondered. He struck another match.

"Oh, Rose, thou art sick!"

No matter how many matches he struck—no matter how many.

"Oh, Rose, thou art sick!"

Where ever did the voice come from? Was it a revelation from heaven? Was it a prophecy? Whatever, the words kept hounding him. Endlessly, endlessly . . .

Notes

1. Presumably Tokyo, Yokohama, and Hachiōji.

2. From the Chinese poet Tao Yuan-ming, who lived from about A.D. 365 to 427. The phrase refers to the secluded home and garden of a retired scholar-official.

3. The writer is said to have named the dogs after two disciples of Saint Francis, Frate and Leo.

4. Refers to a ghost story in the eighteenth-century collection *Ugetsu Monogatari* (Tales of Moonlight and Rain) by Ueda Akinari. It tells of a man who returns home after seven years' absence to find at first that his home and his faithful wife are safe, only to wake the next morning to find them gone. At his side is the tomb of his wife.

5. Unidentified. Possibly not by Goethe but by another German poet.

6. 1644–1694.

> By daylight,
> The firefly has,
> A neck of red.
> Blyth translation from *Haiku*, Vol. 3, by R. H. Blyth. Hokuseido, 1952, p. 219.

7. 2 Corinthians 6:10.

8. The old name for Tokyo before 1868. In the Meiji Restoration of that year the power of the Tokugawa shogun rulers was terminated, and the name of the city changed to Tokyo for the capital of the new administration in the emperor's name.

9. Refers to the Akita breed, often considered frightening in Japan.

10. From Kanagawa to Hachiōji.

11. Refers to a work of Novalis (Friedrich von Hardenberg), German romantic poet of the eighteenth century, about a minnesinger's wandering search for a blue flower, a symbol of infinity and eternity.

12. From the Japanese translation used by Satō. A direct English translation from the German would differ slightly.

13. Quotation from *Rose Leaves*, poems of the Tang Chinese poet Chu Guang-yi, A.D. 700–760. English rendition by this translator.

14. Quotation from *Poems of the Rose* by Qi Dynasty Chinese poet Xie Tiao, A.D. 464–499.

15. From a poem of William Blake, "The Sick Rose," 1793. Included in "Songs of Experience" and reprinted in the *New Oxford Book of English Verse, 1250–1950*, chosen and edited by Helen Gardner (Oxford University Press, 1972), p. 483.

Okinu and Her Brother

(OKINU TO SONO KYŌDAI, 1918)

I once lived in the village of N in the district of T in K prefecture. When I think of it, I get a strange feeling. I wonder today what put the idea into my head to live for whatever reason in such a remote country place, and it all seems too fanciful. At the time I seriously intended to spend my whole life in that village. Only two years ago, it was. Still, it seems more than ten years in the past. Maybe I aged more than ten years in less than a year of life in the country. I was so lonely in that village. . . . I wrote an account of my own state of being at that time in *The Sick Rose* or *Gloom in the Country.*

I felt so lonely. The village itself was such a lonely place. That pleased me in a way at the time. It was less than twenty miles from Tokyo, Yokohama, and Hachiōji. There was scarcely any transportation to the cities. People who should know say the area once produced railroad ties. N village was more than two and a half miles off the Kanagawa-to-Hachiōji rail line. If you missed your train, you'd have to waste three hours waiting. When you think of it, the train was no kind of convenience. The villagers could only go by rattletrap carriage to Kanagawa; failing that, they could walk. From the neighborhood of my house it was about two and a half miles to the carriage stop. All the same, the villagers didn't think it inconvenient at all. Those villagers lived such a simple life. When you think of it, how strange to have an inconvenient, desolate country place so close to Tokyo, where we now are. When I first happened to look on this area, bouncing along in a carriage, I was astonished. Suddenly and before I knew it, I saw a world unfolding before my eyes, a world of roadside rice paddies, farm fields, marshes, bridges, clumps of trees and woods, mulberry fields, forested hills, and peach and pear orchards. I thought that here so close to the big cities this place was created as contrast. It was charming, and it made me think the more.

There in this corner of Musashino the plains ran out. The land seemed poised to become mountains. Commonplace hills lay piled in succession over and again. There are places in those hills where stone arrowheads left by ancient peoples are said to turn up after a heavy rain. The upstream basin of T River opened out a bit here into rice fields. In the distance behind the southern hills some of the mountains around Fuji could be seen. From some places the pure-white solitary summit was visible. Various peaks of the Chichibu Range lay like layers of clouds—indeed in summer you might think they were nothing but clouds—lay dim and dark on the western horizon. Old thatch roofs were clustered at random along one side of the straight road or removed from the road and clasped in the bosom of a hill. They were examples of how people in ancient times had chosen a place and said, "I'll make my home here." I lived in one of those houses.

At first I lived in I section of N village where I rented a room in a temple. Three months later I rented a house in K section. K was a mile or more up from I. It was that much more inconvenient.

When we moved from I to K there was a woman who showed us the house, who helped us move our things, and who washed the sooty shoji doors for us in the ditch in front of the house. She was a diligent and obliging worker. From that connection she came frequently to visit. My wife (we later separated) had no companions, and she often chatted with that woman or gave her laundry to do.

"She really is a kind person," my wife said, often praising her.

Her name was Okin. She was the wife of the village cooper named Mampei. In age she was about thirty-five or thirty-six, or perhaps younger. But to be honest, she was an ugly woman, so whatever age she was didn't matter very much. She was swarthy. Her face was shaped like a chestnut. With that plain, flattened face, the head was large and the chin was missing. She was fat. Her husband Mampei had a face like a grasshopper. He was gaunt. However probable such people may be in the country, you would never see their type in the city. Mampei said he liked dogs, and he used to come to see my dogs. He came rarely, but Okin often visited. On the long, autumn evenings she would come through the continuous autumn rains, carrying something grown in her garden. She would talk of anything. Okin loved to talk. It was one such rainy night. Suddenly Okin began to tell the story of her life. I didn't ordinarily know what my wife and Okin were talking about, but this evening I happened to be sitting by the brazier, and I heard Okin's story. It was more interesting than I expected. I was impressed, and I listened to the end. To all appearances the woman was not unusual; I wondered how she had endured such an extraordinary fate. I watched her face attentively with a feeling that I was staring into the depths. I was truly impressed. It would be wrong to say that Okin was trying to excite us, but her story drew my interest. That seemed to make her happy. She said no one had ever listened to her story so attentively, and she thanked me. After that she came whenever she was free. How many times, time after time, she repeated the story of her life. To think of it, I am a patient man. Although I came to the country seeking solitude, in less than half a year I could no longer be satisfied in such lonesome country. I was so homesick (both in body and in mind) for a place I knew not that I fell into a mood of irritation at every occasion. Okin's story came in the end to anger me. When I saw her face, I wanted to escape. How tormenting it became to hear that story again and again. I can recount Okin's story almost in her own words.

*   *   *

Okin was born near a sacred place called M in Yamanashi Prefecture. Her mother died when she was six. She seems to have been raised in a temple in the village. Okin called the chief priest of the temple familiarly by his title of Oshō-san. At that time she thought of herself as an orphan because her father had died before her mother. Her now-dead mother had told her so. Even as a child she seems to have wondered vaguely whether Oshō-san weren't her own father. When she went to the village school, the boys teased her every day, calling out, "Hey, the priest's kid. The priest's kid." At first she thought the other kids were saying that because she was being brought up by Oshō-san. At the same time, although without knowing why, she suspected that maybe Oshō-san really was her father. That Oshō-san was indeed her father as she suspected the child Okin soon learned. That was when Oshō-san was on his deathbed. Her aunt told her (her mother's brother's wife, she was). Okin was eight years old at the time.

Really an orphan now, Okin was taken in by her uncle and aunt, her mother's younger brother and his wife. Her uncle lived in a village thirty-five or forty miles from the temple. They had no children. She was treated lovingly by the couple. A year and a half went by.

It was at dusk one day. A young man she didn't know called at her uncle's home. He had a citified manner you would not see in the country. He wore a hat. He entered wearing his traveling clothes. Her uncle talked warmly with the young man. As she watched them, Uncle called and said, "This is your older brother."

This was the first she learned of a big brother. She served sake to her uncle and the young man he called her brother. It must have been autumn. Somehow she remembered there was a fire laid in the hearth. Okin stared curiously at the two. She realized they were speaking of her. For some reason their voices grew gradually louder, and the two appeared to be quarreling. Her aunt came in to calm them. Her uncle was a gentle man who rarely got angry, but this time he was very angry. He persisted even as his wife tried to calm him, and he shouted, "You ran away from home when you were a child. You didn't show up when your mother died. You didn't come to your father's funeral. How dare you cross my threshold?" Then, "Why should we turn this child over to a scoundrel like you?" he added. "She's our child now. Brother? Older brother? What authority do you claim by that?" Uncle shoved Auntie aside. Brother stood up. Brother was a very big man.

"I was in tears already," Okin said, "but, when I saw my brother stand up, I was so frightened I shuddered and stopped crying." No matter, Okin had to go with her brother. He told her, "I'll take you to an exciting city, not like the country here."

The place he took her was Hachiōji. Okin lived with her brother in the second floor of a house. Only one old lady lived in the house. When he took Okin, Brother also received from the old man all Okin's belongings that her father and mother had left her. Brother must have deceived the honest aunt and uncle with his smooth talk. When they got to Hachiōji, Brother took off right away that night from the old woman's house. He left the child Okin alone and went somewhere unknown. He was away for three days. There were more times he would not return for three or four days in a row. When that happened, the old lady would trudge up to the second floor saying, "What a pity. You've got a bad brother. He didn't come home again tonight, did he? You must be lonely. Come downstairs now and sleep with Granny."

The old lady would tuck her into her bed that evening. Okin did not think of herself as particularly lonesome even though her brother had not come home. She had not yet lost the feeling of fright at her brother. She had not had time to gain any affection for him; he was never home. But there was a reason she wanted her brother to come home. Here is why. On the nights he did not return Okin had to sleep in the arms of the old lady. Even if she didn't want to, she had no choice. On the second floor if she awoke in the middle of the night, she could not go back to sleep alone for her fears. When she slept with the old lady though, the same conversation would always ensue. . . . As Okin told me, mimicking her speech:

"Your brother is still roaming around doing bad things. There's a woman, I tell you. It made Otsune worry so much that finally she died."

"Grandma, who died?"

"Otsune did."

"Otsune?"

"Yes."

"Otsune, who was that?"

The old lady would reply, "My daughter, she was."

Then she would talk on about her daughter Tsune. Finally she would add, "To think of it, Otsune was pathetic. You are pathetic. I am pathetic. I am the most pathetic of all."

So saying, the old lady would sob loudly. As she cried she continued talking.

"Grandma, can't you stop that talk!" Okin would say and begin to cry, too. She would cry herself to sleep.

The old lady was all bent over. In her dotage she was like a child. She grumbled on the same way to Okin every night.

"My daughter, she was. . . . To think of it, Otsune was pathetic. You are pathetic. I am pathetic. I am the most pathetic of all."

Impatient, the old lady would sob aloud.

"Grandma, can't you stop that talk!" Okin would say, crying.

The old lady never failed to say these things. Night after night she repeated over and over the same thing in the same words. Come nighttime, it was more distressing than anything for Okin to hear this talk. It made her desolate. It frightened her horribly. To listen was so painful that she longed for her brother's return, the brother she did not care for. He rarely came. Occasionally, when he did return, he hardly stayed at all. He would open Okin's chest of drawers that he had brought from Uncle's home and would take out his mother's and Okin's kimonos. Then in the evening he would go out somewhere: not just two or three days, but for a week he would not come back. Once after being away for about ten days he returned abruptly with two strangers. The two began carrying the chest down from the second floor. Brother followed them out promptly and again did not return for some time. Then suddenly he came. This time he was unaccompanied. Looking at Okin, he praised her saying, "You took good care of things while I was out." He had never said anything like that before. Brother invited her to go to town with him. Since moving to Hachiōji Okin had not once been to town. No one had offered to take her. The doddering old lady stayed home every day, so Okin went to town at her brother's invitation. They walked around various places. When they reached a certain place, her brother, walking silently until now, stopped suddenly. Taking Okin by the hand he said to her very gently, "You're going to be a different child from today. O.K.?"

Dropping these words, brother slid open with a clatter the front shoji door of a house directly in front of them. Taking Okin's hand, he went in. He sat on the raised door frame and said, "Hey dad. I brought her."

On looking in they saw two men in the house talking about something. "When brother called, the two glanced at me—Okin."

One said, "Oh, that child? Big for her age isn't she?"

The other said, "Yeah, she'll do at silk spinning in a couple of years."

It seems that brother and the two men had settled the matter earlier. "Well, I leave her to you," she thought her brother said, and he disappeared somewhere by himself. The man who had looked at Okin and said, "Big for her age," became her father for a long time. As father he wielded the power of a bad father over Okin. Even up to now for Okin in her thirties, this foster father has not once been of help. That first time he didn't offer a cup of tea. He didn't even have her sit down on the raised door frame. In fact, as soon as her brother was gone the other man, who had said, "She'll do at silk spinning in a couple of years," took her and placed her in service at another house. She was ten at the time.

The place he took her was a house in a village near Hachiōji. The family was in the hand-loom weaving business. In addition to Okin there were about ten female employees. They were all girls in their teens. Okin was the only small child. Of course she could not run a loom. Nor could she reel thread. She could do nothing. Her only jobs were, when someone had completed a stripe of warp threads, to carry the batch of long threads to the warp beam, and, when they were being wound onto the wooden spindles of the loom, to help the person who was holding down the spindles and winding the threads, and to insert bamboo slips between the layers of winding thread. Or when the girls who were running the looms dropped a shuttle by mistake, Okin's job was to pick it up. The older girls made fun of Okin. When the supervisor wasn't looking, the girls would deliberately drop shuttles and make Okin pick them up. First here and then there the same thing would occur. Finally someone would kick Okin in the head as she bent down to retrieve the shuttle. Everyone jeered and laughed. Then when the master came in, they would quickly feign a deathly quiet, like mice listening to human footsteps, and continue their work. The cause of the uproar was Okin, they would all say. "What are you crying about?" the master would scold her. He'd beat her. At noon, at snack time, in the evening the girls made nothing but lewd talk. Ostracized though she was, Okin could not help but edge up close. The weaver girls were quick to notice when she did, and they taunted her with, "Okin's only a child but she's got a man," and, "She wants to hear man talk." Okin didn't know how many times a day the weaver girls had made her cry like this. In the end she took to hiding alone in the rest periods in closets and corners where the girls could not find her. The weaver girls felt lonely when there was no one to tease because Okin wasn't there. They hunted her out. Pampering her cleverly at first, they brought her back to the others. Then they would torment her in various ways. They would tease her about her dirty appearance. "She's a beggar child. She's got no spending money and no home to go to for Obon Festival. She's only got one kimono. Hey, beggar child. Beggar child. Beggar child swarming with lice. Everybody, if you go near, you'll get lice." They jeered like this at Okin. They mocked her. Actually what they said was true. She had no one to give her spending money. When the Obon Festival came and the girls all dressed up and went away, Okin had no place to go. She had no other kimono but the rags she wore. When it changed from summer into fall, she had no change of clothes.

There was an old woman in this house, too. Noticing that no one cared for Okin, the woman inquired about the child's welfare. She began to look after Okin. Finally as autumn was ending the old woman noticed that Okin was still wearing a simple, unlined kimono. She took apart an old threadbare, plain blue unlined kimono of her own and used it as lining for Okin. When it grew colder, she took it apart again and inserted cotton padding. When she noticed that Okin's head was littered with straw and thread, she helped her wash her hair. There really were lice nesting in the hair.

The old lady was so kind to her. The weaver girls seem to have grown tired of teasing Okin. The taunting was not so severe as before. But her period of relief was brief. It happened one day: One of the weaver girls said she had lost a five-sen nickel coin. As soon as she said it, another girl declared she, too, was short. Still another said she had seen Okin buying and eating candy. Then and there they all suspected Okin. "I've had to take lots of bitter treatment up to now," Okin said, "but far from stealing from others, I haven't even picked up anything dropped in the street." (Indeed, I believe what she said is true. She was an honest woman.) In response to these suspicions she gave honest answers. Unable to believe this had cleared away the suspicions, she cried for a long time on a pile of straw in a storeroom. She was so sad and vexed that come night she snuck out of the house and fled aimlessly.

She returned alone to Hachiōji.

The village was quiet as the middle of the night, but, when she reached Hachiōji, it was a brightly lit early evening. She walked idly around Hachiōji. She thought to find the house where she had lived with her brother, the house where the old woman hugged her and cried every night. Nowhere could she find it. She may not have rightly remembered the house or the road that led to it. When she thought she had the right neighborhood, the house was never there. The night was growing late. Becoming bewildered, Okin had a sudden idea, child that she was. That house her brother took her to for five minutes once and from where she was sent into service. She would go there. She would ask them where her brother lived. With that thought she looked for the house. She found it. When she went in, the man from before was there. "What? You're back now?" he scolded her. Sobbing, Okin told him what had happened in as much detail as a child could manage. All he said was, "Is that so?" Then, "Your brother is not in Hachiōji now. But don't worry. You can stay here. I'm your father now, so it's all right not to go back to that bad place." He spoke with surprising kindness.

The next morning the master of the house she had fled the night before came to take her back. The man who called himself her father was angry when he saw the visitor, and he shouted, "You take a person's child. You call her a beggar child. You accuse her as a thief. As a child it's only right that she can't endure it. How dare you come here so shamelessly to take her back? Look what you've done, even if it was a mistake, and especially because she came home you regret that a good girl was called a thief. What do you mean by showing up here?" Overhearing this gave Okin a really good feeling. Hearing it, too, the man who had come to fetch her shut his mouth and left without Okin. Nominal Father beamed happily at his family and laughed. That day Okin received a twenty-sen silver coin from that father. Never before and never after—that was the only time Okin received a thing from that father. He was in such a good mood. Only long afterward when Okin reflected on that father's subsequent behavior did she understand the reason for his good mood on that occasion. When he delivered her into service at the hand-loom house, how many years of advance salary payment for her term of service had he received? When Okin fled without completing her term of service, foster father thought, "Well done." He must have then decided to place her in service somewhere else to collect double wages. The twenty-sen coin could be called Okin's reward. That very day indeed, the day after she fled, Okin was promptly sent into service at another house.

The house she was taken to was again in a nearby village. It was a house of silk spinners. She soon learned to reel thread. Okin liked that. Silk reeling stands are usually mounted in line in one large room. In Okin's house there were fifteen or so. Here, one after another in a row they were driven by the power of a large water wheel. Because Okin was a child, she got scraps of bad thread to reel. Here she was not abused so much. No one became a companion, either, but that was all right with her. The child seated next to Okin was sweet and gentle. Here, too, Okin was the smallest. This child was perhaps the next smallest. She taught Okin a lot about reeling thread. What the child's name was Okin could sometimes almost remember. The forgotten name would rise in her throat, but she could never get it out. The child was quiet and pensive. All day long she said hardly a word, but she had a habit of humming quietly. Okin could still hear the tune ringing deep in her ears. She could not remember the words at all, though. The child had a bright, pretty face. Okin was strangely happy beside that child. Then one day it happened: the girl suddenly disappeared. The overseer noticed that no one was seated next to Okin. "Where did the girl go?" he asked. Okin did not know. "I don't know," she said. He asked everybody. "I wonder what happened," everybody said. One said she had seen the child drinking water from the bucket at the well a while before. After a couple of hours the child had not returned. By then it was evening. It grew dark. Everybody worried even more. Some said maybe she went home. One of these they sent as a messenger to the girl's house. The messenger returned late and said the girl had not gone home. The girl's father, worried, too, came back with the messenger. Maybe the child was lost; maybe she had been spirited away, the villagers said as they assembled and organized a search through the night. No trace of the child could be found. After exhausting all means, there was nothing to do but leave it at that, all thought. Nothing was left but sundry rumors. A day passed after the child disappeared, and then on the third night a sudden loud thud resounded and the entire roof trembled. Startled, all gathered in the garden. They thought at first it was an earthquake. Then from the garden they saw that standing dimly white on the thatch roof was the shadowy figure of the lost child, missing since the day before yesterday. Again they were startled. They fetched a ladder and brought the child down. "Then it was interesting," Okin said. According to the child's story, she was carried off by a goblin. As she was drinking water at the well a large man appeared suddenly and carried her into the sky. He carried her to the middle of some unknown mountains. A lot of similar goblins were gathered there in the mountains. When they saw the child, one of the goblins said, "That's a good child. We should let her go."

"Oh?" the goblin who brought her seems to have said. He took her once again up high and flung her with a jerk on her sash. When she noticed where she had fallen, it was the roof of the house. The child became even gloomier and said not a word to anyone for a week. Yes, that's so. She was fifteen or sixteen at the time.

"That was the first time I saw anyone who had been carried off by a goblin."

That's the way it was. Still there was no change for Okin. She remained in service reeling thread at that house until the spring of her fourteenth year. Then father came for her and released her at last from the house. Okin was sorry to take leave of the house she had grown accustomed to. She became maid in a small restaurant near the red-light district of Hachiōji. From the beginning Okin had no intention of staying in this house. She had unpleasant experiences from the maids and from the guests. She was scolded by the mistress for being clumsy. The guests deliberately used code words that were hard to understand when they ordered. They enjoyed seeing her confusion when she failed to understand. They would give her various orders. When she went down to get them, there was no such thing. The people who ordered would double up laughing. Okin did not understand what was so funny. To think of it now, they were all obscene. She was scolded for a fool by the mistress. There were three adult maids in the house, but all they did was sit with the guests. When it came to carrying and taking orders, always there was only Okin. Although the house was small, there were unreasonably many guests. How many dozens of times a day did Okin have to run up and down the stairs. How tired her legs became. People who have not experienced it simply cannot understand—no matter how you try to tell them. Because it was that kind of house, the nights were very late. Mornings were comparatively early, though. The first one to get up in the morning was Okin. The mistress wakened Okin from her own bed. Okin prepared everyone's breakfast. She showed admirable patience, I must admit. However, it soon reached the point that she had to flee the house.

Why it reached the point that Okin had to flee Okin never said. Instead she explained in detail what happened next.

She decided she had to flee no matter what. But this time she would not—she could not—flee to that father's house. If it came to fleeing, she decided she would have to flee to her uncle in Yamanashi. Still, she had no money at all. Bad foster Father must have taken all her pay. The guests gave money to the older waitresses, but no one said a thing about giving to Okin. Nor did they

think she wanted money. Okin thought she might have accumula-
ted from fifty to seventy sen in coins. But even if she had money,
she could not figure out how she could get a train to Yamanashi,
how she could board the train, or how she could find her uncle's
village. In the first place she had forgotten the name of the village.
She could clearly recall the sight and scene of that village. If she
went there, she would recognize it, she thought. Okin was confused. Evening came. She thought she would have to escape this
very evening. Saying she was going to the public bath, she left the
house. She carried a towel and a rice-bran bag in her hand. In that
house when you went out to the public bath, they gave you bath
money and bran for scrubbing. She always carried all the money
she had from before. She brought nothing else with her. She worried about the long distance to Yamanashi and had not yet determined to go. How many times did she walk back and forth, thinking, in front of the bathhouse. She could not make up her mind no
matter what. Suddenly someone called, "Where are you going?"
When she answered, "To the bathhouse," the other person said,
"Oh," without appearing suspicious. At that moment she made up
her mind. Okin did not herself understand why meeting that person precipitated the event. As soon as the person passed from
sight, Okin took off at top speed in the opposite direction. When
she started hurting, she walked. Now and then she ran again. . . .
When she could run no more, she walked. . . . Absorbed in a
dream, she walked. . . .

When she came to her senses, she saw she had fallen asleep in a
place she did not know. All was smoky white. Gradually she came
to see where she was. It seemed to be mountains. She was lying on
wet grass. What made it white was mist of a summer morning in
the mountains. Her surroundings emerged by stages as the fog
lifted slowly. When it had fully cleared, high peaks soared abruptly
before her eyes. Light from the morning sun burst onto the crests.
Okin looked around, and from the narrow mountain road leading
through the trees a white-haired old man wearing a deerskin work
skirt emerged alone and unexpected. The old man did not at first
see that Okin was there. He walked briskly up to where she was

lying and then quickly jumped back two or three paces. The old man stared as if he could not believe his eyes. After a bit he was the first to speak:

"You—what are you doing in a place like this?"

Okin stood up and said she was going to her uncle's house. The old man asked, where was Uncle's house. When she could not answer, the old man kept repeating, "What village? Well, which one? What village is it?" He mentioned two or three names of villages that seemed to be nearby. They were all names that Okin did not know.

She spoke daringly, "It's in Yamanashi."

"Yamanashi? Where did you come from?"

"From Hachiōji."

Again the old man was surprised. He jumped back two or three steps just as when he first saw her. In a voice that startled her into jumping, he shouted, "You're possessed by a fox. Look at that! Look at those eyes!"

He poked his finger at her face as a child would do. Okin was startled. Then in a relieved tone he said, "Oh. O.K. now. The fox has gone. What eyes it made. I was really amazed."

He approached her again, talking as he did. Coming here from Hachiōji you won't end up in Yamanashi. You come out in exactly the opposite direction in Kawagoe. If you want to know which is nearer, Kawagoe is nearer than Hachiōji. The road here from Hachiōji is not something for women and children. He explained all this in detail, and, when he learned from Okin that she had walked through in one night, he was even more astonished. "You were possessed by a fox. There are bad foxes around here," he nodded to himself. He repeated over and over how frightful Okin's eyes were when she was possessed by the fox spirit. As he talked he led her home to his own house. Blooming there were large mountain lilies as tall as Okin. She was about to touch one when she noticed she was still clutching in her hand the towel and bran bag from last night. Maybe she really was possessed by a fox. Even Okin came to think so. When she had run off at top speed and turned to look back from time to time, no matter when or how many times she looked she saw right behind her each time the two strings of glittering lights from the Hachiōji red-light district. No matter how she walked and walked the lights never faded. As the lights flickered in the distance, Okin walked on and on in single-minded absorption with that distance. At the moment the old man said, "You're possessed by a fox," the fox spirit must have dropped out with a start. Okin thought so. The old man thought so. The old man's house was a solitary cottage. He worked alone as a charcoal maker. Okin stayed at his house for a while at the old man's urging. He felt sorry for Okin. He comforted her. "In the fall I go down from the mountains. I'll go to Hachiōji, and there I can search out someone to take you to Yamanashi."

For some reason Okin was much comforted just by the old man and his wife.

Up to now Okin had been talking almost without stopping for breath. Suddenly she broke off.

Then she added, "Well, to wind it up, that's about it. I may be out of order to say so, but that's how I came to be here. The man that my brother turned me over to was an out-and-out scoundrel, according to what I heard later. He was said to be a gambling boss who would bet on anything. That man, he brought me utter misery. He was my parent. My parent, he said. He hounded me wherever I went. Just five or six years ago he was still alive. When I came to this village and decided to register my domicile here with Mampei, my domicile seemed to be still listed with that foster parent. I didn't know what he would say, so I consulted someone who advised me to wait until I was twenty-five. At twenty-five we entered into free marriage."

Okin used the words *free marriage.* Probably she had heard people say that in those days.

All she had said was, "Well, to wind it up . . ." But I soon came to understand how Okin had made a living and how she came to this village. Okin hardly concealed it from us. We could surmise perfectly well. We could get by without speaking the harsh words. Without actually asking we heard from nobody in particular that when she first came to the village she was waitress in a kind of country teahouse that used to be there some years ago. The villagers never said she was bad. Everyone said she was a kind, good, openhearted woman. Even the wife of the priest at I Temple, that woman who had to say something about everyone without distinction, said so. When we remarked that Okin had been helpful to us, the priest's wife said, "That's because she is a kind, honest, good person." Okin seemed to see herself as a good person, too. She tried to be good. That is, Okin spoke as follows: "Because Okin has experienced many things, people who are suffering attract my attention." Okin's house was on the road from Hachiōji going toward Yokohama. It was on a little rise on that road. As Okin worked around her house, she would catch sight of unfamiliar people passing on the road below. They were trudging along, looking careworn and barely lifting their heavy feet. Without asking, one knew for sure these were people without money and weighted down with worries. In a world with better ways to travel, why would an ordinary person want to trudge this road from Hachiōji toward Yokohama? Okin often saw people like this. One time she noticed a young man and woman walking together. Another time it was a man carrying a baby. Once it was a young woman resting in the shade of a tree by Okin's house and not about to start out again after an hour or more. She wondered whether the woman weren't pregnant. Another time it was an old man who came into the house and asked for a glass of water. Looking discouraged, he asked Okin how many miles was it to Yokohama. Okin always had a word or two to say about something to all these people. Okin well knew the power of a kind word at a time like that. She would give them three sen or five sen or sometimes a rice ball or a potato, whatever she happened to have at hand. If she was asked, of course she gave, but, even when she wasn't asked, she gave. "Excuse me, but would you like this?" Okin would inquire. The other party would stare at her first and then reply, "Yes, please." Nearly ten people out of ten would react the same way. When she handed it to them, they would respond gratefully in various ways. They would say they would surely never forget such kindness. Some would compulsively ask her name. They were going to Tokyo, they would say, but, when they got home, they promised they would surely send a thank-you note. There were three or four who said that. She had not yet received a single thank-you note, though. Okin did not want thank-you notes. She did wonder sometimes how these people made out afterward. She remembered her own past. "But," she said, "the world is full of gossips. There may be people who have seen me give five or ten sen to persons like that. For Okin who lives as nothing more than a beggar herself, it's beyond her station to give alms like that. I've heard people talk that way. I always try to hide it from people. Sometimes I had to run after a person three or four blocks to hand over the rice ball after I made sure no one was watching."

That's the tenor of what she said. Some cases she told me in more detail. Because they didn't relate to her own life story, and because she did not repeat them over and over but told them only once, I don't remember them very well. It is too bad that I can't relate them now. Anyhow, Okin was that kind of woman. Abused by a harsh world, she was always good-hearted after all. What's more, she was outspoken. Out of character, sometimes she told corny jokes. On those occasions I felt I had encountered the tea-house waitress in Okin. "But really," someone said, "Okin is basically a fickle woman. Her liking for men is troubling. On top of that, Mampei is a man of unparalleled goodness. Even now Okin is said to be intimate with a straw boss who comes to her house. Every evening she goes to his mountain hut. Meeting someone on the way, she will say she is going to the mountains to get wood scraps to make a bucket. Or she'll say she is going to the mountains to build a fire in the bath for the boss man. Recently during the S Festival a group of young people working in the mountains came partying by the hut about 2 A.M. and saw that Okin was still there. Every night she comes home late with the boss man, but Mampei never says a thing about it. Such stories are still circulating widely —that's because Mampei sometimes takes off with his tools and spends a month away wandering around on odd jobs in neighboring villages." I heard these rumors about Okin.

Even though we didn't ask her, Okin once explained that these rumors were all trumped-up lies.

"My life is like a novel," she said, continuing her story.

The brother that Okin was separated from—indeed abandoned by—when she was a small child she had never seen again. She didn't know where he was or what he was doing. Not only her brother: news of her uncle and aunt had ceased abruptly. She could not remember the name of the village where they lived. There was no one near who would know that she could ask. For more than twenty years she was totally bereft of relatives. She thought her uncle and aunt might have died.

Three or four years earlier, though, she unexpectedly had a chance to meet them again.

It was the beginning of summer that year: someone she had never seen or known suddenly called at her house. He looked like a peddler and said he came from Yokohama. At first she thought he was a peddler, but he carried nothing to sell. He had come to look her up on purpose. When he saw Okin he said, "Excuse me, but I've got something to ask." Where was she born? he asked. Then suddenly he blurted out, "Don't you have a brother you haven't seen for twenty years?" She was astonished. She hadn't thought of her brother recently. If she remembered him at times, it was never with the thought that she could or would see him again. When she was asked by this strange fellow, she could make no ready answer. She stole a hard glance at his face. She could not make out, though, whether this was or was not her brother. She had utterly forgotten Brother's face. If it were her brother, he should be a somewhat bigger man, Okin thought as she recalled the ancient quarrel between Brother and Uncle.

The stranger looked at Okin, who could not answer, and he said, "The person who asked me to search you out thought from what he had heard that there was no mistake about who you were."

So the man wasn't her brother after all, Okin thought. Learning that was weird. What do you suppose her brother was doing now? What was his scheme in sending someone to find her? It would be good to avoid worrying Mampei. . . . Suppose her brother had done something bad, and he was a person who might well do something bad? Maybe this fellow was a policeman. She suspected so. Her heart was thumping. It cannot be, and yet, even if she tried, she could not deny knowing her brother, she thought. Suddenly a strong feeling welled up that she might see, that she wanted to see him again. Her life flashed briefly before her. The man said, "Yep, that's right, isn't it?" He spoke of the man who commissioned him to find her, the man who must be her brother, as a chief priest. This supposed brother he said was in the A Temple in the Noge district of Yokohama, where he had become chief priest. He told her that Brother wanted to meet his younger sister, on whom he had inflicted such misery, as soon as he could find her. Brother's age and other factors mentioned all coincided. There could be no doubt that he was Okin's older brother, she concluded. Still, Okin felt she could not yet believe what the man had said. Suppose there was someone else in the world with a life exactly like hers, and there was a priest inquiring after this younger sister, she wondered at last. Mampei had gone that day to U's home to fix a bath bucket, and Okin went to meet him there. She conferred with him on the way home. Without meeting that mysterious brother how could she know whether he was real or a fake, and so that very day she left for Yokohama with the man. She worried about what she should do when they met, if both she and her brother had forgotten each other's faces? It was, happily, her real brother. The moment she saw Brother's face, the face she could not recall no matter how much she thought about it on the way, she exclaimed in wonder, "That's him all right!"

Neither happy nor sad, she stood blankly in the dirt-floor entrance to the priest's quarters.

Brother asked not one word about Okin's later life. He spoke in rapid succession, calmly but only of himself, and apologized to Okin at every word. He was a big man after all. He looked to be over fifty. As a child he had been a boy priest in his father's temple, but finding it disagreeable he fled the temple. He became a wandering actor in the country. He took to gambling. He became a policeman. He spoke at length of all these things. He told her politely but not in sequence about how, not so much in the beginning as over the last four or five years, he had most wanted to see Okin, as she had of course earnestly wanted to see her brother and her uncle. Although he could keep track of Uncle's address along with his own, he could not find Okin's. Brother himself had repeatedly gone to Hachiōji to look, but sadly he had almost given up hope.

As Okin listened to her brother she learned for the first time that she had another brother. She learned, listening, that this older brother was from a mother different from theirs, and he was about forty years older than they were. The brother was in Tokyo, a priest of high standing in the famous N H Temple in Asakusa. He was much respected. "In that he differs from me," Brother said. A fine, gentle man, wholehearted and without deceit. Brother had consulted with this older brother about the search for Okin. "When I tell him I have found you, how happy he will be," Brother said to her. "You must meet him some day." But Okin didn't think she wanted to meet that brother at all. That was not unreasonable. Although he could be called brother, he had a different mother. This was the first she had heard of him even as a rumor, to say nothing of see him. There was too much difference in their status. She would rather meet Uncle and Auntie. When she heard from her brother that he thought they were still alive, she felt like jumping for joy. She could not say a thing, however. A feeling of reserve toward her brother somehow kept her from speaking. Brother talked at length about Uncle and Aunt. They were still alive. In Yamanashi but no longer in the same village, Uncle was a forest ranger for a hydroelectric company in the mountains. "Although I had long thought I really should visit Uncle, I didn't have the time for one thing. Then when I tried to think over my own past, I felt terribly embarrassed at the thought of seeing Aunt and Uncle without first facing Okin again," he said. After he had left Okin in Hachiōji he had been back to Uncle's more than once. In those days he roamed around Yamanashi and Nagano. All this he told her in brief. Although he later sent letters, he did not visit again: "I thought if I could find you first, I could have you go and extend my apologies. But I gave up when I couldn't find you. I thought perhaps you had died and I decided I should go myself. Now that I've found you, I'd rather have you go first," Brother said. "I could go, too, but the Bon Festival is coming up and I can't get away soon. Fortunately, a man I know, an engineer for the mountain company, is in Tokyo on a purchasing mission. He should be back in Yokohama by now. I heard he would be returning to the mountains in two or three days. If it's not inconvenient for you, how about going with him? If you go, I'll send a message to your husband. Or at your convenience you could go at another time soon. Do you want to go home to the country first? You could come back soon with your husband." So Brother conferred with Okin. As she listened to her brother, Okin's face wetted with an unexpected stream of tears. The first she knew, the tears were dropping into her lap. In the carriage on the way Okin had pondered and wondered, if it turned out to be her brother, would she say this or would she say that, but, when she arrived and faced her brother, she could not say a thing. She forgot what it was she had been thinking to say. Why had that evil man become her foster father? What about the old lady in Hachiōji? Had someone named Otsune been Brother's wife in those days? She could not ask anything like that. She said nothing whatever about the old days. She spoke only to answer about her husband Mampei and to explain that, although it had been nine years, the two of them had no children yet. As the night grew late, Brother at last fell silent.

Suddenly in a tone of great importance he asked, "How old are you?"

"Thirty-three," Okin answered. Brother was silent.

Then from Okin came the question: "You, Brother?"

"Forty-three," he said, then fell silent and thoughtful again.

. . . Because there was the chance she wanted, Okin accepted Brother's proposal to leave at once to visit Uncle and Aunt in the mountains. Brother readied several gifts for them. He provided a new summer kimono for Okin. He ordered and had it sewn in one night. He arranged for the engineer to escort her, and they departed for Yamanashi. They left the train at K station shortly before Kōfu city. They walked about five miles up a climbing mountain road. At evening he stepped into a house by the side of the road with a grape arbor in front. He was a silent man who spoke hardly at all to Okin on the way. He knew nothing therefore of why Okin was going to Uncle's. When they arrived, he didn't say, "This is it," or anything. But as soon as Okin went in, she thought this was it. In the house were an old man and an old woman: no one else. The engineer greeted them as he lit a cigarette. The woman served tea to both of them. Okin stared at the man and woman. Both looked very healthy with full heads of hair. Entirely white they were. They were undoubtedly her aunt and uncle. No question about it. What should she say? What she had prepared to say became totally useless when she entered the house. . . . That is, the old man and woman who were her uncle and aunt took it fully for granted that she was the engineer's wife. They addressed her as, "Madam, Madam," and treated her exactly as they did the engineer. "You probably don't need to go farther up today, do you? Why don't you and your wife stay here, even though this is a poor little cottage. You can go on in the morning, when it's cool." They urged this on the engineer. The engineer said that after this brief rest he would go on. The moon was out tonight, and it was bright. "That's all right for you, but your wife as a woman must surely be tired," the aunt said. Auntie's voice was exactly like it used to be. "Well," the engineer said, standing up impatiently as if he were embarrassed here. "Can't you possibly stay?" the old man and woman said to the engineer and Okin in parting. Okin was deeply troubled by the farewell. Helpless and bewildered, she followed the engineer out of the house.

The engineer turned and said suspiciously to Okin, "Wasn't this where you were going?"

Okin collected her wits. Immediately she went back into Uncle's house. She forgot to thank the engineer for guiding her here.

As she entered she called out, "Uncle, Auntie, I'm Okinu, who left you twenty years ago. It's Okinu."

Her spirits suddenly welled up at these words. Without thinking, she fell down in tears.

"Okinu is it? Really? It's not a dream?" It took a while for Auntie finally to say this.

"Still alive?" Uncle said at last.

"My eyes are misty, and I can't see clearly," Auntie said. She cried. They all cried. Even in the dim evening light, even after lighting the lamp.

*　　*　　*

"My real name is Okinu. Everywhere I go it becomes Okin." She explained this finally, as if she had suddenly thought of it.

Gloom in the City

(TOKAI NO YŪUTSU, 1922)

*P*EOPLE in the neighborhood looked at the house and thought it strange. Two people only—a young husband and wife —lived there with their two dogs. The wife went out every day in the morning. Her gaudy clothing was no common form of dress. The wife looked to be about twenty. Once she had left, the house to all appearances was vacant. Not one panel of the front shutters was ever open. But the house was not vacant—*he* lived there.

The small one-story house was set halfway up a hillside that for some reason was called Ghost Hill. The name was not inappropriate for that narrow, unpleasant, sloping street. It was neither a blind alley nor an outskirt to the metropolis, but most people had no business with that street. No one but those who lived in the neighborhood even knew of its existence. His house was midway up the slope. It was a house where all the day long the sun never shone. Instead, the dry winter wind swirled clouds of dust off the slope and through the house.

He opened the front door wide and looked out with a dreary feeling. Not a single ray of sun was shining; dust clouds clattered grittily against the shoji doors. Although he had not opened any of the shutters in front, clouds of dust streamed in on the cold wind that came through the cracks. With no sun all day and with no housekeeper there, the house was all the more dim, dark, cold, and desolate. Not saying a word all day, he sat burrowed into the movable *kotatsu* heater that his wife had prepared for him by a window before she departed. He did nothing in particular. Every day he thought of various things. It was all rather detached. For his heart and his senses to be touched, he needed a resilient heart. His heart, though, had no resilience left. Among his trifling thoughts the one that pressed on him most forcefully was indeed, "Why doesn't the sun shine on this house?"

That was the trivial truth. Wasn't the fact that there was no life left in him wholly the result of dwelling in a house untouched by sunlight? He complained of that to his wife one night. Thinking he was talking like a spoiled child, she consoled him by saying there were times the sun did hit the house. When she left every morning at about nine o'clock, the sun was shining on the front window shutters. On hearing his wife say this, he rose with her early the next morning. He opened a front window to see, and there at the edge of the upper left panel of the shoji was a triangle of sunlight just the shape you could make by putting together the thumbs and forefingers of both hands. Although it was the winter sun, it glowed with the particular brilliance of the morning sun, boldly and brightly, on the sooty, silvery-gray shoji. When he slid the shoji window open, the rays of sunlight, piercing in iridescence through swirls of dust to strike in a triangle, illuminated a layer of white dust and reddened the brown tatami floor. Like a child from a backyard tenement greeting an unexpected guest of honor, he gazed in astonished rapture at the surprising sunlight flowing into his home. The sun spilled through a little crack between the discrepant roof lines of two two-story houses across the street. He looked toward the sun. It must have been fifty days since he had seen the sun from his house. The sun's rays crept moment by moment over the old tatami until, to his gratification, the patch of sun no larger than a hand had grown in ten minutes to a triangle of more than three feet on the slanted side. He squatted and watched the small spot of precious sun. Sunlight that lit up half his shoulders spread at last to cover all. Then moment by moment the rays of sunlight on his shoulders appeared to shrink. In ten minutes they had disappeared, and there was not a beam of sunlight anywhere. The sun had struck his house—the house he was convinced the sun would never touch—for twenty minutes out of a whole day! After that he got up every morning with his wife to enjoy the twenty minutes of sunlight. About to eat breakfast with his wife, he slid open one panel of the front shutters to bathe himself in the stream of morning sun. Twenty minutes! Then he crawled back into bed. He drowsed in the easily woken sleep of a dog. When his wife went out in the morning, she made the rounds of the stores to order supplies for his evening meal; when the delivery boys arrived, the dogs sleeping by the kitchen door, lightly like their master, would let out a bark. He would open his eyes. In this condition his day became noon. Sometimes he would finish the breakfast leftovers for lunch, or he would skip lunch completely. . . .

To say a little more about the relation between the house and the sun: for nearly an hour one afternoon a little ray of sunlight shone onto the fence directly facing the window where he happened to be nestled in the *kotatsu* heater. Literally within arm's reach of his window, the fence stood on the boundary between his house and his neighbor's. He noted from the sun's reflection a faintly warmish light in the dusky two-mat room. Taking a good look, he saw that, because it was his neighbor's fence and not his own and because the nails were all pounded through from the other side, the points of the nails protruded into the sunlight. On a whim he went over to his wife's mirror stand and picked up a rather large mirror. He wrenched the nickeled feet around backward and focused the circular part onto the protruding, sunlit nails in the fence. The sunlight was reflected from the mirror onto the wall above his desk in the little room. He stared for a while at the tiny spot of sun above him and then raised his hand to block the narrow streak of light. The sun struck his hand. Staring at the sunstruck hand, he alternately clenched and opened his palm like a baby. At length he arose from the *kotatsu*, and, letting the ray of light strike his face, he looked at that little sun in the mirror, the mirror in the sun. He stared intently for a while. He did that simply out of tedium, but, when he noticed what he was doing, he was stirred by an ineffable sense of the absurd together with a feeling of melancholy. At that moment he wondered whether he were in jail, or, if not that, whether he were crazy.

*　　*　　*

He chanced to remember the house in the country where they lived until two months ago. The garden of that house, the shaded roses in the garden—how symbolic even now were those rustic shaded roses of barely six months ago. That's why they were so beautiful. But for him today there was nothing to entrust with his dreams. It was a gray city, a house the sun never touched, a season where all sounds were vanishing into winter. He was a literary youth with no talent and no accomplishment. . . . No, he was husband to a minor actress in a suburban theater. . . .

The day straggled into dusk. The sun set especially early in the house it never touched. What made this house alone appear so dark was that the lights were not yet lit. In the restlessness of a long twilight he searched in the brazier where the embers had died for a live coal no bigger than the tip of his little finger to blow into flame. He resumed his straggled thoughts, left straggling from before. . . . Will my whole life rot away, will I be no more than the husband of an actress in a suburban theater? . . . Maybe so . . . If so, that's O.K. Forsaken by my mentors and my friends after all their goodwill, maybe I've really got no talent. . . . Who would put any hope in a man who, of his own accord, has lost his scant self-confidence?

His wife said he'd be stimulated if he went back to the city, and she took him back there. At first when she came home late at night, she would ask whether he had accomplished something that day, but recently, he thought, she hasn't even said that, has she? . . . People have completely forgotten the me that everybody said was "perhaps a man of talent." That's not unreasonable. Haven't I been losing moment by moment my own feeling of being "perhaps a man of talent?" Well, that's all right. It's good that I awoke early from such idle dreams. Still, how sad I'll be if I have to live my whole life in this sunless house.

"A nobody?" He murmured the trite phrase aloud as he thought of it. A nobody—a man of the shade. A man not of the world; a person shamed by the world. He thought about that, but the ordinariness of the words *a nobody* didn't have such a powerful sound for him. The literal meaning of *shade*, "a person who must live in a sunless place," was frightful to him.

Raised in the south, he was sensitive to the cold. As flowers cannot bloom in the cold, so a man's fancies are likely to freeze in the winter. For one whose character could barely survive in the intoxication of his fancies, the dulling effect of winter on those fancies was most depressing. In winter, therefore, he always set aside an idle hour for basking in the sun. Yet the sun never shone on this house. Growing up in a middle-class home, he had never experienced winter in a sunless house. It made him feel entirely wretched that he had to live in such a house. So he thought, it doesn't suit me to have to live in a sunless house. It is not only me whom it doesn't suit; it wouldn't suit anybody. No, not just humans—don't dogs long for sunlight, too? Whether it's for one or two winters or the condition continues longer, won't I become fully accustomed to such a sunless home? People can get accustomed to any bad condition. . . . Isn't that one of the saddest things about people?

As he stared intently into the coals that were beginning to glow red and burn, he dwelt on these vacant, dispirited thoughts aroused by the hysteria of evening, when suddenly the room became light. The electric light was on, and it illuminated the dirty lunch dishes left scattered on the small table pushed into a corner. At the moment the light came on, he noted absentmindedly that it was five by the alarm clock on the buffet. Looking at the clock face, he thought, it is still five and a half hours before my wife comes home. How restless and yet how boring was the half day since he awoke, barely before twelve.

❊　　❊　　❊

"I went by your house two or three days ago. I thought of calling out, but the door was shut and on looking I saw that the dogs were asleep on the porch. Life in your house is like a novel, isn't it?" one of his older friends had said to him. . . . His friend's house was in a residential district less than a block from his own. Returning home from walking his dogs, he sometimes stopped in. There on occasion he would run into a Western-style oil painter, who would look hard at his face and say, "Interesting. Definitely pictorial. The condition of your hair and the look of your beard— not one thing breaks the harmony! I'd love to paint your face using my blues and blacks as basic colors." He knew why people said things like that. The stagnant, turbid, chilly atmosphere of his house exuded into the street and affected passersby. The exhaustion of his spirit, showing wretchedly on his face, attracted the attention even of strangers. "Life in your house is a novel." "I'll paint your face using blues and blacks as basic colors." Those words had the same effect on his nervous state as if he had been told, "Your whole life is an interesting case of decay . . . because you are a defeated person." Although he thought that it was a warped view, he had to admit it was natural for someone to find that failing in him.

His wife's mother sometimes came to visit. "With all your mysterious, conceited manner," she would say, "you've got no way of earning a living." She was reluctant to trouble this strange son-in-law who, if he wanted to talk about money or anything else, would turn aside as if he were asking at someone else's behest, even though it was his own business. Smiling sourly she would insinuate, "The only work you can do is to be caretaker for the dogs in someone's mansion." Various things such as these that people had said lingered in his heart. Sometimes the shame of it all would suddenly rise to the surface of his feelings. It made him knit his eyebrows and screw his cheeks into a bitter smile. That happened every night when the light went on, and, as he looked around the suddenly illuminated room, he recalled . . . "Coming to look at your house is like looking at the house of a speculator who is failing rapidly. The bureaus and braziers and buffets are not appropriate to the house, and the wife is not yet worn down with housework." Those were the words of his friend Emori Shozan. The expression, so typical of Shozan, amused him. But when he thought of Emori Shozan who once said those words, his wry smile soured as it gave way to more solemn and bitter feelings.

*   *   *

Emori Shozan was without exaggeration a failure, he thought. . . . As soon as he thought it, he realized the very thought placed Shozan lower than he had fallen himself. Wasn't that an unwitting way to console or to boost himself? If so, that was utterly mean, he reflected. He wasn't the only one; everyone who knew Shozan looked down on the elder friend. Shozan concealed his age, and no one knew how old he was. He was at least a generation, ten years, older. When he spoke about anything, he often first explained that he was about to set out in the swim of literary trends and movements of an earlier era. All his younger friends smiled when they heard this. According to Shozan, he was acquainted with the two or three great masters of the earlier literary era. Two or three stories from the hands of these masters had just been published in appropriate journals. That gave him pleasant memories. Since his first venture into literary life, he had firmly believed in the principle of naturalism in art, which put value on experience. He not only believed it; he served the principle wholeheartedly. When his mother had died about twenty years before, he had come into an inheritance of two thousand yen, not a small sum for those days. He resolved to spend his life perfecting the talent he believed he had. For a novelist, everyone said at the time, the experiences of life were more important than scholarship or character or anything else. To buy the experience of life as well as to enjoy his youth, he spent years wandering here and there among summer resorts and hot-spring inns so long as his money lasted. Shozan's experience at length became rich. Then when the time came to use that rich experience in a first attempt to launch himself leisurely into the literary world, the literary trends (indistinguishable from popular fashion, groundless and changeable) had shifted from the principle he believed in to a course almost completely counter to his thinking. However, if one's maturing brain develops in the atmosphere of one set of principles, without doubting, and if those principles start to evanesce, the blind believer is long tormented by his ghostly ideals. Those who are weak or those whose beliefs are most firmly rooted are haunted by those ghosts for the rest of their lives. Indeed in later years when his beliefs became embarrassing to him, he could in no way change them. When Shozan learned that his younger companions, one after another, had adopted ideas from a newer age, he understood with tolerance. His own ideas, word by word, bespoke their antiquation. With inborn goodness the humble Shozan received all his younger friends in courteous language. Was this somehow the kindness of a mentor leading his juniors, or, looked at more malevolently, was it Shozan's concern that, if he carelessly spoke so kindly, the younger ones would not talk back as equals? Shozan would often talk of the plots of stories he was thinking of writing. If anyone listening were to say, "That's interesting," Shozan would reply happily, "Is it interesting? Oh, do you like it? How about it? How about trying to write it? You may have this material. . . . There are lots of other experiences I'd rather write about." The fact that Shozan in pride at his own experience wanted to offer material to others was celebrated talk among the friends. Behind his back they laughed and mimicked his tone of voice as they conjectured about his state of mind in wanting them to write about his experiences.

Four or five years earlier Shozan had somehow become acquainted with Ozawa Mineo—the *he* who is the central character in this story. It seems that Shozan sought to make friends as widely as possible out of necessity for his livelihood. Only friends that were younger than he served this purpose. Shozan used to come often to meet him—perhaps he was too new a friend—and beg for money. After mentioning some job opportunity, he asked for a summer dress coat he needed for that purpose. When Shozan learned how little *he* was receiving in allowance from his father and how little money there was in the house, he appealed for the loan of several books. Just as *he* was about to ask Shozan whether it weren't natural for job applicants to appear in shabby clothes, he decided there was something valid in feeling unwilling to apply for a job or a loan in too shabby a dress. No matter how odd it seemed, he went along with Shozan's request without showing the least sign of reluctance. Of course the job didn't work out, and Shozan showed up at his house wearing the silk-gauze *haori* jacket that he had obtained from the secondhand store. Holding the collar in his fingers to show off the coat, he expressed his gratitude in the polite words *thanks to you*. He disclosed that he did not get the job and that the position of reporter on a country newspaper would be beneath him anyway. Ten days later, when *he* was out on an evening stroll, he was caught in a sudden shower. Hurriedly boarding a streetcar, he ran into Shozan, who was clutching in his bosom the silken coat carefully folded up in a newspaper. "It'll shrink if it gets wet, you know," Shozan said. Feeling that Shozan would make an admirable character for a story, he offered his friends the topic of Shozan's summer coat.

Later, when he abandoned all his friends and moved to the country, he of course had no occasion to meet Shozan. On his return to the city, relationships with his other friends remained as distant as when he had been in the country, and social contacts were resumed only with Shozan. That is, it was Shozan who came frequently to call at his house—the house in the shade. The decline in Shozan's livelihood seems to have accelerated during the time— less than a year—that *he* had spent in the country. Shozan had picked up an infectious disease somewhere in the old days when he was wandering around searching out life's experiences. As a result his hair became thin, his face dusky, and his thinking uncertain. He soon tired of things and his body invariably ailed in one part or another. In this condition, the poverty of Shozan's dragged-out existence went of course without saying, but, although he had been making various drawn-out apologies over the past two or three years, he never tried to borrow spending money from *him*. Looking at *his* present living conditions, Shozan understood at a glance that it would be useless to raise the question. Nowadays Shozan came frequently to call with no expectation of material benefit. Truly, it was pure friendship! he thought. That made him fearfully sad and solemn. Shozan no doubt had found the atmosphere in his house easier and more comfortable than anywhere else because Shozan saw his junior following down the same path he himself had taken. But then Shozan on occasion confided in him more candidly than before about his feelings and his life. For now he wasn't seeking anything more than consolation. Two or three years earlier at the beginning of the relationship he had to look down on Shozan, and even now he harbored the same feelings. Yet Shozan treated him without reservation as his best friend. He found that somehow hard to bear, strong in self-respect as he was. But what connection was there in fact between the possession of self-respect and a person with a future? Shozan had his self-respect. And yet? "And yet how much I must differ from Shozan," he thought. He believed that, vaguely, but then it was normal to think on. . . . "But no matter what you say, there isn't anyone else, is there, other than Shozan, any friend who pays any attention to me for any reason, who meets and talks to me at all about human life and art? No, there may be. But everyone is wrapped up in his own work. That's entirely natural. For that reason Shozan is my only friend. . . . No, there is another."

His other friend was an errand boy who worked for a second-hand bookstore. A youth of about twenty, he showed up one day just as *he* was thinking he had some spending money. The boy had a pile of books and magazines that one of the store's customers was selling by the lot at no set price. Recognizing that they were all literary publications, he asked how much the whole batch would be. Altogether two yen eighty sen at best price was the answer, so he bought them up, and the boy proceeded to offer him opinions on a whole range of artistic, human, and philosophical subjects. Did he know the philosophy of Bergson? Learning that he was not acquainted with it, the boy gave him a general outline. He didn't understand the explanation at all. He could not decide whether that was because the boy was talking nonsense or because his brain had lost the power of comprehension. There was nothing for it but to listen in silence to the boy's exultant explanation. The boy seemed to find something satisfying in his attitude, and he began to show up at the house on a weekly basis. Two or three times thereafter the boy dropped in while loitering on errands for the store and pressed him cleverly with names like Tagore and Bergson, as he had the first time. Sometimes the boy brought books popular with the reading public and lent them with the recommendation that he try reading them.

"I don't like being an errand boy for that secondhand bookstore.

There are lots of things I'd like to try to write, and anyway I'm just reading and writing without letting the proprietor see me. Please look at some of this. I envy you, always sitting in front of your desk," the boy said.

Although he had naught but disdain for Shozan or the errand boy from the bookstore, whenever the conversation turned to the arts, he (with his instinctive affection for the arts) could not but express enthusiastically some fitting opinion of his own. After they had left, he felt a lonely void in his heart, a feeling that his self-respect had been wounded for nothing. When he went out to walk his ever-chained dogs and there was no one left in the vacant house, he wondered whether somebody hadn't come to call, somebody who said he wanted to talk about something other than money, and there wasn't anybody other than those two, Shozan and the bookstore boy. He felt he should go home at once and see.

* * *

The arts are really a marvelous thing. Such marvelous things are rare in this world. You can explain by saying you don't find anything else adequate to compare the arts with. Let's liken the arts to that marvelous fever that afflicts every person severely or slightly: the emotion of love. Those passions resemble each other closely. The young person unrequited in love will usually turn to hatred for his loved one. . . . As time passes this may change to longing, and in order to forget it is normal to look back on the lover who is the object of desire with feelings at least temporarily of hatred, resentment, or contempt. If the artist on the other hand finds himself in some worldly distress on account of the arts, he will still be happy and proud that it's all in the name of art. Saying how much he loves the arts, he will never turn to hatred, disrespect, or neglect for them. When he's discouraged from feeling that his talent is weak or that he doesn't fit the times, his devotion for the arts becomes deeper and more magical. It's a kind of religious conversion. Maybe you can say it is like the faith of Job, who cried out, "The Lord gave, and the Lord hath taken away." In the case of religion most people think this is not possible unless one is a devout believer. In the case of the arts almost all who aspire to participate will cherish the feelings on their own without having to perform any particular service. Of course there are those who find the arts of no account, but for Ozawa Mineo at that time his whole life was of no account. If he abandoned art, there was no other place in life for him to go. That was a little different in effect from a religious devotee in doubt about his gods and agonizing over whether to prostrate himself before the devil. . . . No matter how you try to explain these things, they are incomprehensible to anyone not born with the instincts of an artist, not bewitched by the unknowable spirit of the arts.

The father with a son who embraces these mysterious, undefinable feelings in most cases pursues the same sequence of measures in dealing with his son. Father and son feel discontented with each other, but finally out of love the father gives in. He grieves for having an eccentric son, and, then, becoming resigned, he lets the son go his way. Ozawa Mineo—the *he* who is the central character in this story—had chosen his own way in precisely this manner. His father was a doctor practicing in a country town. His grandfather was a doctor. In this family of many generations of doctors, his father had wanted his oldest son, *him*, to become a doctor, too. But considering his character as a youth, Father had changed his mind. Father owned some fairly good reclaimed land in Hokkaido, and, if he sent his son to an agricultural college, he might be able to manage that land. Father turned over in his mind various hopeful fancies for his son, but, as the son grew up, he became addicted on his own, and not through outside influence, to reading poetry and fiction. When Father realized that his son's ambitions were tending toward literature, he had to allow the boy to follow his desires. Father was not completely without understanding of literary things. *He* was clearly more fortunate than other literary young people in having a perceptive father. But you shouldn't forget that under any circumstances a father and son are father and son. Father had allowed him to pursue the study of literature; Father demanded the son become a scholar. He did not approve at all of the son's becoming an artist. The son had not the least intention of becoming a scholar. . . . *He* believed scholar and artist were different things for him. He had betrayed his father's hope for him to enter a public school, and with barely an apology he had entered a more easygoing private school instead. Once again ignoring his parents' wishes that he at least graduate from that school, he soon withdrew in mid-course. Then without consulting them he had taken as wife a woman totally unknown to anyone in his family. What's more, there was nothing they could discern that he was going to work at in any way. It bothered his mother to hear in the course of events that the sons of her husband's friends would be coming home from their schools for summer vacation; some of them would be graduating next year from medical school; others were in their second or third year at the university; yet others would be returning next year as bachelors of medicine. She was ashamed before her husband to have borne an indolent son like *him*. . . . She harped on these things when he came home from afar now and again to ask for money. His father, however, didn't say a word about that. He spoke instead of more reasonable and hence more scathing concerns: "You've said for a long time that you are an individualist. You act that way. When are you going to do something for the family, as a member of the family? To rely on the family while pursuing only your own convenience—does that make sense? The 'Blending of Japan and the West'—that's you to a tee. It's the blending for your own convenience of Western individualism and the Japanese ideal of the family." He would crack bitter jokes like that. Or, "You got married without duly consulting me. At the time I asked how on earth you proposed to support a family. You made no answer at all. I thought that you were entitled to your share. I'm sending you money because I think it's a father's duty to support a child who hasn't the strength yet to be independent. I don't feel that duty extends to support for someone who takes a wife on his own accord when he can't earn even a bare living. But to say so doesn't mean that I'll let another family's daughter starve. You and your wife may not be able to maintain a standard of human dignity on the scanty monthly allowance I send you. Doesn't a policeman raise a family on a monthly salary of twenty-five yen? What I'm sending you isn't much, but it's more than a policeman's pay. Everyone lives by the sweat of his brow. That's the normal state of human life. You're living in idleness.

What work are you doing? Even if you are doing something, I wouldn't know whether it had any value. I don't understand the arts or literature. If you were going to school, I could tell your progress by your academic record and promotions, or, if you were doing something that was being discussed in the world and it was recognized by the intellectuals, there would be a way for me through those intellectuals to gain confidence in your talent. I'm not in the position of having excess money or giving you what you'd like. I have two more sons after you. If I continue paying your school expenses in full without any time limit for as long as you want, I won't be able to do as much as I want later for your promising younger brothers, will I? You've proved so unreliable I don't see what purpose your expenses have served. Having chosen your own path with confidence in your own ability, shouldn't you be indifferent to poverty? If you can't make a go of it at literature, aren't there lots of other things you can do, like being a streetcar conductor or a policeman? Of course if you do those things, you aren't destined to glory for yourself or your family. But for a man who is not a complete idiot or a madman to do nothing, even without our urging, is more shameful than taking on a low-status job. It's unpardonable before the world." After Father finished this speech, he turned toward Mother where she sat. "I'd like you to listen to this, too. Don't you be giving him money behind my back, even though you think things look bad. There's something called the parental love of a cow for its calf. That applies to you. In its love the mother cow licks the calf inordinately, not knowing there are other ways to express that love. . . ." Every word his cultured, healthy father had to say was reasonable. "Until twenty-five. I'll cover it until then if you're going to school, and, because I look on it as if you were in school until twenty-five, I will continue the same monthly allowance. After you're twenty-five, though, you'll be in trouble if you look to me for support. I won't support you at all. . . . Your lack of purpose and decision irks me. In the *Analects* Confucius says, 'Now you limit yourself. . . .' You give up your own strength. There must have been men like you among Confucius' disciples. Great courage and drive are what's wanted." That's what his father said. His mother said sometimes, "It's all because of your attitude. . . ."

It ended when he turned twenty-five this January.

His wife and his wife's mother were rather suspicious of why in his poverty he received no money from his father. A hint of that crept into their talk now and then. From his point of view there was really no reason to receive money from his parents any more. . . . One couldn't go on begging forever just because they were his parents. He understood that his father had made up his mind and would no longer give money no matter how dire his poverty. He felt that strictly speaking it was neither logical nor very moral for him to depend on the unstinting love of his parents, a love he did not cherish to the same degree. So long as his father continued to believe in his talent, he could presume to think of his father as his artistic patron. Now that his father had given up on his talent, and because *he* was rapidly losing faith himself, and because he was not a crook, he could not broach the question of unpaid bills to ask for money.

    ❊   ❊   ❊

He noticed the room had become dark from the smoke of his cigarette and smoke from its ashes, smoldering where he had dumped them in the fire. If he opened something, a cold wind would blow in, he thought apprehensively as he squatted stolidly by the brazier. He felt his head was just like the room—dark, forlorn, and wretched. Self-pity, or self-scorn, or he knew not what it was . . . Perhaps if he brooded hard about it, he might be able to identify the sensation: a feeling of regret coming from birth, or rebellion against nobody in particular, or rather an ending that mocks everything, or merely an ever-restless irritability, an introspective state of mind that could not doubt he was a man to be pitied. It was all these various feelings—they were neither vigorous nor violent at all—as if he were staring with arms folded at the dimly black, disorderly movements recurring in his heart, like watching a street scene at dusk. In the weakness of his spirit he was always taking the pulse of his mental state. He had no time to think of anyone else, even his wife. "Even though I may have talent," he thought, "when on a whim I try to write a short piece and then think it over, it turns out to be nonsense without the slightest connection to real life. . . . For example, a maiden light on her feet and skilled in the dance is presented at a king's palace. She is so light they are afraid she will fly away some night while asleep. They bind her hands and feet firmly with chains. Then, still feeling uneasy, they pick flowers that bloomed that day in the palace garden, and every evening they charge the air of her room with the breath of those flowers. Then . . . again, maybe there's an unfamiliar cavern that I find while strolling on a moonlit night. Becoming interested, I enter the cave; the interior is brighter than the outdoors. A Chinese maiden is playing there. Biting into something I think may be a lotus seed, I look more closely, and it is a cocoon. I split it neatly in two with my fingers and eat the insect that is inside. . . . Or . . . I wrote two or three of these totally meaningless things. 'What's that?' I said, scolding myself, ripping and crumpling the unfinished manuscript. I think about how disagreeable these wholly unsound elements in my fancies are, and I'm ashamed that I found them interesting even for ten minutes. Why don't poverty, love, other aspects of life, and human feelings and thoughts resound powerfully in me as they do in others? It's because life itself is bad; but how is it bad? . . . It's because nothing can be done about it. . . . Because I've no great courage and drive . . . If I think these problems over again and again in a circle, what do I end up thinking? I call out in my despair. I am helpless and can say nothing. . . ." He felt the shadow of Emori Shozan forever flickering in those reveries.

*   *   *

Whether from thinking in a general way about sundry unproductive things, or whether from concentrating on one thought alone pursued through a labyrinth, his mind was totally exhausted. The night was late, and the traffic of people passing had ceased completely on the lonely back street, when the sound of wooden clog geta on the frozen ground resounded keen and cold in his ears. The two dogs chained in the narrow back garden also heard and seemed to recognize the sound of the steps. They jangled the chains on their necks and whimpered and barked in soft, short yelps. An intermittent, awkward whistle responded from outside the house.

Soon the front door was opened with assurance, and a voice called out, "Leo! Fratty! Fratty!" The names of the dogs. The door closed. His wife was home.

The lively young woman, cheeks brushed and reddened by the cold wind, squatted down briskly, facing the brazier, and spread her hands in their black gloves before the fire, without, however, saying anything in particular about the cold. At once she began to talk rapidly and laugh noisily about one or two silly things that had happened that day out there on the streetcar or backstage. She pulled off her gloves and the long white scarf that hung down to the floor. Reaching out one hand, she opened the shoji door behind her, picked up the copper kettle of boiling water, and took it to the kitchen. There she quickly cleaned up the dirty dishes on the dining table that had been shoved idly from the kitchen into a corner of the sitting room, and, when she had finished washing the dirty bowls, she put them back in the sitting room. She asked her husband whether he had fed the dogs. He had not, and she went out again to the garden with food for them. The two then ate their own dinner. When that was finished, she washed the dishes again and laid out things for the morning. . . . He—uncommonly cold and idle as he was—watched with astonishment at how his wife managed things so quickly and nonchalantly after returning from a full day's work. She did come home late at night; was that why she managed so diligently? he wondered, as he watched attentively. He had to feel tender toward her. Although he always had words to express his complaints cogently and quickly, when it came to words of affection to express his tender emotions, nothing would come easily. Somehow it was always uncomfortable for a man of his temperament to say such things, try as he might. He never had even one word of sympathy for his wife. Instead, with a sour, hard-to-please look he paid her no heed, as if he had no interest in his cheery, talkative wife. Realizing this, he would sometimes say something more cheerful and chatty than she. Whatever he did, his wife was relatively indifferent as she was accustomed to his capricious character from living with him for the past three years. She seemed to think he was unhappy for no particular reason.

Indeed there was no reason for him to be unhappy. Yet he was for now oddly and inexplicably dejected. The mood assailed him often when he faced his high-spirited wife on her return late at night, or when morning after morning he watched blankly, half asleep but wakened by the little noises of her dressing quietly, careful as possible not to wake him and then leaving lightheartedly, or when he watched her sleeping soundly and snugly beside him as he lay sleepless night after night. Among the feelings he had thus far experienced this was most akin to envy. It was not a common kind of envy—not once had he fancied that feeling about his wife. Yet as a feeling resembling envy grew a bit each day, he thought he began, little by little, to understand the likely cause. He saw it was a kind of envy after all. A person with nothing to do, a person who does not know what he wants to do, a person who seems unable to do anything—when that person watches someone near to him who has a job or a profession attack that job with joy and zeal, then you have envy. In other words, the envy of one who has no livelihood for the one who does, isn't that it?

He told himself, "It's not that I'm happy idling. There's nothing for me to do. There's nothing I can do happily. It's all right to be unhappy. There's no profession I can do even against my will. Haven't I already thought many times about becoming a company employee or a news reporter or something?" Indeed he had now and then tried to consult friends or mentors, but not one of them took his request seriously. Even if they took him seriously, the honest ones would answer, "It's useless. What can you do?" When they said that, he believed it really was useless. People who didn't speak so bluntly would scoff at the idea, saying, "But you're an artist by nature." So after all, he had to think the cause of it was "because I am an artist by nature. . . ." Neither alive nor dead, neither awake nor asleep, he lay beside his enviable wife who could sleep soundly because she was tired from a day's work. He lay there like a shadow with weight and volume in dull and desultory self-reflection.

*   *   *

"That's the reason I've recently come to want a profession so much. Anything will do. I'm ready to try anything. Was it Nietzsche, or who was it? who said, 'A profession is the spinal cord of life'? Somebody said it, and here am I like a jellyfish. I'd like to find any profession, anything that would change my life to fit a profession. Even if it has no relation to the arts, if it's a bank employee, for example, that would still be O.K. An ordered life would be good, where you go to work at precisely nine in the morning and come home in the afternoon at four on the dot. If I try to do my best at a job that is ridiculous for people like us, and if my life becomes completely harmonious and I grow accustomed to it, and as a result even if it becomes no more than idle fancy to think of writing a novel, that's all right. It'll be like a sieve to winnow me from being an artist. After all if I'm going to stop being an artist, it's best to be sifted out by the fastest kind of sieve, isn't it? Anyway, my life now is submerged as by a flood. My body and soul are both useless in this state. . . ."

Once, catching Shozan just when he came to call, Ozawa Mineo appealed to him with enthusiasm for a job opening. When he said, "My body and soul are both useless in this state," and he noted it was Shozan by chance he was talking to, he thought it was ill advised to speak that way in front him. Good natured as he was, Shozan might be apathetic and pay no heed. What's more, it made his wretched self angry to confess his gloom so earnestly to Shozan as a confidant. It was a complete change of tone for him. In self-scorn he said flippantly but intentionally, "If I do say so, where would I get a job? Not more than one place, to be sure. . . ."

"Ho. What kind of place would that be?" Shozan, hitherto grinning without apparent interest, now interposed with sudden curiosity.

"What? Oh, well, a stagehand at a modern theater. Yes, yes. When my wife went into the theater, I understand she asked the director, Mr. Ōkawa Shūhan, in passing if there weren't some kind of work for me. Shūhan seemed to know that I paint as a hobby, and he asked her whether I'd like to help out on the scenery. 'Of course that doesn't require as much talent as writing scripts for plays about wickedness,' he said. 'It's pleasant work and it's not every day. If you do it for fun, you can earn some pocket money,' Shūhan said, as he urged it on my wife. Just for a time. But I wasn't convinced. The wife was a minor actress, and if the husband helped out backstage, both husband and wife would be retainers of Ōkawa Shūhan, and I didn't want that. It isn't so much of a problem now, though. . . . Of course I would like some pocket money. Or rather, I can't stand the boredom of sitting tight like this every day. The day I start adapting to life as a scene painter in a suburban theater may not be the day my life turns worse instead of better. No, I can hardly say that would be worse than my present life. It might be about the same. I think that would be all right. What I want is an improvement in my life. If I can't get that, at least a change would be good. That's why I recently asked my wife to take my application to be a scene painter to Shūhan. She said that was a silly idea and she would have nothing to do with it."

"Well, when you showed real enthusiasm, Madam decided she didn't want you to do it. How about trying to write something instead?" Shozan suggested. He then continued, "But it wouldn't be so bad to try out that world, would it?" It was a typical Shozan thought. . . . Such a valuable new experience in life would be an incentive for his work, Shozan added. His manner of speaking, though, did not really encourage him to become scene painter in a small theater. Shozan was simply keeping the conversation rolling. He understood as soon as Shozan opened his mouth that Shozan as usual had seized an opportunity to tell him of a plot for a novel he had not yet written.

"I've been thinking of an episode about an unfortunate artist like that." Shozan's story was of a young artist who became a panorama painter in Asakusa. At high noon one midsummer day when the artist was working on a high scaffold, he became suddenly dizzy from the dazzling light, the steaming heat, and the stink of paint, and, falling from his high perch, he was knocked unconscious. As he lay there unable to move, another artist climbed up to the high scaffold to continue the painting. The second artist discovered why the first one liked to paint the high parts, which everyone else disliked, and the probable reason why he lost his footing. Boldly exposed through a nearby open window as one looked down the line of sight from the scaffold was the spectacle of a room in a brothel. . . . Shozan related the plot and began as he always did to expound on his work, a work for which he had not yet written a single line. "What? It's just a trivial thing. I plotted it out more than ten years ago. Of course I got some ideas from some real-life facts. At the time I was trying to write like Zola in a naturalistic style with an interesting plot. I planned to write a novel called *Asakusa* using only the Asakusa entertainment district for material. I intended to write independent short pieces one by one and then collect twelve or thirteen into a full-length book. . . . Well, did you read the story I wrote called *Oyoneh* in the journal *Martyrdom* three or four months ago? Ugh. It brings out a cold sweat, but that was one in the *Asakusa* series. Oh, it was shameless of me to write that. . . ."

The piece called *Oyoneh* was picked up out of sympathy by one of the little magazines. Somehow it seemed to be written about Shozan's own life experiences. As Ozawa Mineo had some interest in what this boorish man had done in the old days, he thought he would like to hear the plot of *Oyoneh*. When Shozan had earlier asked him whether he had read it, though, he thought if he had to listen to another Shozan story plot just then . . . So, carelessly and half-heartedly, he indicated he had read it. Shozan's manner of speaking showed that *Oyoneh* was a work that had his confidence as a passage from his own autobiography. Shozan ran on loquaciously but in his usual humble tone. Not wanting to make a carelessly irrelevant answer, he had no choice but to be evasive.

Yet, although he pretended to listen to Shozan's talk, in his heart he was thinking to himself, this Shozan was not without some talent. No, maybe he was not a great talent. How many there are of much less talent, himself included, who become passable writers by following transient fashion. . . . As he thought these things, he gazed intently through the darkness of unlit twilight at the face of his older friend confronting him wearily across the *kotatsu* heater—the flat, featureless face of a small man, but not that of a youth. . . . Well, for this little time had he forgotten his own concerns?

It was a warm, springlike day. That gave him courage. How much it would help him if the weather stayed like this for ten days. This was unseasonable warmth, so he decided he had to go out that day. When he started out, he could not decide whether to wear his overcoat or to take it off. It was an old coat, five years old. The collar was dirty, and the hem was frayed. On a day like this there was nothing odd about going out without an overcoat, but, when he took the coat off, the silk of his only outfit was wrinkled, and the collar of his *haori* jacket was shabby. When he noticed that, his enthusiasm for going out was crushed. As he looked out from his window at the purplish, springlike sky brought by the warmth, he happened to remember fifteen years ago when he badgered his mother about his school cap being so old, and he was severely scolded by his father. . . .

"A scholar, whose mind is set on truth, and who is ashamed of bad clothes and bad food, is not fit to be discoursed with."[1] That's when his father taught him those words. The words are true enough, but, if your dress is too shabby, doesn't that make for a servile mentality and a faltering way of walking? Somehow he had lost pride in his intended way—the way of the arts. Now he was about to go out as a mere job applicant. Yes, it's Shozan's summer coat. That's completely true. Whether he tried it with the coat on or with the coat off, it was equally pitiful, so it was all the same whichever he did.

He walked with his coat in his hands. . . . That is, he carried the old coat with the better inside folded outward to conceal the torn and dirty parts.

Well, what was Ōkawa Shūhan's manner of speaking? He was not totally unacquainted with Shūhan, but he did not know him all that well, either. He had not seen him for more than five or six years. . . . The enterprising Shūhan had recently taken advantage of the new currents raging in the theater. With his adventurous spirit and with the wit and looks of the most popular actress of the day for the courtesan roles, he had become a brilliant upstart success. Shūhan enthusiastically presented his company of actors and actresses in various cafés and had attracted public attention. Couldn't you say that Shūhan and he were café friends in those days? . . . He had still been in school then. The gang of idle students in liberal arts at the expensive private college used the school only as a place to muster. Almost every day and all day they went here and there from one café to another. As long as they had money, each acted independently. When the money was gone, they pooled their funds and ordered one cup of coffee for the group. Often they would chat there for hours until they were tired and sad. . . . Because Shūhan's plays were the so-called modern theater entertainment for onetime students, the people who pushed their way into any play on free passes came not to see the play but to loiter around the corridors with an expression like they belonged there. One of his friends at that time had long since become a writer on the literary scene. Another had gone abroad. The least promising ones had become schoolteachers. He alone was left with no one to mingle with. . . . He, as the last of his group, and Shūhan would recognize a familiar face and exchange greetings. Once in a while they would happen to be seated at the same table and would engage in some idle carefree chatter. From this kind of relationship with Shūhan he then chanced to marry an actress from the modern theater world, an actress employed in Shūhan's troupe; he had thus created a new relationship. Now to face Shūhan and ask for a job helping to paint scenery, even if there were a job available, seemed uncommonly pretentious. Needless to say, it was definitely not pleasant. Because his wife would have none of it, he was going to do it by himself. He had to admit that his wife was justified in refusing. If Shūhan was sensible and didn't embarrass him too much, it would be all right, but . . .

As he walked and in the streetcar, he thought about these things —about his friends back then and how he came to meet his wife. As he neared the theater, the thought of saying he had business with his wife in the greenroom gave him an odd feeling of defeat.

On his own he had suddenly decided to call on Shūhan, and he had said not a word of it to his wife. She would surely be surprised. Actually his wife was not likely to understand how keenly he wanted to escape from this life and why he was emboldened to become an assistant scene painter. Perhaps no one else would understand, either. Like his wife, everyone might think it was no more than a passing fancy. Halfway at least it was precisely that—a passing fancy. But his intent was fully serious. For a person like him the passing fancy and the serious intent were intricately entwined and difficult to disentangle. . . . Wasn't that the common characteristic of the so-called romantic? As a romantic he believed only in the seriousness of his own intent, but the world saw only his fanciful side. He thought about himself as if he were an author studying the hero of his story, while he walked, staring at his feet kicking up dust at every step until he mounted the stairs to the second floor of the theater.

He opened the door. Inside it was dazzling bright. He had come through a dim passage into a six-mat room, where sunlight was streaming through a window in the middle of one wall and flooding the tatami-mat floor. The sunlight on the floor was reflected into four mirrors on stands lined up below the window, and the reflection from one of the mirrors had struck him in the eyes the moment he opened the door. Blinking and looking down, he asked, "Is Segawa Ruriko here?"[2]

Some women who had been chatting without noting that someone had entered the room now turned around as one. The oldest and least attractive asked in a gruff voice who he was.

"She's my wife." He spoke crossly. Three women stared unsparingly at him. One of them motioned him to a gaudy muslin cushion next to her—that was Ruriko's seat. A man sprawling there sat up and pushed the cushion toward him. The man stood and went out, leaving the door open. He may have gone to look for Ruriko. Awkward in his relations with other people, he took a seat in embarrassment amid the three women he was meeting for the first time. He lit a cigarette and looked around the room at the clutter of women's clothes—in reds and blues—tossed untidily where they were taken off, or hung on the walls, or rolled up carelessly almost like balls. In response to his moroseness the women stifled their conversation, stared at themselves in their mirrors, and repaired their stage makeup, which was already complete.

"This is really a sunny room, isn't it?" he said unexpectedly—not just to be sociable, but without thinking, because he had not sat in the sun for so long.

"Yes, it is truly hot today." The older woman answered and picked up a dropped cigarette. She reached out her hand to light it at the brazier in front of him. There was no need to develop this awkward conversation because Ruriko appeared in the open doorway, her hair bound up for a wig, the corners of her eyes painted with long red lines, and her greenroom clothes slipped on over her bathrobe. He looked up for a moment sternly at the disheveled figure of his wife. She looked dubious about her husband's unexpected appearance in the greenroom.

"What do you want?" She spoke as she closed the door.

"It's O.K. Nothing," he replied.

"Did you come for the fun of it?"

"It's O.K. Why would I come for fun?"

The conversation seemed so ludicrous that the three women laughed without restraint. He and his wife could not help laughing with them.

Then he asked, "Is Mr. Ōkawa in? I think I'd like to see him. No, it's nothing. . . . Actually, I thought I'd ask him myself about that matter."

"Really?" She said just that and stopped. Then saying she would show him to Shūhan's room, she had him get up. The two stood in the hall and exchanged a few words about whether it was useless to make the request of Shūhan now, or, if useless, whether it was even all right to try. She then pointed to the door of Shūhan's room, and saying she had to dress, she disappeared somewhere.

He knocked lightly two or three times on the door that his wife had indicated. The last time he knocked a little harder and heard from inside, "Yes." Surely it was the voice of Ōkawa Shūhan that he remembered from some years before. Despite the response, no one moved from inside to open the door. He opened it himself and went in. The moment he glanced at Shūhan's face he thought it would have been better not to come. Such a glowering expression Shūhan had, as if reproaching him suspiciously for entering. Even after Shūhan recognized that *he* was the intruder, he did not alter an expression of disgust that might be called hostility. He merely dropped his gaze to the square paulownia-wood brazier, where his hand rested. He picked up the tongs and pointlessly stirred the ashes.

"It's me, Mr. Ōkawa." Thinking that Shūhan had failed to recognize him, he attempted to introduce himself.

"Ah, yes. Good to see you."

Shūhan responded stiffly and nodded at him to take a cushion facing the brazier. Whether in apology for leaving it at that, Shūhan took some care to conceal a rather blank air of annoyance. *He* was confused about what to say.

Shūhan spoke: "What business brings you here?"

Hearing these words, he was even more confused. . . . The expectation vanished that he could talk familiarly with his old nodding acquaintance. He did not understand Shūhan's attitude toward him; it was as if they were a couple of unacquainted dogs meeting in the road. He wondered whether he hadn't stumbled into a confidential conversation between Shūhan and his mistress in her quarters. He got the idea from noting that various utensils and personal effects were arranged neatly about the room, that the room had a different atmosphere to it from the similar greenroom he had just been in, and that the room had an intimate, settled duskiness because the window was hung with a thick curtain entirely shutting it in. The only door was the one he had come through. There was no sign of any other person in the room. As he thought it over again, maybe Shūhan was displeased that the scrubby husband of a subordinate actress had come in behaving as if he were the equal of Shūhan.

Conscious of that feeling, he spoke in a self-mocking tone to the man who sat ensconced before him in two-ply silk pongee. "You've been very helpful to my wife. I wanted to thank you in person. . . ."

"Oh, thanks for your trouble in. . . ." Shūhan spoke like this, but there was not the slightest change in his facial expression, even as *he* would cynically have expected of Shūhan.

"And," he added, "actually I have a little request. It's just that— once when Ruriko asked, you said I might be able to help paint scenery. . . ."

"Oh. Is that it? Yes. Well, that is . . ." Shūhan cut off his words in the middle, looking oddly discomfited. After a few speechless moments he suddenly resumed speaking rapidly. "You could put that in a letter—no, you might consult me again in a month or so."

Shūhan spoke incomprehensibly and stood up. Sticking his head out the door, he shouted for someone in a loud voice. "Tanaka! Tanaka!" Without waiting long enough for an answer he called again. "Hey Tora! Tora! Are you there, Tora?" A young fellow— probably Shūhan's houseboy—appeared, bowing profusely. Shūhan said to him, "Right away . . . No. O.K. I'm going out by myself." He seemed to be saying he wanted his troublesome guest to leave quickly. Sure enough, saying he was rather busy just then, Shūhan showed him out the door.

Before returning home he went back to the actresses' room to get the overcoat he had left there. A solitary young actress was sitting there blankly, looking dejected in the stage costume of a young lady and unexpectedly lonesome in the midst of noise and bustle. When she saw him, she said Ruriko was onstage now. Ruriko had left word that, if he would wait a bit, she'd be back. They could have lunch together and then go home.

"Tell her I went home at once." He spoke brusquely. Then as he started down the dark stairway, the steps suddenly became light. The electric light had snapped on over his head. . . . It was early for the lights, he thought, but then it did seem that time.

*　　*　　*

After the first of February Shozan came frequently to visit. Shozan was a practical man about these things, and he took care lest too-frequent visits trouble the other party. Until recently he had been calling only once every week or ten days, but now he started coming every other day or so. He would sink down and talk for hours. In coming so often, the timid Shozan appeared ill at ease. He would apologize and volunteer that he was on his way to look up something in a nearby private library. When *he* asked what Shozan was looking up, Shozan answered vaguely in a way to make one feel bad about asking any further. That suggested that Shozan's library visit was perhaps untrue. In any case, Shozan's calls at his house became almost daily, long-lasting ones. Because the two were basically not very compatible, they would often fall silent, unawares, with nothing to talk about. On the pretext of walking the dogs, he would leave Shozan behind and, asking him to look after the house, would go out leading the dogs. When Shozan made a move to go home, he would try his best to detain him. Shozan would do as he asked and would settle back indefinitely.

One day Shozan came as usual in the evening. Settling down as always across the *kotatsu* heater from him, Shozan took something from his pocket and said, "Here." As he spoke, he opened the small paper package he had taken from his pocket and handed it to him. "This is nothing much. Please give it to Madam. I thought she'd like it, so I brought it. It's called a pigeon pipe. It's like a toy from olden times. It's called a Hiromae pigeon pipe. I think the primitive shape is rather elegant. What? I got it in Tokyo. It caught my eye as I was looking through a toy store in Kanda. This is interesting, I thought, so I bought two of them, a larger one and this one. . . . What do you think the two cost? The larger one was six sen and this one was four sen. I gave the larger one to Mr. Iwata's daughter when I went to see him the other day. This one, being so small, is rather interesting for its clumsy workmanship. Try and blow it. It makes a tasteful sound. . . ."

He took the supposedly elegant gift, the bamboo whistle crudely made in the shape of a small bird, and he tried blowing it.

"How about that? Interesting sound, isn't it?" Shozan said. "You could call it a dreamy sound. . . . There's an episode about that in a story."

"What? An old legend?"

"No, no! It's an episode from my life."

Shozan began his story: "I bought this recently around the end of January one evening when it began to snow. I returned to my lodgings late that night after buying it." Shozan's lodgings—*he* had never before been much interested in someone else's life-style, and, anyway, Shozan was always moving around, changing his lodgings from here to there. He had never specifically asked Shozan what kind of house he lived in and what his living arrangements were like. As Shozan began in an orderly way to relate the episode, he described his lodgings briefly. They were like *his* house halfway up a slope, and like *his* house untouched by the sun. All the day long not a single ray of sunlight reached the four-and-a-half-mat room that Shozan rented for three yen a month. The northwest window that should have received the sunlight looked directly onto a cliff thirty or thirty-five feet away. That was Shozan's room. In the next room of six mats separated by a single sliding door the morning sun shone briefly. At five yen a month the room was rented by a factory worker in an arsenal. From way back the young fellow had often received visits from a woman who seemed also to be a factory hand and who stayed over with him.

After buying the pigeon pipes on a whim, Shozan strolled for a while along the street of secondhand bookstores. It was late. The snow became heavy and it was very cold, so he stopped for a drink at a local bar. His lodgings were close by streetcar but rather far to walk, but, rather drunk, he walked. He did not have enough money to drink all he wanted, so he was merely tipsy, and by the time he reached home he had sobered up from the sake completely and was unable to fall asleep easily. He sensed that as usual the woman was next door with the factory hand. In his boredom he thought he would try out his new whistle. He blew lightly two or three times. He kept on blowing. "Hoo, hoo." The sound faded in the still night air, when . . .

"Something's there."

"What?"

"Wasn't that a cry just now?"

"No. It's not so. . . ."

Shozan heard the conversation in the next room. . . . "As I thought, 'She's there. And still awake.'" He stopped blowing the pigeon pipe. Although the man's voice said, "It's not so," he felt the two were straining to hear something, and he wanted to blow again. Deliberately, he sounded faintly, "—Hoo, hoo."

"There it is."

"Yeah . . . What is it?"

"—Hoo, hoo, hoo." Shozan blew again.

"It's strange."

"I wonder what it is. It seems to come from under the eaves."

"I don't like it. I'm scared."

The man said something like, "Silly." He seemed to get up, and there was the sound of a window shutter opening.

"Oh, it's piled up a lot," the man said in a loud voice. A creaking noise suggested the man had climbed onto the windowsill. "No. Nothing there."

Shozan suppressed the impulse to laugh and was silent for a while. Then when he thought the man was snugly back in bed, he blew again for a bit. "—Hoo, hoo, hoo-hoo." The man and woman seemed surprised. "That is to say," Shozan concluded, "if you hear something late at night, it makes you feel lonesome and uneasy as if you were shut in a dim and shadowy place." He blew the whistle again as he wound up this episode from his life.

He listened in silence to Shozan's story. Shozan recounted the occurrence so casually, but in its depth the brief tale struck him as the embodiment of Shozan's misery and isolation. Of course Shozan spoke with nonchalance and but fleeting interest. Perhaps Shozan himself saw no more than the outward appearance of a slight incongruity. Listening to Shozan's words, though, he had to feel that an intricate shadow was lurking there. When he thought about these complicated feelings that Shozan boldly pretended not to notice, the story of the pigeon pipe and the snowy evening gave him the feeling of reading a humorous tale—a kind of humor that profiled human life so that one was compelled to laugh.

Shozan was still a bachelor at thirty-five or thirty-six. At various times in the past, his young friends used to tease Shozan, by suggesting in jest that he should get married. Shozan would reply seriously that he intended never in his life to take a wife. When asked why, he would simply reply, "I won't say now, but you will understand for yourself after I'm dead." He remembered that at the time one of the friends had said in rather innocent spite, "By the time that guy's dead, who's going to care why he never married?" He pictured the form and the feeling of Shozan blowing his pigeon whistle alone and late at night while he listened to the whispers of the man and woman beyond the sliding wall panel.

Without thinking, he said, "Yes. That's interesting. One could certainly make a story out of that."

Shozan listened to his words, and a good-hearted smile played about the corners of his mouth. But just as they exchanged glances, he saw momentarily a look of anger in Shozan's eyes. In an instant the smile at the corners of the mouth and the anger in the eyes commingled, and the whole face turned to a sour smile. Shozan did not say, as he usually did, "Do you think it's interesting? Well, here, I'll give you the story to write." The sour smile hovered briefly on the face, but he said nothing. As he looked at Shozan's face, it struck him for the first time that he had said something to be sorry for. Seeking to apologize, he said to Shozan, "For us both, it's not that we can't write the story. It's like being the person written about in a story, isn't it?"

Then he told Shozan in detail of his recent visit to Ōkawa Shūhan in the dressing room at the theater. Shozan appeared to listen with comparative interest, but, as the story ended with Shūhan turning a deaf ear, Shozan spoke in the tone of an elder, as if recalling from his own deep experience. . . . "There are a lot of people like that."

"That there are," he said. "I thought at the time that Shūhan was a coarse chap who was vain about his own success, but later I heard from my wife that he has been worried about something recently. He's been finding fault with everyone at the theater. . . . They say he's learned that his mistress has taken another man."

"Oh. His regular mistress is Tachibana Sujaku, isn't she?"

"Yeah—and so the splash reached even me."

Shozan and he laughed together, their voices mingling vapidly. . . . Life, after all, left no choice but to laugh.

*　　*　　*

One night Shozan arrived quite late. Ozawa Mineo wondered whether it weren't his wife coming home. Recently, though, she had been late in returning. It was too early for her, he thought, and it did turn out to be Shozan. . . . After ten-thirty—never before had he come so late. Still, he seemed to have no special business this evening. He asked as he sat down whether Madam was home. He came late because he hoped to see her again after such a long interval. Shozan seemed to have come down with a violent case of the calling sickness.

There is no specific illness named "calling sickness." It is a condition of nervous depression. The curious practice used to be popular among those in Shozan's group. When someone reached a dead end and lost the ability to endure his isolation, he wanted desperately to see a friend's face. He tried going to see the friend, but the talk there was not congenial. Again he racked his brain for a friend he wanted to see that very day. He went to that friend's house, but there, too, he found no peace. Feeling a kind of desperation, he spent all day going from one friend's home to another, near and far so long as they lasted. When one of his friends had fallen into this sick state of mind, the condition infected the others in the group, who could find no composure in their own inner lives. When A, exhausted with the calling sickness, visited B, B would catch the disease. Together A and B would call on C, and the condition would be aggravated among all three. A, B, and C would go together a long distance to visit D. . . . The lives of the friends were mutually corruptive. At least one among them was always suffering from the illness, whether lightly or severely. Sooner or later that one, impatient at being alone and feeling that life, his own and his friends', was devastated, would roam the streets sadly seeking the troubled face of a discouraged friend—a face that in an hour's time would become for no reason as gloomy as his own. . . . The condition continued like a plague for some time until life at last was but a dead end. Some of the friends had gone home to the country to become elementary schoolteachers. Another had wandered off to Manchuria. Thus had the plague abated. The evanescent crowd mentality was dispelled only with the breakup of the group. Because *he* had a wife and did not spend all his time roaming around, two groups at least of the calling sick would barge into his home each day. There all would rendezvous and materialize into a club for the calling sick. His desire to escape from the crowd of the calling sick had been another reason for him to flee the city and live in seclusion in the country. He was physically and spiritually devastated by the calling sick. These friends were from a later time than the group acquainted with Ōkawa Shūhan. They graduated from their calling sickness about the time he escaped to the country. Some found peace of mind—that is, comparatively speaking, they found something to be enthusiastic about. With others the disease became more serious. Like *him* they developed misanthropic tendencies and no longer wanted to see a friend's face. Only in Shozan did the disease seem to linger on unchanged over two years. Sadly today, though, there was no friend left for Shozan to infect. These days Shozan seemed to be making the rounds of several friends a day. . . . He went alone on the circuit of his busy friends. He relayed gossip about various friends, but the gossip was all about people he had seen just yesterday or today. Shozan's friends at the time had scant contact with *him*. The gossip that Shozan troubled to bring thus failed to blossom into conversation. *His* own subject of conversation with Shozan was already determined, and, because Shozan showed up almost every day, the predetermined topic became ever thinner. He had heard utterly everything about Shozan's "extraordinary story materials." That evening Shozan began to recite the story of his novel *People of the Ravine*. He had heard the outline of that story before.

Shozan appeared to notice this in midstream. "Well, I really am going to write it. How about you, too?"

Shozan wound up his story sounding like a host urging a guest to have a piece of cake. He muttered that he had plotted out *People of the Ravine* some years ago, and he really did intend to finish writing it.

"Still, I can't write in peace at my present lodgings, and I have no place to move. . . ." Shozan grumbled on about this.

Was Shozan hinting at the possibility of coming to live with him? Did Shozan want him to say, "Won't you come stay at my place for a while?" This interpretation did not seem overly suspicious. He pretended not to notice. Shozan knew that earlier, when *he* was not so destitute, Tada, who later wandered off to Manchuria, had moved in as a free boarder. If that intractable man had lived with him, didn't Shozan see himself as a much better housemate? There was no argument about that. Shozan was a nice, affable fellow, not to be compared with that young scoundrel Tada. Laying aside for the moment the question of how impossible that would be for his own life-style, he imagined life with Shozan if Shozan simply acted himself. That would be too distressing for him as he now was. His older friend was too appropriate a partner to live with him now, wasn't he? It is often said, "People will lend money needed for pleasures, but they don't want to lend money urgently needed for subsistence." That's the difference between Tada and Shozan, the difference between "money needed for pleasures" and "money urgently needed for subsistence." Still, people have a strange and irrational way of thinking. There was really no room for him to be moved too much by pity and sympathy for Shozan. . . . While he was musing on like this, he could not venture to guess Shozan's intentions. He could only try asking Shozan about the family who lived downstairs under Shozan's unpleasant four-and-a-half-mat room with the window facing north onto a cliff.

According to his answer, they were a couple aged about fifty and their niece of sixteen whom they had brought from the country and adopted. The three lived in two rooms of six and three mats, respectively.[3] They made their living by renting out the second floor and by tying hemp as a home industry. Shozan explained in some detail the work of tying hemp.

"But," Shozan continued. "they're always up until late at night. They go to bed after twelve. Of course I'm up even later. When I go to the toilet at night, I have first to pass by the girl's bed, and then I have to slip through where the husband and wife are sleeping. That's not a very good feeling. . . . Of course that's not the reason why living there is unpleasant," Shozan said finally, after a pause and a quick, halfhearted laugh. "Actually," he said, correcting himself as if something were the matter. "It is just that I am three or four months behind in my rent." How like Shozan. It made him smile without thinking. At any rate, every time Shozan delayed payment with some appropriate excuse they would persist in pressing for payment. That was not unreasonable. After all, they were people who needed what little money they could get. The more Shozan defaulted, the more awkward it became for him to slip into the house. On the pretext that he was looking for a job, they would wait until the end of February, but, to be sure, there wasn't any work that would suit Shozan. When he came home in the evening, some member of the family who would be up working until midnight would surely greet him. They would be polite enough in greeting, but in fact they would ask him right out whether he had found a job. For Shozan, who had no ready answer, that was unpleasant, and he chose to avoid it by always coming home after midnight when they were all asleep. He would open the front door as stealthily as possible and step through the three-mat room—the stairs to the second floor went up from the same room where the girl slept. As he tiptoed by, a cough invariably resounded from the larger room next door where the old man slept.

It seemed he had done well to caution himself on that point—in aspiring to write a naturalistic novel, Shozan caught the trivial details and related them lightly. The details appeared consistent with the story of the pigeon pipe that he had heard earlier, and the circumstances of Shozan's life had emerged more clearly. Driven out by his loneliness, Shozan not only made the rounds of his friends' houses; he stayed and talked late into the night in other peoples' homes because he found it hard to settle down in his own lodgings. . . . As *he* mused like this, he remained silent and made no effort to reply when Shozan interrupted his tale. Shozan, too, fell silent for a bit as if savoring his condition. Then, with whatever intent, he spoke, "Excuse me for asking, but about how much does Madam Ruriko earn in a month?"

"Forty-five yen, I think it is," he snapped back.

"Forty-five yen. You people make out all right, don't you?"

"Well, let's see. . . . If my wife brings in forty-five yen, it's not really enough for us to live on. What with her lunch and dinner money, streetcar fare twice a day, office functions and sociability at the theater, monthly installment costs for kimonos, most of the money is gone. Often there's only five yen left. That's just enough to carry the interest at the pawnshop."

"Then how do you keep the house going?"

"That I don't know—I just don't know at all. Maybe it's my wife's mother, or maybe her good management. . . ."

"You're really happy-go-lucky, aren't you? Like it's not your business at all—I envy you. However troubled you say you are, it's all the same."

Again the two were silent, lost in their respective thoughts. There was the usual sound of footsteps and a whistle. It was his wife come home. . . . Already it was twelve o'clock. Recently she had been coming home no earlier because of a play performance.

He understood fortuitously that night that Shozan's illness had now become serious. That was when his wife closed the door as always on her return, and there was the sound of something falling over with a clatter. They listened and realized it was Shozan's cane. Shozan said something evasively. He realized a bit later, though, that Shozan probably needed to lean on his cane as he walked because the joints in his legs pained him from the illness. It appeared that, not wanting to have the cane seen, Shozan stashed it outside the door without bringing it over the threshold. Shozan was to stay at *his* house that night. "Noodle shops and quilt rental stores stay open the latest of any business in the city," Shozan remarked in his usual Shozan manner. What's more, he knew of a quilt rental store in the neighborhood. The man had come to the house that evening with the intent of staying over night, and it seemed certain that he had hunted out a quilt rental store on his way there. After the wife had gone out to order noodles and quilts, Shozan untied a parcel he had been carrying under his arm and took out a strange, long, slim, cylindrical object. Then he felt in his pocket and pulled out a body warmer. "I use an old man's thing like this because my stomach hurts," Shozan said as he took the object from the package—a refill stick of hot ash—and inserted it into the heater case. At this an inexpressible feeling of sadness for Shozan flashed through him. At the same time, though, he worried that Shozan might be moving in to settle down in his house just like that. You could think that Shozan was prepared somehow with all his daily necessities carried in that small parcel. If so, you couldn't throw him out point-blank. . . . Then he chanced to recall a manuscript for publication of some dime novel that the boy from the secondhand bookstore had urged him to write. If he could do a foreign adventure story, a rough summary or translation, however inaccurate, or an adaptation, the job should be worth about thirty yen for two hundred pages. *He* didn't read foreign languages at all, but Shozan could. Shozan had gone through middle school in the old days. He asked whether Shozan weren't interested in trying his hand at the manuscript.

"Well, if there's that much money in it," Shozan said.

"I could pay the rent since last November. I could clear up what I owe where I eat. In addition, it would cover the fare for me to go and live on an old acquaintance who has set up practice as a doctor in Shiogama. Yes, he's a friend that would help me if I went there. Sure I'll do the manuscript," he said proudly. Shozan's joy at the news of the dime-novel manuscript was touching.

* * *

One day *he* got his first haircut in three months. He also went to the public bathhouse for the first time in a week. Bathing and haircutting were for him the highest form of Buddhist "suffering and emptiness." When he had his hair cut, his eyes swam and his head felt smothered from the rear. When he took a bath, the act of soaking himself in the hot water was not so much to wash his body all over as it was to exhaust that body. He sank down into the bath, in short, only so that, naked in the hot water, he could continue the same rambling and oppressive train of thought. He did not think that cleanliness was any special virtue. Whether his body was dirty or not was no great problem in a man's life. Whether the body was scrubbed clean, whether the beard was shaved, whatever was done with the hair, you could say it was not something a person like him paid any attention to—that is, a person with an uncrowded mind, or rather a person who is not absorbed in things like these. Living his life absentmindedly through the day, he rarely thought of things like taking a bath. If the thought did strike him once in a while, in the next instant a totally different idea, usually a somewhat less focused idea, popped into his head. As he pursued the new idea, the desire for a bath vanished before he knew it. By then it was evening. He found it unpleasant to bathe in the evening. To watch a muddle of motley bathers jostling, washing, and scrubbing down their unattractive bodies, that gave him a strange, dreary feeling. He was unsettled and oddly disgusted at being seen in the middle of the crowd, scrubbing off dirt that was caked on his body for days. If he was going to bathe, he much preferred the unpopular hours around 10 A.M. and 1 P.M., but he was always asleep at those hours. . . .

Indolent as he was, he went that day after a long interval for a bath; then he went on for a haircut—for no special reason, or perhaps on a whim, or rather because the weather was good. Actually the weather had turned warm. A couple of men bathing with him were having a consultation on flower viewing. . . . Yes, yes, the flowers are blooming. The swallows have returned. People are smartly dressed in lined kimonos for the first time of the year. It's about that time. . . . Completely immersed in the hot bath and gazing at the yellow sky through the high glass window, he mused on these unexpected events. Perhaps in relation to the season, or perhaps for one thing because his body was warmed right through, he felt there were some pleasures left to human life. Because it was nearly one o'clock when he got up, there weren't more than four or five people in the bath. A bush warbler was singing incessantly from a cage mounted at the top of the partition betwen the men's and women's baths and near the bath attendant's seat. The pleasant, melodious song echoed from the high window of the deserted bath chamber. . . . The old bath attendant enriched his life by installing there the warbler's cage. That's what *he* thought. Maybe human life after all was no more than the accumulation of trivia. Isn't it a foolish and irrelevant dream to think there is some special abstract thing called human life apart from the little things of daily living? People in whom that dream persists for life are called artists and poets, but, for me, lacking talent, maybe I'm awakening little by little from that dream. . . . He felt rather vague about that. Passing over the thought without any deep analysis, however, he noticed as he was dressing himself that his hair hung heavily over his ears. He decided to go for a haircut that day. He had the change from the fifty-sen silver coin he had brought for the bath. He thought, though, that the barber might be angry when he saw that crazy long hair. No, the poor color of my face might make him think I was an invalid who had been in bed for a long time, he mused. Worrying about all those things, he looked at his face reflected in the full-length mirror. As he dressed, he thought that because it was so warm he ought to pawn his overcoat and order a new lined jacket instead. Would the overcoat cover the cost of a new jacket? Because he ought to have a new jacket, it would be good to trade the coat. He really did want a trim new *haori* jacket, but . . .

To take a bath so soon after rising, to think of getting a haircut, and then to think about his clothes—these were indeed strange and positive feelings for him in his current condition. . . . That's how far he had become dispirited in character and devoid of interest in human concerns. The spring season was very subtle in the way its power affected two-legged, wingless creatures. It called forth a blithe spirit even from a man like him in his present condition.

Definitely that was a day rare and energetic for him. As soon as he was home from having his hair cut, he felt like taking the dogs down to the Kudan Plaza. He wanted to see how much the cherry blossoms had budded out.

The two dogs, Fratty and Leo, were fully grown. Fratty looked like a full-blooded Akita and was a splendid, powerful animal. One day as he strolled through the neighborhood enjoying the sun with Fratty, a passing young blade called out to him. First he praised Fratty repeatedly. Displaying his varied knowledge of dogs, he expounded that Fratty's build would be ideal if he were about half an inch taller. He guessed at the dog's weight, and then asked whether there surely weren't many fine dogs in the neighborhood. On inquiry, the young gentleman disclosed that he had finished veterinary school in March of that year. He was thinking of opening a practice in the neighborhood and had come to look for a place.

Actually, Fratty was that good a dog. He always took Fratty, as his favorite, for a walk on his chain. Fratty had a jolly disposition and was never fidgety. From the time they were in the country both husband and wife were naturally inclined in their affection toward Fratty, but he cautioned his wife never to treat Leo less favorably than Fratty. Leo had a very nervous temperament and was smart and expressive. When anyone looked at Fratty's form and behavior and then turned suddenly to Leo, they would ask whether Leo were female. You could say that Leo was coquettish like a woman. Where Fratty had a stupid look, Leo's clever coquettishness could be considered cute. What is more, when Leo was small he was much trimmer in shape, but as he grew larger his body grew long and low slung. He became excessively fat and otherwise not much to look at. Trotting along next to Fratty, he looked shapeless. Although he walked Fratty on the chain, he always let Leo run free. Leo had a quiet, gentle disposition and there was little need to worry about fights with other dogs. For another reason you had to admit that, as appearances go, Leo was not a very grand dog. If Leo were as fine looking as Fratty, he would probably have kept him on the chain as he did Fratty, and heedless of the minor inconvenience he would have walked with a leash in each hand. . . . That was a time when fighting dogs had become popular and when people were being singularly careful about dogs in general. Everyone who passed by as he was walking Fratty would keep an eye on the dog. If a small dog ran up barking, Fratty pretended not to notice. It was that way when they walked, and it was even more so on reaching Kudan Plaza. Here in the big open square the neighborhood children brought their pet dogs for exercise. Fratty's noble appearance was most conspicuous. When the children with small dogs saw that Fratty had come, they hauled in their dog chains and hid their dogs. Tired of playing around, the children gathered about Fratty and cheered.

"Hey! He's a good dog."

"Darned if that ain't a real big one."

"He's strong."

All the children praised the dog. One of them, an errand boy from a wine shop who had joined the group while dawdling on his rounds, was profuse in his praise for Fratty. Pushing out front by himself, he patted Fratty gingerly on the head.

"Yeah, he's sweet. Look how gently the son of a gun wags his tail." The boy talked on excitedly. Suddenly he noticed Leo timidly eyeing the group of children, completely ignored by the crowd.

"Huh? How about this mutt? It's shaped like a pig. Hey! You! Pig!" Intending to praise Fratty more effectively, the boy spoke abusively of Leo and turned a fawning look at him, the owner of the splendid dog. Not knowing that he was Leo's master, too, and in an excess of mirth after all the sporting around, the boy chased the cringing, nervous dog away. As he ran, Leo kept turning his eyes toward his master, pleading for help. When the boy first began teasing Leo and calling him bad names, he had failed to say that the ugly animal was his dog, too. The boy also failed to notice that was his dog, and he chased Leo around and around. Leo bravely refused to leave his master's side, and the dog kept dodging around his master and his brother Fratty.

"Hey!" he snapped at the boy, "stop that bullying."

The boy paid no great heed to the words. He seemed to become more annoyed the more he chased the dog, and finally he lifted his foot and kicked Leo. The dog at last turned tail and ran away from *him*. Chasing and failing to catch the fleeing dog, the boy picked up a pebble at his feet, aimed and threw at the running dog. Hit or not, Leo let out a howl and, taking off at top speed for home, looked back again and again at its master. Yanking suddenly on Fratty's chain, *he* strode at the boy and grabbed him abruptly by the collar. "Hey there!" he yelled. "What are you doing?—What are you throwing stones for!" The exuberant boy was struck with terror at his unexpected behavior. The boy was dumbfounded and unable to understand the reason. He stared at the boy's crying face.

"That's my dog!" he declared.

He felt his face was distorted like the boy's. Weakly, then, he released his tightened grip. With a totally different and rather gentle glance at the dazed and petrified boy, he walked away briskly without looking back—walked in the direction that the cowed and terrified dog had run, looking backward as it fled.

As he walked, his spirit was deeply depressed by that look from Leo: "Why didn't my master protect me? Why was my trusty master silent when I was bullied for no reason? Help me. Pity me." *He* mistrusted the whole incident, but those eyes of Leo's, begging mercy from the master he trusted to the end. The suddenly terrified eyes of that simple, playful, childish boy, who was innocently flattering him. Two pairs of eyes so similar, showing an injured soul, wounded for no understandable reason, yet making no resistance. The cause for Leo's look, the cause for that boy's look—they came from him. "That's it," he thought as he walked. "That's it. All because of *his* indifferent attitude. All because I would not tell them that I, the owner of that wonderful dog Fratty, was owner also of the ugly dog Leo. There was no reason for me to get angry at that boy. . . ."

The day was growing dark. He walked head down on the lonely, slowly darkening street, lined by houses on one side only. He was right in his thinking but he perceived that he was too hysterical. By self analysis he decided this was a reaction to his strange, overly cheerful feelings of the morning. Still, he could not subdue the hysteria. On reaching home he called Leo at once. Leo had come home alone, but the dog either feared him or was angry. Leo hid back under the veranda and would not come out. He brought food from the kitchen and shoved it at Leo, but still the dog would not come out. He was annoyed that Leo was sulking, and he thought of throwing a stone under the veranda. Then he thought again. . . . Either Leo was sulking or Leo thought he had done something bad but didn't know what. Leo feared for that fault and feared the more because he did not divine the reason. Maybe that was why the dog would not come forth. He ought to leave Leo alone until the dog recovered its spirits.

He went to his room. He was distressed as if he had done something wrong. "I really am a show-off," he thought. ". . . I'm that way with Shozan—because Shozan leads a miserable life and I'm ashamed to be friendly with him. Whatever can be the reason I'm ashamed to be a good friend of Shozan. . . ?"

*　　*　　*

Suddenly then he was absorbed in the idea—a continuation of his earlier hysteria—the very idea of Shozan: the only person that he could call a close friend, the only person he had until now to scorn.

What was it about Shozan that made him ashamed of his friend? Was there something out of place about the man? What was strange and out of place about him? Was it the oddly polite manner of speaking? Or the oddly proper and good-natured attitude? Or the fact that the artistry that Shozan so highly fancied was unrecognized by the world? Or was it that nothing was left of the mother's legacy, long ago squandered youthfully and haphazardly for the sake of a talent that proved unreliable? If you thought of it that way, everything about Shozan was strange and out of place. But suppose he was now—as *he* thought on about Shozan—suppose this same Shozan was a highly renowned writer. . . ? Toward all his juniors Shozan was kind; he was polite. He was modest, rich in common sense, with a gentle personality. Yet he was really enthusiastic about his own artistry. Couldn't you say he had ventured everything for his art? That's it. If Shozan were only—if only he were a success! All the things that seemed odd about him would then be counted as strong points. When you look at it that way, he thought, the oddity is just that Shozan is unlucky. To speak of his talent: yes, maybe it's not really so great. . . . No, maybe it's not great now, but you can't say that he lacked such talent long ago when he was young and looking to the future, casting off that shining vision. We don't know whether that talent has been worn down by his bad fortune. Bad luck does not as a rule foster a man's talent. Don't we perceive as much when we think of the rose that the sun never touched in the garden of my former country home? "If it's a rose, the flower will bloom." Then if the rose is in the shade all its life, who knows whether it won't wither and die before it blooms?

Without his realizing it, his thoughts up to now were not entirely devoted to Shozan. Deliberately he thought only of Shozan. It was too dreadful for him to think about himself at this juncture. He therefore continued to think of Shozan. . . . But now Shozan was no longer a real person. He was a symbolic person. . . . Shozan was a man everyone thought was without talent. "Yet actually," he said to himself, "I can't be expected to know what manner of man Shozan is. You can't say I held him in high regard from the first. Even as a friend I haven't found a single work of his that I read with satisfaction, have I? When Shozan says, 'Here's a work I'm proud of,' his very words seem strange, and I don't want to read it. Yes, shouldn't I have received the magazine *Martyrdom*? Why haven't I tried to read his story *Oyoneh* even yet? If that were the only one, that would be all right. But because I haven't read one thing of his with satisfaction, haven't I had a low opinion of his talent from the beginning?"

He stood and went to his desolated desk. There he shuffled

through a nearby pile of old magazines, tattered pamphlets, and useless old manuscripts. He could not by any means find the issue of *Martrydom* with Shozan's story *Oyoneh* that he thought he would try to read right away. He stopped the search. Before he knew it he was deep in thought about himself. What he happened to recall at the moment was the rose that bloomed in the shade of his country garden and with that recollection came memories of his gloomy life in the country. . . . It hadn't occurred to him before, but wouldn't that be worth writing something about? Maybe he could write it up. Next time Shozan came he'd talk with him about it. Heretofore, he never imagined talking to Shozan about anything he was considering. That night, however, he felt differently about Shozan. . . . "Yes, what is there for me to be ashamed of in being Shozan's friend?" he asked himself. "Just as Shozan tells me everything, shouldn't I tell him everything, too? Think of it: if I unconsciously make myself feel a bit superior by scorning Shozan, that's a heartless attitude. It's the first step toward failure! . . . No, without my noticing it, that may not be merely the first step, but an even further descent toward my own failure, inwardly as well as outwardly. . . ." For some personalities there is a pleasure in self-rebuke.

*   *   *

Speaking of Shozan, the man had not shown his face for more than two weeks. He had gotten the contract to do the manuscript for the adventure story, and he had dashed off something on it. His demand for payment was called unreasonable before the work was fully finished, but he did get some advance payment. Thanks to that and, although it was late, he did finish the job after the end of February. As Shozan reported this, he produced a splendid original edition of a book more than two inches thick—a book, though, that would sell at a night stall for fifteen sen. The foreign author may have been hardly more famous than Shozan; indeed the author had a name not known at all. It was written in a style presumed to be Stevenson's, who was popular at the time. As Shozan opened the lavishly illustrated book and showed Ozawa Mineo a picture, he said, "I put this story together at your request." Judging by the pictures, it seemed to tell of pirates and pirate battles awkwardly and tediously enacted from *Treasure Island* and *The Gold Bug*. After he finished the conversation and left, Shozan did not come again for some reason. Was he engrossed in his work? *He* thought so, until the reason became clear. He was to hear that reason later in a conversation precipitated by a postcard sent through the mail.

—A postcard. He knew at once from the absurdly serious hand and the circuitous statement of a simple matter that it was from his wife's father, a lower-level bureaucrat in the Ministry of the Interior. The card was written on one side. The gist was, "I've got something to talk over with you. Can you stop by on your walk tomorrow afternoon? If tomorrow is not convenient for you, we can come by your house in the next day or two. . . ." That's all it said. It was signed in the name of his wife's mother and dated March 23. Without going he knew what the business was. It was sure to be the question of what he was going to do at the end of the month.

As he fiddled with the postcard, crumpling it and smoothing it, he wondered how many times a letter had come to this house since he had moved here. Wasn't this postcard the only mail in four months? Maybe there was one other. . . . It was appropriate. He himself had neither business nor inclination to write anyone for a long time. There was no one that he could expect to hear from.

*   *   *

Accustomed to solitude as he now was, it was unusual for him to want to meet someone that evening. As he toyed with the postcard in his hand—the postcard that said, "Come, I have something to talk to you about"—he knew without a doubt that the topic was his prospect for making a living. The thought came naturally to him, intensifying his feeling that he wanted to meet someone. Anybody would do. The boy from the secondhand bookstore, who had not come by for some time, would do. Shozan, if possible, would do. If Shozan were to show up by chance, they could talk earnestly of poverty. "No, I shouldn't be afraid of poverty. I certainly couldn't say something like that, though. I would rather talk about the arts. What I finally noticed today, my life in the country, the rapport between my feelings and nature that I came to see without realizing it . . . If I could talk with Shozan about that, wouldn't Shozan surely recognize the subtle story was just like his own thinking? If so, wouldn't he encourage me as always to write it quickly? No, if Shozan really sees and believes this to be a subtle story, no matter what he says won't he inwardly feel jealous or hostile toward my plan to write up such an elegant work? Then, too, he may not understand the story at all. No, this was certainly not something to write with the likes of Shozan in mind. . . . But supposing it were written, who would ever print it? . . . Or rather, could I really write that admirable story where somehow the feelings are clear but there is little probability of coherence?"

In order to forget tomorrow's talk, he thought over various approaches to the story that had occurred to him but had yet to take shape. He felt strangely proud, but right away he had to admit that his confidence was without basis. Still, the artistic excitement led him to think of trying to write some headings for an outline. He realized he had not been at his desk for more than two weeks, and he knew he did not have even one sheet of writing paper. He didn't have money to go out and buy paper, either. After the bath, the haircut, and the purchase of a pack of cigarettes all he had left of the fifty-sen silver coin was carfare money for tomorrow. Off and on he had written two or three lines, or five or six pages, and then thrown away the unfinished work. The cover of his wicker trunk was full of these scraps. He took the trunk out of the closet and looked for the paper. One by one he turned the sheets over and smoothed them out.

By coincidence the magazine *Martyrdom* was mixed in with the papers. How hard he had looked for it. Shozan's favored story, *Oyoneh*, was included. He stopped smoothing paper long enough to scan *Oyoneh*. . . . He may not have done it from any good feeling for Shozan. For an artist who was thinking of writing a new work, it was surely appropriate to examine the work of a personal friend for material that might inspire his own perilous self-confidence.

He ruffled loosely through the pages of *Oyoneh*. It was a longish short story. He thought it might be eighty or ninety pages. The woman named in the title was the heroine. A young man named Kunikichi was presumably Shozan. Apparently it was one from his collection of Asakusa stories. . . . It concerned the relationship between a young woman from a very low-class house of assignation, where questionable Asakusa women received their clients, and a young patron named Kunikichi who frequented the house. The man eventually moved in to live with the woman. She was a girl hardly seventeen. The woman she called mother was a widow of not yet forty. The story's theme was the pattern of events between the girl and her mother on the one side and Kunikichi on the other with the resulting inner complications for Kunikichi. It had the marks of a sweet story, but the girl, soon corrupted by affairs around her, left Kunikichi for another lover in less than six months. In his jealousy Kunikichi began to move out of her house, but lingering attachment was stronger than jealousy, and he could not leave at once. Because the girl's mother was sympathetic to Kunikichi, he was not turned out. Bickering was endless between mother and daughter over the mother's sympathy for Kunikichi. The man with his unending affection for the daughter fell to the temptation of the mother. The next morning he fled without hope or aim from the frightful house that had guaranteed his livelihood. . . . That was the plot of the story. He started to skim it, but Shozan's writing required careful, devoted attention. As a writer, Shozan was no fool. He was a veteran with the pen. Here and there he used words that gave a glimpse of blighted mental states that were not easily moved nor idly upset. As a man Shozan made a strange impression, but as a writer there was nothing strange about him. He found no reason at all to scorn Shozan. He read the story through, but, when he thought it over again, he felt, as a critic who was not easily satisfied, that he was not satisfied. Then he sensed the discontent gradually giving way in the end to sympathy. Shozan's style was fully developed. He achieved a certain undeniable standard of success with the psychology. At least it was the work of a man who sought moral discipline for literature. He absorbed all there was to absorb. The work in return was freed of immaturity. But why was the vitality lost with the immaturity? You might think the refinement was written into such base material simply because the passion was so weak. Although the unfortunate Shozan was a writer without name, he had here written the work of an old master. A most subtle old master! An oddity as a man, Shozan was in no way odd as a writer. . . . A work without a fault one could point to anywhere. How can good art be made of merely that? What was most unfortunate—the ideas of a little Tolstoy were set into the plot of a little Zola. Shozan had written with all the freshness at his command, but for the literary establishment it was three years— just three years too late. . . . That's what the work made one think. There are authors and works like that in the real world. . . . What a contradiction of life it was! The unfortunate Shozan had given him such encouragement, and yet the weakness of a colleague is one source for a man's pleasure.

*　　*　　*

The title was "A Tale of the Rose That Will Bloom." . . . No one had ever tried to write that story before!

*　　*　　*

He picked up his pen and started to write. He wrote on and on. He wrote without sleeping. The next day he continued to write, almost forgetting the postcard that had summoned him. . . . He was a slow writer, but, surprisingly, he had written seventeen or eighteen pages by evening. When he read them over, he could only despair at what he had written on the back of the scrap paper. He remembered how it was in the house in the country when he had sometimes written poetry late into the night. By the next morning the color and smell of the words had evaporated into the night, and the writing was delirious and without meaning. That strange frenzy persisted even now.

"It's no good!" he said to himself in a loud voice.

He sat at the desk for a long time. He recalled the words of a man, a sculptor in clay, of strong personality and large frame. The man had said, "I comprehend a thing only when I realize that I am without artistic talent. . . . That's the only way." What was the real sense of those words? Was it pretense, or perhaps a paradoxical display of self-confidence? He couldn't say. He thought over those words spoken vehemently several years ago as the sculptor was flipping through photographic reproductions of Rodin's works for him in his studio. If his self-confidence were to be crushed by his own pronouncement that he was without any talent whatsoever, and, if he were to do that now while still a young man, his life would be worth living no longer. The world teems with hordes of people without talent, and that may be why his own loss of self-illusion came fortunately in silent, steady stages. Thus was a person's self-confidence chipped away slowly, piece by piece. The individual didn't notice it was happening. . . . He considered these things as he sat as his desk. His thoughts, as always, progressed by natural sequence into self-criticism. He had to sense, vaguely, that his ridiculous self-assurance was dripping away before his eyes like sand through his fingers. Whatever one tried to do, it all came out the same: it was just an active way to wear down one's own self-confidence. Where there was no real talent, wasn't it rather stupid to go on believing in the dream forever? . . . "For those who aspire to the arts," he thought, "won't many of them see their dreams and their confidence for the arts extinguished along with their youth? I'm just at that point now. If I can't do art, what else can I do? Is human life something anybody can get through one way or another? A life lived like that is frightful to think of; yet no other way is given to those who have no talent. A man's hopes for his life are always to believe in his own ability and to dream of tomorrow. . . . When you put it that way, take Shozan, who, having lived for more than twenty years believing he would soon achieve something, has been thinking and experiencing all sorts of things and writing aimlessly. Outwardly it seems to have brought him no happiness, but isn't it valid to respect him just for that? Even if his anguish is slight because he lacks the wisdom to understand himself, I don't know whether he is to be laughed at or to be envied. . . . Not only Shozan but anyone who lives out his own life—shouldn't that person himself be worthy of full respect? The lives of those who have talent should be respected expressly for that talent. Shouldn't those without talent likewise be respected for living through their life with no talent? . . . For someone like me, at the start of life, I feel

like I'm already out of breath. . . . The youth that people praise is a
burden that I cannot endure. . . ."

> I am sick of malady
> There is but one thing can assuage:
> Cure me of youth, and, see,
> I will wise in age!

—He thought these things as he ran through his mind the
dimly remembered verse. "That's it. Youth may be the very thing
that throws a man's life into hysteria. What I need now is the clear,
serene life of an old man. But what about my present life? Youth.
Wilted youth . . . I wish thirty years would flash by in this instant.
No, it would be better if my whole life passed in the instant. I
have not the heroic, positive will to die right now, but I shouldn't
be so alarmed either if death were to come unexpectedly and suddenly. . . ."

Realizing that he was foolish through and through, he wondered
that he did not know how much was poetic exaggeration. He was
fixated on the thought, but it gave neither relief nor solace. When
he saw rather that it muddled his head, he thought he might try to
freshen his spirits by going over to his wife's family home. However, it was almost eleven o'clock. He went out the gate and whistled for the dogs. If he didn't take a walk when he was so needlessly
agitated, he would never be able to sleep, he thought. Although
there was hardly a thing worth stealing in the house, he could not
leave without someone there. Anyway, he had no place to go, so he
walked the dogs up and down the deserted street in front of his
house. The sky was springlike with a hazy moon. He walked looking at the moon. That country life—since yesterday it had floated
before his eyes, but he simply could not portray it. He recalled it
anew as he gazed at the moon, and he felt a strong yearning for it.
Why didn't he stay there longer? What's more, why didn't he end
up as a resident of that sepia village? What purpose did he have in
returning to hang around the city? He savored those feelings with
deep emotion. Gradually his spirits calmed. Tonight, when his wife
returned, they could talk of the country, talk about that hill, and
the well, and all that. If they did, surely something new would

come to his attention. . . . Thinking on like this, he shortly reentered the house.

He climbed into his laid-out bed and thought he would read over once more the pages he had written. Again, though, he found the writing showed a lack of ability, and he stopped reading. He laid the manuscript and the pen neatly next to his bed. . . . Just as his inspiration may have been no more than a fit, his despair might also be but a fit. He would try again leisurely to write. "There is no reason for me to decide I cannot do a thing," he said to himself. He consoled himself until suddenly he wondered whether Shozan would sleep if he were thinking like that. This trivial idea struck him as unbearably ludicrous. His own loud laughter rang in his ears. This guy is some strange fellow, he felt, as if looking back at himself from afar.

Lost in all these thoughts and feelings, he suddenly heard a short bark from the dogs, and he gathered that his wife was home. The dogs customarily barked that way when they heard her footsteps. His wife would whistle in response. That evening there was no whistle. The footsteps sounded far away. Like the ears of a man in jail that are very keen to sounds from the outer world, his own ears were as sharp as those of his dogs. Slowly the footsteps neared; they were not those of his wife. The steps on the rarely traveled road approached his house, and the sound of the wooden geta suddenly faded. Along with the stealthy steps of the geta he could hear a slap-slapping sound like rubber sandals. Two sets of uncoordinated and disorderly footsteps passed his house. . . . He was inclined to think his wife had not come home. . . . In less than ten minutes another set of footsteps sounded, this time from the opposite direction, from the top of the hill, not the way his wife always came home. This time they did not tiptoe in front of his house. . . . The door was opened. Unlike what was usual, the dogs could get no response to their fawning whines. They did not bark. They knew exactly whose footsteps those were. The dogs had been that way, too, when the footsteps passed ten minutes earlier. Because suspicion made him uncomfortable, he refrained from calling out to his wife. What if suddenly he were to ask her casually, "Isn't that a nice hazy moon tonight?"—wouldn't she surely say yes without thinking? Then suppose he were to grin and say, "It's a night for a man to walk a woman and a woman to walk a man. That's for sure." What kind of a look would his wife give him? . . . He looked down and thought to himself, "Say, does this fellow have bad ears. . . ." So he pondered to himself. He remained silent and pretended not to know his wife was home. Attentive and distrustful, he listened to his wife moving about in the next room.

Probably she was leaning back quietly in front of the brazier, he thought. She said nothing, thinking he was already asleep. Suddenly he had another thought. . . . Last night his wife had accidentally seen the postcard from her family. On her way home from the theater she may have stopped by her family home to consult with her mother. Her mother may have walked this far with her. Now his wife might be distressed and worrying over household matters. . . . That's it. . . .

"Hey," he called through the sliding door panel. "Did you come home by a roundabout way?"

"Oh, you're up," exclaimed his wife, startled.

"No. Why did you come that way?"

Not getting the answer he expected, he fell silent again and then added, "You came from the top of the hill tonight, didn't you?"

"Oh, you knew that?"

"I knew it. I know everything. I could hear your footsteps perfectly. . . . Anyway, you did come by way of the lonely hilltop."

"Well, it was a warm moonlit night. I met someone I knew on the streetcar. My friend got off at Shinmitsuke, where I did, too, and walked with me this far through the lonely street."

His wife spoke without hesitation. . . . A tale half true, or one-third, he thought. If he hadn't heard the footsteps coming earlier from the bottom of the hill, he could believe what she said was the whole truth. He neither said nor asked anything further. He just picked up the manuscript from his bed and crumpled it up.

"What are you doing?"

He answered her question calmly: "Oh, I'm tearing up another botched piece of writing, like always. . . . It's not your fault."

After saying so he got up and went into the next room, where his wife was. Displacing her from the front of the brazier where she was sitting, he went through the drawers one by one.

His wife looked dubious. "What are you doing?"

"Sleeping pills. There ought to be one left."

*   *   *

His wife's mother was sitting with her back turned on the sunny veranda. He walked through the gate and caught sight of her through a break in the bamboo fence. She seemed to be sewing. He walked directly in without saying a word. The house was so small that five steps beyond the door you were standing in the middle. It was his wife's family home. His wife's mother turned and looked up at him standing there in his usual grumpy way.

"Oh, you've come at last. I thought you weren't coming, and I'd have to go to you—as soon as I finished this."

She was sewing. "Look at this," she said, holding it up for him to see. It was a lined silk kimono in a wild red and black checkerboard pattern. It appeared that the finished kimono would have a black satin neck band. He spotted the cloth for it next to the woman sewing, as he picked up a cushion, laid it out, and spoke.

"That's awfully flashy for a kimono. Who ever can that be for?"

"Whose is it?" she said laughing and holding it up. There wasn't a touch of malice in her smile, but the manner of her laugh left a coarse impression. . . . When his wife's mother smiled like that, he always found it disagreeable. She glanced his way with that smile and then looked back at her hands working the needle. "I don't like this pattern very much. First off, the material is poor, isn't it?"

"Yes," he said. "I don't like it, either. Who's it for anyhow?"

"Oh, really?" she said again, glancing at him doubtfully. "Wasn't it your choice? I thought you asked me deliberately because you knew."

"My choice. Not at all. Well, then, is it a kimono for Yumiko?"

When he understood it was for Yumiko—his wife—an unpleasant feeling welled up from the depths of his heart. Yumiko was earning her own pay these days, but she had never made up a silk kimono on her own discretion, nor had she ever failed to consult him about anything to do with pattern or taste when she bought something. He did not know when she had bought this material, nor had she said one word to him about how it should be made up. Even granting that, what about this particular choice? He thought that, if the taste was fitting, it didn't matter how conspicuous the attire. Although this fashion was proper to a girl, a recent student graduate, would a careful woman for any reason choose something so out of keeping, the attire of a geisha—a cheap-imitation geisha at that? It made him angry; it suggested that she was posing as a superior artist although she was attached in a minor role to a suburban amateur theater. In response to his silence Yumiko's mother continued her work without any special notice. It was to all appearances no different from his usual grumpy silence. When she came to a pause in her sewing, she poured tea and began her promised consultation. First she took out something like a strip of paper from a roll. It was an itemized list of amounts of money advanced from time to time for her daughter's household. She explained it to him at length, as if calling up the recollection of each instance. Indeed all that money did seem to ring faintly in his memory. It didn't matter anyway. Whatever could be done about it in the end, he wished the conversation would come to a conclusion. The very idea that money matters of all things had to be precise was incomprehensible to him. This garrulous woman could not open her mouth without pursuing precision in money matters as the natural course of life and, what's more, without doing so in systematic circumlocution. Still, he thought the conversation was even more tedious than the usual month-end review. He just kept thinking he wanted more precision about the footsteps last night and the checkerboard kimono today, when the other problem, about which he cared nothing, reached its conclusion.

"Well, Mineo." She spoke his name to press him for a reply. He took little interest in the problem and had said hardly a word. Taking two or three puffs on a long pipe, she continued.

"Well then, Mineo. As I just said, the amount you two have borrowed totals one hundred and ninety-six yen. Roughly two hundred yen. Of that amount fifty yen is money I borrowed at the end of the year for you from someone I know. It comes due this month.

If I can give them an excuse, they'll put it off a week or ten days. It's your loan, but, because we've got some money—my, we're temporarily taking the role of your father, aren't we?" She vented her habitual grievance at his parents' coldheartedness toward the two of them. "The loan was for our dear daughter and you. It was given neither to provide luxury nor to allow waste. Not just two hundred. Even a thousand if we had it—we can't help but do it. If you had a firm objective, no matter how long it was, or if you could think of some other way. But so long as you don't, and it continues like this, it will ruin us all. . . . Anyway I think it would be better for now to settle things up to date. If I do say so, though, it really bothers me that there is no way to do that. If you have any thoughts on it, I'd like to hear them." She spoke without insistence, not particularly expecting any answer. Instead she forced a slight smile and resumed speaking at once. "It's your business and I know it's indiscreet of me. I talked with your father-in-law recently. What Father said—be quiet and listen. I don't know whether you will agree or not. That place in the country that you bought to live in—if you were to mortgage the fields for two or three hundred yen, you could get a three-hundred-yen loan. With that you could clear up your present loans. While the remaining money lasted, you could try your best to work. How about that? Still, the remaining amount would not be more than one hundred yen at best, not enough for two months in your present condition. You could close out your present house—it seems you don't like it anyway. The inconvenience for you is even more regrettable because Yumiko is not there in the house. If you did give up the house, you could let Yumiko stay here for a while. . . . Of course it's up to you. It would be all right for you to come and live here, too, but in this house there's no place to put a desk. It would be inconvenient for two couples to sleep here. Daytime would be all right, but at night Father's like that—he chants Noh dramas until 10 P.M. You say you don't like that, and you'd probably be annoyed. If it's not distasteful to you, wouldn't it do to find temporary lodgings nearby? You could move Yumiko into the lodgings, too, but in the first place, a couple costs more. Then it is strange for a married couple to live in a rooming house. Of course, if you were to say you wanted to, that would be all right. If you want to find lodgings for yourself or for the both of you, there is a place within a block. You turn in at the side of the bakery that makes bread for the army. The old man there is a singing friend of your father's. He's very friendly, and I went there yesterday to inquire. It's a very nice room, light and south facing with sunlight all day. It's four and a half mats big but very nice. He said it was seventeen yen. If you look it over and don't dislike it, how about closing out your house at the end of the month?"

So far he had been listening quietly, but now he had to say something. He had no particular idea what to do. In short, anything was all right.

"Yes, anything is all right with me."

"You are a helpless one. You say anything is all right even though it's your business."

"Uh-huh." He smiled wryly along with his mother-in-law. What they were proposing was generally all right, but he asked, "Well, have you consulted Yumiko about this?"

"Four or five days ago I had a message from her that the theater manager's son had died, and they were collecting condolence contributions at the theater. She had no money and asked for five yen. I arranged to take her the money, and at the time we discussed the matter briefly. She said, if it was all right with you, she'd like to do it."

"What? Four or five days ago? She didn't say anything to me about it, about meeting you or anything." He felt this added new detail to his strong displeasure at his wife. Whether the mother noticed his expression or not, she spoke in defense of her daughter.

"She thought you'd be annoyed by the subject, so she left it to me. Anyway, if you think it's all right, can't we confirm the decision? Because we're going to do it this month and there's little time left, I'll come tomorrow and help get things together."

"Oh . . . but since you make it so soon, is it all right that I don't have the money yet?"

"Well, if you do intend to raise money on the country place, and it can't be done right away, we'll trust you until it can. We'll take care of it for you. . . . Because every month is a loss under present conditions, once it's decided, it's better to do it within the month. So far as mortgaging the country place, Father says it's only a thought. After you've looked it over, Father says he wants to stop troubling you about it. There's no use thinking it over any more. . . . It's the prejudiced choice of the pauper."

The two pondered in silence.

"I wonder what's with Emori Shozan. Well, that's how it is." She had changed the subject to break the unpleasant silence. "Yes. He hasn't been to your house recently, has he? He hasn't been here recently either. Around the twentieth of last month he was coming almost every evening. Did you know that? He's very good at Noh chanting."

"Chanting? Really? He has that hidden talent?"

"There's nothing hidden about it. He's an expert. A fine, seasoned voice. He sang 'Wisteria Gate' with a singing master who comes here. The instructor admired him. Later the instructor said that, if he'd practice hard, he would be able to do the first lessons to perfection. The next time Shozan came, Father told him, 'Say, Emori, because you sing like that, why don't you give up your poverty and become an instructor of chanting? He could help you find students, that's what he said.' Father is straightforward, and he spoke more than enough. Emori laughed at the time, but then he stopped coming. Maybe he didn't like it, huh? . . . We really don't understand the intentions of either of you two."

If she saw a completely commonsense guy like Shozan as eccentric, surely she could have no idea what he himself was like. But then he didn't understand himself either. . . . Whatever art Shozan undertook, he did it with refinement. The fact that he had never once blown his own horn about it added a certain pleasing shade to Shozan's personality, he thought.

*   *   *

The three-o'clock afternoon sunshine of an early spring day dazzled his eyes when he came out of the little north-facing room with its one window, where they had been talking. His feelings, too, were overwhelmed by the dazzle. As he walked down the busy street, staring at his feet, his eyes were drawn now and then to the gaudy decorations in the shop windows on both sides. . . . They were that colorful. It was the kind of day when everything that struck his eyes made him wonder whether everything in the world were so bright—wonder whether it were all right for everything to be so bright. It was a day to make one think spring had really come to the world in these last two or three hours. His spirits, idle from the stagnation of winter, began to quiver a bit. As they did, he felt his fatigue grow heavier. Not only his feelings but external circumstances were gradually pressing in. Like it or not, he had a presentiment of crumbling, as if his dead-end life had at once breached a dike. . . . No, rather he felt it was the forebodings of fact that were casting a heavy, albeit small, shadow in his heart. . . . To return to his dirty, dimly lit room and hunker down alone thinking over his too-appropriate problem—that would be terrifying, or disagreeable in a ghastly way. He turned his feet away from home and immediately climbed an embankment at the side of the road. It was part of a ruined old castle wall in the center of town. He walked leisurely across the young, green grass like a man with nothing troubling his heart. Although he tried his best to avoid those things he wanted not to think, the shadows spread moment by moment through his heart. He stopped walking and stood still. He sat down on the grass, and after a bit he lay flat on his back. The sky was purplish rather than blue; not a cloud was to be seen. On such a beautiful day he thought how annoying it was to have to be suspicious of his wife. When, he thought, have I ever talked seriously with my wife? Since we left the country and came to the city, I think we've almost never talked to one another seriously. When they did talk, the wife spoke only of her things and he spoke only of his. With her going out early in the morning and returning late at night, even later recently, there was simply no time for it even if they wanted to talk. When had he ever thought seriously about his wife? Actually, he hadn't felt like talking to her for a long time. No, recently he often forgot her existence entirely. All he thought of was his work, and Shozan in relation to it. Didn't he talk more to Shozan than to his wife? Didn't his wife, too, spend more time and talk about more things with other people—whether men or women he didn't know —but with others rather than her husband? Different worlds had opened up for each of them. Surely there could be nothing unnatural about that. It was not unreasonable for him suddenly to look with grave concern and suspicion at the wife whom you might say he had forgotten entirely until yesterday, literally until he heard the double footsteps echoing last night. Well, chastity should not be something that everyone can demand of anyone. Like all gifts it is given only from the goodwill of the other party. If she lost her goodwill toward him and so would not give the heart's finest gift, to be faithful, who could blame whom? Wasn't it wrong to expect gifts through compulsion? . . . To be able to think this way freely, or with some degree of indifference, wasn't that because he had already lost his passion for her? Or rather he could think somewhat rationally because this was still a case of mere suspicion? So long as he could not see the facts gradually becoming evident, he could not by himself measure how much passion he still cherished for his wife. . . . Well, he had to admit he had cooled off to that extent. In this condition, then, what right did he have to force chastity on her merely on the grounds that she was his wife? If he were to confess his doubts to her, and if there were some kind of appeal he could make to her, would it be right to do so? Or if he had already lost that much passion, would it be right to give her some warning as a friend? Warning? What kind of warning? He felt there was nothing he ought to say. If it was a common banality, she ought to know it herself without his repeating it. If she were going to leave him, she could go. He hadn't the enthusiasm to run after. If so, what tormented him so much? It wasn't affection, was it? Was he just thinking of his honor as a man? That was close to it, he thought. If he had come to hate her, it was not for anger at the betrayal of his love. It was a mean resentment for destroying his honor—common, ordinary honor. As she destroyed his honor as a man, didn't the business cast away her common honor as a woman, too? If so, what would embolden her to such conduct without regard to her own honor as a woman and anyway in full knowledge that the honor of the man she loved would be willfully disgraced? A new passion stirs in her, no doubt. The thought came to him with an awareness of jealousy sprouting in his heart. No, if he truly thought the problem began only with jealousy, not just newly sprouting but from way back, wasn't that a roundabout way of making him despise himself? . . . This point absorbed him for a long time. At the same time, the suspicion was no more than mere suspicion for him. The grounds for doubt were too flimsy: she might be coming home late recently because she was walking around every evening with someone; the vulgar checkerboard kimono might be the choice of a new companion; you might think she wanted to close out the house in preparation for leaving him. Over and over he wondered whether all this weren't a mirage arising from his own shameful distrust. "Maybe so," he was thinking, when he was struck by an idea: it was something about life in jail told to him by a socialist once imprisoned for his activities. Many of the inmates were tormented by suspicion that their wives were being unfaithful during their absence. They saw it in their dreams. As the feelings grew worse, there were often cases when the husband suddenly reprimanded the wife who had come to visit. He turned the story over in his mind, and, "Yes," he thought, "it's been a morbid life of mine for the last two or three years and maybe my mind has become just as morbid as a prisoner's. . . ." That made him inclined to believe his wife. If she betrayed his confidence, that would be no shame to him, only to her. He thought so.

He listened to the streetcars rumbling by just below the embankment. He had been there nearly two hours absorbed in thoughts unfitting to the beauty of the day.

*   *   *

As he thought along like this, he reached but one decision: he would say nothing about it to his wife. It was just a matter of folding his arms. There was no other way for it. If there were anything else he could do, it was only to observe her as calmly as possible. For someone who knew not what to do, the only thing he could do was to watch closely and learn clearly, without missing a thing, all those circumstances about which he knew not what to do. Once he was driven into a corner where he had to say something, he had to be able to state in an orderly way his suspicions of when and where and his observations of what happened at what time. That way he could let her know when the time came that, although he had earlier remained silent, he was not to be considered a fool for not knowing. When his thinking reached this point, he felt unbearably wretched and miserable at having chosen unwittingly to be so combative and thoroughly negative toward his wife. "But," he thought to himself, "I don't really intend to get my assurance through energetic spying. To settle my doubts I'll use only those facts that strike my attention in what my eyes and ears pick up naturally, just as I have been doing all along." . . . This excuse he gave himself was not at all promising. By temperament she was good-natured, and, whatever she did, she would not be able to cover it up very well. She would give herself away quickly. The thought struck him with a flash that made him feel how strange and pitiful was his wife. If these feelings were to strengthen, he might say to his wife, "Hey, I've pretended not to know anything, but actually I've been watching you. If you've done anything wrong, you've been clever in avoiding any cause for my suspicion." Like an actor rehearsing the lines for his role, he murmured the words to himself. If he did say these things to his wife, it would not likely be from love or mercy for her. He would have to admit it was craven, cowardly evasion because he did not like to confront things head-on. . . . "I really lack the strong spirit of a realist," he thought; "the spirit in which a man, climbing at his normal pace, counts the steps up the scaffold where he will be beheaded. If I could stare unblinking at all human nature with neither surprise nor sorrow but impervious to the fogs of exaggeration and sentiment, that I could call a kind of salvation. Let it happen, whatever it was to be." That invocation was half a pretext for him to give up. Let it happen. Wherever you went there was no way out. For him, let it happen. Whatever it was, wherever you went, there was only a dead end. . . . He thought of himself sometimes in the first person, sometimes in the third. Time and again when he felt his brooding thoughts were unexpectedly emerging onto a broad avenue, they swerved suddenly back into the dark byroad of suspicion over his wife—and yet the thoughts ran on. If the event that was tormenting him had occurred, when did it start? In tracing back his memories a new thought occurred to him; he should have thought of it before. It was that day he went to call on Ōkawa Shūhan at the theater. . . . In the dressing room his wife had been rather cool to him, he thought. No, not so—his wife was reflecting back his own unconcern for her that stemmed from his feeling of awkwardness. Although he felt that he wasn't giving proper consideration to how flustered he was at going into an unfamiliar place, he could not doubt that any coolness was because she was busy and the time for casting roles was imminent. When you looked with suspicion, everything looked dubious, but if the affair had already started by that time, she would not have told him that Shūhan's attitude that day could be explained by the fact that Tachibana Sujaku had taken a new lover. If there was anything for her to be ashamed of that resembled something she might fault in someone else, she wouldn't be likely to mention it unless absolutely necessary. But he did not know that. The average person sees someone else doing before his eyes the very thing he has done himself. Then very calmly, as if he had completely forgotten his own action, he carelessly utters the very criticism that should be directed at himself. . . . This may be counted as one of the important differences between the common man and the man of some cultivation. Doubts about the self as well as the reflex action of the conscience are almost totally lacking in women. The fact that his wife criticized the Sujaku affair severely would be no proof at all that she had not committed the same fault. . . . His thoughts were a black structure that he was erecting and tearing down again and again, but as usual they had no end.

There in the darkness his eyes discerned anew the irritated expression, the strained face of Shūhan reportedly deserted by Sujaku.

She hadn't come home yet. There was nothing special to say to her when she did, so one could not have said that he was waiting. Still, it was a problem for him that she wasn't home. With the light of the match that lit his cigarette, he looked at the face of his alarm clock next to the bed. Quite a lot of time had passed since the other clock struck twelve, he thought. By this clock, though, it was only fifteen minutes past the hour. . . . She always came home late, but in order to make it look less late had she set the clock back? The thought flashed through his mind.

*　　*　　*

He awoke from a light sleep, thinking he heard a noise in the house. From the light leaking through the many chinks and knotholes in the door, it seemed to be rather late in the morning. Wearily he slid open the door next to his bed. The sound of dishes being washed came from the kitchen. His wife had not come home last night after all. She must have arrived a little while ago. The clock by his bed said it was just before eight. He felt it would annoy him to call out to her, so he lay there blankly in his bed for about ten minutes, eyes open but not fully awake. Unable to go back to sleep, he lit his last cigarette. He had a piercing headache, perhaps from lack of sleep. Deliberately he had not called to his wife, but the silence made him curiously angry. To admit as much and say something now would be all the more vexing, but, if she were to notice he was awake and then say nothing to him, he felt he would have to scream at her. To scream would be all right, but he did not know what words to scream at the wife who came home only in the morning. He thought about trying to scream something without knowing what to say. If he really did, he realized it would be a terrible thing to do so early in the morning. Would she answer him back with something furious, or would she burst out crying? It had to end in a quarrel. . . . Only half a year ago he would often quarrel violently with his wife. Had he now unwittingly lost the ardor for quarreling? Now he was terribly frightened to quarrel with her. When they began to quarrel, his wife's facial expressions were indescribably disagreeable. Her words were like a play script. Her facial expressions and bearing, you could not fail to think, reflected a deadly seriousness. When he suddenly recalled the looks of his wife at those times, he was acutely aware of the words *husband of an actress*. Surely he could write about that, he thought, as he threw the totally burned-out cigarette stub into the ashtray.

Carrying the fire shovel heaped with coals, his wife went from the kitchen into the next room. Strange, he thought, and in the next moment he noticed that last night his wife was wearing the kimono her mother had made for her. Whether it was becoming to her or not, it was strange, and it made him feel she was an unfamiliar woman. His wife gazed at the coals in the shovel and then sat down and dropped her eyes to the fire she was feeding with charcoal. He could not see the look on her face.

"Oh, you're up?" She spoke as if she had just noticed him. He did not answer, until after a bit he said, "I'd like another cigarette."

He crumpled up the empty pack without a sign of much feeling and tossed it at the foot of the sliding door.

"You don't have to be so sarcastic. If you ask me to buy cigarettes for you, I'll buy them." She spoke only a little sharply and went out to buy cigarettes.

The two sat for a bit saying nothing. Then facing each other in silence they ate breakfast. Hearing the nearby clock strike ten, he suddenly remembered the alarm clock that had caught his attention last night. He went into the still-unmade room next door and fetched the clock from his bedside. He put it on the sideboard and compared the time. Suspicious, he thought, but it was not even five minutes slow.

"I've got the day off."

What was he thinking of in putting the clock there, his wife asked with a glance at it. Her voice was so soft it expressed the burden of the long silence. He had to say something in reply:

"Why?"

"Some trouble. . . . I was told to take the day off." He had no idea what the trouble was but did not ask. She looked disappointed at getting no answer to her statement. Continuing on her own, she said, "Miss Sujaku, you know, she's quitting. Quitting as an actress. I hear she's leaving Mr. Ōkawa." He listened in silence and learned that Sujaku was withdrawing from Mr. Ōkawa's theater troupe—a company whose box-office success rested almost entirely on Sujaku's popularity. With Sujaku gone all the others would naturally be dismissed by their employer. It seemed that Shūhan had known this for some time, but he wanted to preserve company unity for a while so he did not let out a word to anyone until last night. Then after last night's show he announced it to the troupe.

They discussed it late into the night, and everyone ended up staying overnight at the theater. . . . That's why she didn't come home last night, she explained. As if to suggest that he wasn't very interested in her talk, he bit intently at a tiny hangnail on his thumb while resting his elbow on the brazier.

"So what was the result of your conference last night?" He asked after a pause, as if it had just occurred to him.

"Well . . ." She cut off her words and glanced deliberately at his face, testing the expression. Then abruptly she said, "I'm thinking of quitting as an actress."

Her words and her look could be taken as a sounding out, a gentle plea for his opinion.

"What's the reason for that?"

"All those dropped by the theater will go to Asakusa, they say. Because they are being turned loose, Shūhan will place the remaining performers with a show manager in Asakusa. But I don't want to go to Asakusa. . . . If I do, I'll seldom be home. I want to stay home all the time and not go out anywhere."

He didn't much listen to the latter part of her talk. He spoke instead: "You say you don't want to go to Asakusa. It's such a vulgar place, you say. As amusement for the lady of the house, that's not unreasonable. But if the stage and the audience are bad, does that mean there is no external value in the artistry of the actors? If I were you and I liked the play, I'd do it, whether it's in Asakusa or wherever it is. If it's a poor play or whatever, you can still perform magnificently. Didn't the A Theater basically do trashy plays? Just think, was it only the place that failed, or wasn't the quality declining over a long period? . . . I think there are great actors in the suburbs and talent in adversity. . . . In saying so, I'm not telling you to go to Asakusa or not to go there. I don't know why you started in the theater to begin with. You may say it was because you were offered a role, and that was not in my best interest—because I can't help but be displeased at being supported by you and receiving spending money from you. Whatever you think, the theater is your source of pleasure. You're making your own living, but, because you've got quite a lot of spending money to pass out, it's all the same thing. I don't have a single thought of forcing you to be an actress. But then I don't have the thought, either, that you should quit. Yes. Yes." He laughed a little as he spoke. Feeling his wife's eyes on him, he added, "All I want to say is, your thinking is inconsistent and confused when you say your old theater was all right, but Asakusa is bad. If you're going to quit, quit."

"You're not giving me one bit of advice." Her voice had a slight edge.

"Wasn't that advice? Whatever you do is O.K. with me. Didn't I say to do what you want?"

"Yes, but a woman sometimes wants a clear order."

"Indeed. That's one philosophy. . . . But my philosophy from way back has been, Don't give orders to anyone. Don't take orders from anyone." He spoke calmly, even merrily. She remained silent. After a bit she turned to a new subject.

"Have you been to mother's?"

"Yes. I went yesterday. I saw her making that kimono." With a gesture of the chin he indicated the outfit she was wearing.

"What kind of discussion did you have?"

"To give up this house . . . do whatever you want. Do it to everyone's satisfaction. As for me, I don't know what's best to do."

"You. You don't like it?"

"I don't dislike it. Can't we do what everyone wants?"

"It's not a matter of what everyone wants. You're a queer one. If it's not what you want . . ."

"Oh, then it's all right with me. Either way is all right."

"There . . . that's not really any consultation. Mother's not unreasonable when she says you're hard to talk to," she muttered, half to herself.

Even he did not know whether he had been joking or telling the truth. Now he altered his manner of speaking and said in a businesslike way, "I've consulted seriously. Mother's coming soon. She said she'd come maybe tomorrow to help clean up. I like the feeling of novelty involved in moving. But moving itself I don't like at all. . . . For one thing I hope it goes well in an unfamiliar place. Won't it be a carefree life to live in a boarding house, leaving my wife and dogs in her parents' home?" He felt scorn for himself at these ironic words. He stood up. "Eleven o'clock. Well, I think I'll take a walk."

"A walk? With the dogs?"

"I don't want the dogs today."

"Are you going far?"

"I haven't decided. I might go lie on the bank of the castle moat. It's such a nice day."

"If you're going out of spite, why can't you stay home? . . . I'm home today."

"For me, I want to take a leisurely walk when there is someone to look after the house."

He was a man who spoke sarcastically of himself, as both his friends and his wife had observed. Actually he had a rather straightforward but tongue-tied and unhappy disposition. When flushed with emotions of common human warmth, he could find no words to express his feelings. When the ill humor spilled out, he was freer than he knew with contentious words. Some of his friends fancied him a superman, this fundamentally sentimental person. That came from his feeling of isolation; his natural bent reinforced the isolation. Every word that came out of his mouth this day was somehow unpleasant for him. Especially facing his wife, he could not stop. It was a day he had to be alone. He thought, maybe he imagined, that his wife's eyes glistened with tears as she watched him pick up his hat and leave. Or maybe her eyes were that way from lack of sleep last night.

For all that, he had no place to go when he left the house. He suddenly thought he might go to the library Shozan was headed for when he stopped by his house, and there he would read *Anna Karenina*—a book he had earlier started on. When he remembered how big that book was, the idea lost its appeal. While he was thinking of the library, his feet took him by reflex action in that direction. This led naturally toward the big plaza where he had grabbed the collar of the wine-shop boy who was mistreating his ugly dog Leo. Meanwhile he was thinking only of his wife. He wondered whether she weren't crying, alone at home. If it came out of some feeling of defiance for him, that would be rather better. Otherwise she would be waiting in fear for his return. What if, when she saw him, she cried out at once, "Forgive me. It's all my fault." Imagining that, he feared to go home. Then again, maybe she was neither crying nor depressed, but she had sunk into the bedding from which he had arisen and was blissfully sound asleep, making up the sleep she had lost. . . . He imagined that, too. It was crazy. His head was filled with too many visions of things before they happened, whatever they were. . . . Of course if they were pleasant visions, that would be different. As he said that to himself, he chanced to come on a stone park bench. He sat down. Around him were rows of cherry trees fully budded, the branches all pale pink. Looking out across them, he suddenly recalled his wife's words of a little while ago: "A woman sometimes wants a clear order." . . . Clever thing she said. . . . That's not something I would have thought of. It's like something used in a play script. . . . He thought it over again, rose from the bench, and walked straight down a broad, sloping avenue from the plaza toward town. He felt the sun shining on the back of his padded cloak. Chilled as he was, it warmed him until he felt hot. Having nothing to do, he browsed with no objective from one to another of the secondhand bookshops lined in great numbers along both sides of the boulevard. If he spotted the bookshop boy, he thought he would ask whether he had any news of Shozan.

In the window of one shop he saw a rare album of Pre-Raphaelite paintings. He opened and looked at it.

"Hey!" Came a hearty voice and a hand on his shoulder.

He turned and saw a heavyset man, an old friend named Kuno, whom he had not seen for three years. This year he was at last writing his graduation thesis, and he was looking for reference books, Kuno said, adding an invitation to join him in a nearby coffeehouse. . . . With a rather troubled look he followed after his intrinsically kindhearted friend.

"How've you been? Your color looks awful."

"Does it? I haven't been sleeping well."

"Still got nervous depression, eh? Oh, ho, I see."

Kuno's usual booming voice shook and bounced his large frame as if he would blow away anything like nervous depression. He laughed pointlessly. That grinning face with gentle eyes that narrowed when Kuno laughed was mirrored in *his* mind, although walking behind he could not see it. One of his friends had given Kuno the nickname of Saigō Takamori.[4] Kuno had a personality exactly the opposite of his own. . . . He had utterly forgotten about Kuno for some time. Now meeting him by chance, he felt most envious of that personality.

❋　　❋　　❋

The move came, just as his wife's mother had said, to a place less than a block from his wife's family home. His room had a single, low, south window with a sliding glass panel. The glass was not frosted, and there was no covering paper, so the sun shone directly through under the shallow eaves and onto the tatami-mat floor, reaching almost every corner. "It's really a warm room. In winter I live here myself and don't rent it out to anyone," the old landlord said when he showed the room. Indeed it was a good room for winter. When April came, though, it was a room he had to rent. All day long was just like a sunbath. He had yearned so long for the light of the sun, but three days here and he felt his head completely deranged by the flood of sunlight. No, he was really insane—to a mysterious degree. Head and body had become tired and listless. Questions of art and human nature had vanished somehow from every corner of his brain. Nothing replaced them in his brooding, musing thoughts. Although he went to sleep around ten in the evening, he did not rise before noon. Where he had been troubled before by sleeplessness, it was new for him now to sleep like this. When he awoke at noon, he ate breakfast and lunch together. . . . He had no feeling for whether it tasted good or bad; he just put the food in his mouth. When he had finished, he pushed the low table out into the hall, as he did not want anyone to come in for it. He looked for the pillow amid the quilts he had folded up earlier, and, tossing the pillow onto the tatami floor, he lay down again, dead tired. Neither asleep nor awake, he thought this must be the way dogs feel basking in the sun. He considered whether there was anything in the world as empty as this. Literature, wasn't that something like love, or like a kind of fever? he wondered as usual. Hadn't he recovered entirely from the fever without knowing it?

That made him feel a little forlorn, he thought. If he could stop examining everything item by item in nervous search as he had been doing, his feelings might be buoyed, but he could not expect to do that without acting decisively. He was like the stagnant water in an old bog, becoming putrid and putting out bubbles now and then, here and there, from the bottom. . . . That was probably a symptom of nervous depression. He doubted whether a person's state of mind had ever been so affected by climate and place of abode. The currents of anxiety kept flowing through the depths of the stagnant water. These were not his earlier sharp anxieties built up and broken down, one after another, by his intellect. Instead these resembled stiffness in the shoulder, the dull ache of a decayed tooth, stomach discomfort from overeating. They were vaguely dull but would not go away. One of the little things that tormented him was the mortgage loan on the country place. . . . To get it he had to take care of the business arrangements on his own. It wasn't all that much, but he had no talent and no experience in business matters. He had to talk about the business with a man he had never seen or known. . . . He did not know when it would be, but he was quite panicked and sick to death at the thought that it was imminent. As he thought about it, he spoke to himself with a show of courage. "If the man accepts, won't I be fit to become a newspaper reporter? But what if I can't carry this off expeditiously?" He had recently met Kuno by chance, and recalling Kuno's words on that occasion, he dwelt on the idea for a while.

Kuno knew of his straitened circumstances. An acquaintance of his was with one of the big papers. Although Kuno had not graduated from college, the man suggested Kuno might get a job with the paper. Kuno was looking for employment, but neither his circumstances nor his wishes were that urgent, so he did not apply. While he searched leisurely for something else for himself, Kuno could recommend *him* to his friend at the newspaper. When he met the friend in four or five days, they would talk the matter over tentatively, Kuno said. In the week since, he had heard no news from Kuno. Although he thought it was hopeless, he continued to wait for a postcard or something from Kuno. That's what the "If the man accepts"—and so on, was all about. . . .

＊　＊　＊

Weighing heavily among his anxieties was of course the question of his wife. With his tacit leave she had gone to a theater in Asakusa. She commuted there from her parents' home.

"Although we're living apart, it's not far. Coming and going I'll be sure to drop in. . . ." That's what she said, but in a whole week she had come only twice. Once was a day or so after he moved in. She came in the morning while he was still asleep.

"This isn't a very nice room. Can you settle down and accomplish something here?" With a couple of words she left him right away. He heard her fussy voice as if in a dream, still asleep. When he opened his eyes and looked, she was gone.

The second time she came late at night and sat down by the bed where he was sleeping. Her new theater, unlike the earlier A Theater, gave two performances daily, matinee and evening. Morning was a nuisance; she had to be there by nine, and it took an hour or more from her home to Asakusa. She came home late at night and didn't have time to stop in then, she said, running on by herself. Then, as if suddenly recalling it, she asked, "Do you know someone named Yoshizawa? Yoshizawa Komataro."

He didn't know anyone by such a common name. "Why?" he asked. Yoshizawa was manager of the greenroom in her new theater, she said. When he was a student, he had roomed with them for more than six months, Yoshizawa had told her. . . . Yes, he had roomed with a family named Yoshizawa five or six years ago. They had a girl of about sixteen. The mother brazenly pushed the girl onto a well-heeled student from the Kyushu area. The family was Yoshizawa. He was in the theater at the time—something to do with stage sets. . . .

"He was from Osaka?"

"That's right. From Osaka. He's the one. The world's a small place after all."

"Then you won't be able to do anything bad there." He looked up at her sharply, resting on his elbow. She didn't change her expression but spoke after a bit.

"Please don't come to this theater. The manager told me—he's known you since way back. He knows your father well. He said you're just like his kid. It would be just like saying his kid hangs out with the likes of Asakusa actresses."

"That's a fact, isn't it?"

"Anyway, don't come to the theater. You wouldn't like it, either —if you were to meet Yoshizawa."

"I wouldn't mind. I don't remember doing anything bad to Yoshizawa. . . . It would be all right to see him again." He deliberately said something he did not have in mind. He had not previously wanted to visit the theater, and he did not mean to say he wanted to visit it now. He was suspicious, though, of why the woman kept saying, "Don't come, don't come to the theater." Suddenly he had an idea: knowledge of her affair had spread through the theater, and she was afraid if he came, some hints would naturally reach his ears. Yes, her reputation had spread just like that throughout the theater. . . . The husband of a woman with that reputation would inevitably become a subject of gossip, too. Yoshizawa knew the name of the woman's husband. . . .

"You told the manager about your husband when you didn't need to."

"I didn't tell him. Someone else talked too much."

Maybe so. It was just as he thought, without a doubt. Pondering that, he remained silent and wondered what would be next. Why had things changed without his noticing? He suddenly recalled the Yoshizawa girl—surely her name was Oyuki—and the well-heeled student from Kyushu whispering together in the next room on the long winter nights even until 1 A.M. He thought of her as a light-complexioned, naive girl with an unattractive face. . . . Even now something about the student in the next room seemed to irritate him. . . .

"It's already twelve-thirty. I'm going home." She spoke after a period of silence and then stood up. He stared up from his bed at his wife standing before him. He gazed after in distress as if regretting her action in sliding open the shoji door and going out. As the door was about to close, he called to his wife, "Hey," in a low, parched voice. She reopened the partly closed door but stood in the hallway without reentering the room, and said, "What?"

"No. It's nothing." Feeling displeased that she did not reenter the room, he said only that in a voice of dismay. Suddenly he added spitefully, "You're so busy it's all right if you don't come so often." He blurted out exactly the opposite of what he intended originally to say. Disgusted, he turned off the electric-light switch by his bed. His wife left without reply. He gazed from the corner of his darkened room through the unshaded glass window at a cluster of not-very-bright spring stars, and he thought how lonely it was to be a bachelor with a wife.

    ❊   ❊   ❊

It happened one day: the old landlady of the boarding house came to his room to say timidly to the silent, gloomy resident that he had a visitor. A visitor? Here? Who would be coming here on what business? If no one had visited him here, no one would know he was living here, would they?

"For me? Aren't they looking for someone else?"

"No. He said it was definitely you."

"Well, what kind of a person is it?"

"Young—younger than you . . ."

"Huh?"

"A nice-looking man in a Western suit."

Who would it be? He was shocked for a moment at the question. His wife came to mind in a flash. That "young—younger than you, nice-looking man in a Western suit"—he had a hunch somehow that there was a connection to his wife.

"Oh? Well, I'll go see." His voice was filled with the sound of what could even be called determination. As he strode down the stairs, the figure of a man's back in a blue topcoat, squatting in the entryway, caught his eye. At the sound of his footsteps the man, who had already taken off his shoes, swiveled toward him and called out, "Hello!"

"What! You? Why didn't you say who you were?"

He snapped at his younger brother as if to scold him. Then quickly he returned to his room. Brother, not to be left behind, followed hastily into the room. Casting his eyes abruptly around the high parts of the wall, Brother spotted a nail at the top of a post, and there he hung his hat. It was a new, lightweight fedora of bluish gray. Brother sat down, taking care not to let his knees poke out his brand-new trousers. He gazed at his older brother's morose expression, but, because Brother was always like that, he paid no heed. Brother's moroseness that day was something special. Mistrust and misgivings toward his wife, even if over something very trivial, struck Ozawa Mineo as something almost like illness—a mounting supersensitivity beyond even the hypersensitive. He was filled with a feeling, a cross between shame and anger, that was eating into him because it had nowhere else to be directed. When he thought how he could not explain the reason for this special moroseness to the younger brother he had not seen for a long time, it made him more morose. To look at his brother's trim and tidy clothes made his mood more intense. At that moment the old lady appeared, bearing tea and pillows. She greeted the brother with polite words, and he responded in a meek and amiable manner to the effect that he was being a nuisance to his brother. . . . It disgusted him. The social amenities like that endeared his brother to people and spared Brother from his own kind of loneliness. It was a fact: this brother was born with an ordinary personality and went through school without discontent. Thus he could receive from their parents the care that enabled him to sustain an air of the complete young gentleman.

The youthful, innocent younger brother was unaware of his brother's twisted thinking, so in his meek manner he recounted how he first went to Brother's former residence, but, finding it vacant, he thought he could find him by going to his wife's family home. They sent him here.

After breaking off for a bit, he added these words: "Look. It's sudden, but there's a book called *Street Boy* translated by Dr. Mori Ōgai.[5] . . . Dad wants to read it, and he asked me to find it for him. . . . It's odd. A modern theater troupe touring the country came to our area and put it on, it seems. Mother was invited by someone to see it, her first play in twenty-some years. On her return she told father the story: it was about a son like you and the father who got angry at him, mother reported. Father wrote me that he'd like to see what the story was about. What kind of book is it after all?"

"Oh, it's a story originating in the quarrels and fights between a father and his son. The son will not listen to the father. He becomes a beggar, but then of his own accord he returns with his wife and children to the parental home he had fled. . . . It's been running in a magazine serial. It's not come out yet as a book."

That's all he answered. From the rather agitated tone younger brother finally realized that older brother was much more ill tempered than usual. He thought it was because he had brought up the story of *Street Boy*. He took a cigarette out of the case from his pocket, inserted it into a holder, and puffed leisurely. He said to his brother, who appeared unready to say more no matter how long they waited, "I thought I might go home for once, but tonight—" Then he added as if explaining to himself, "Because I'm on vacation I thought I would go right away, but then it was too late. . . ."

"Hmm." That was the only reply. He didn't even ask why.

"You don't have any particular business at home, do you?"

"That's right. Not a thing. Tell them from me I'm getting harder and harder up, and now I'm a beggar like the son in *Street Boy*."

Making no reply, his younger brother said, "Well. Good-bye." He stood up, patted the knees of his trousers lightly, took the hat from the nail, and placed it respectfully on his head. *He* watched from his reclining position as his brother started to leave; then suddenly he arose and saw him off to the front door. As he watched intently while Brother tied up the red laces of his boots, the thought came that it was too bad to treat Brother so uncivilly when he had come so far from Mita to seek him out after he himself had moved without letting Brother know. He said, more softly, "When are you coming again?"

This time Brother answered curtly, as if he were reacting now to his older brother's incivility.

"Oh, I don't know. Before too long. . . . Good-bye."

The landlady, who had come to see the guest off, watched him as he saw off his brother, vacantly and disconsolately. She asked, "Was that your younger brother?"

"Yes, why?" he answered in an angry tone.

Looking scornfully at the landlady, who seemed a bit taken aback by his manner of speech, he returned to his room. Everything was so confused and unpleasant. He had a desolate, uneasy feeling of loneliness, of being deserted by his father, his mother, his brother, and even his landlady. Instead of throwing himself on the floor as usual, he sat squarely at his desk for some reason, absorbed endlessly in these thoughts.

*   *   *

As he pursued this uneasy, unceasing life, the shadow of Emori Shozan faded little by little from his mind until now he had almost no moments of recall. He did not know why his friend, who used to visit every day or so, had not shown his face for three months. If he did remember his friend, he thought no more than, "He's probably getting along somehow like he always does." *He* was so egocentric, or, rather, he lacked the necessary room in his heart and in his life to be a kindly person. . . . To think seriously about a man's friend, to wonder how that person might be getting along, a man must first have a sense of his own well-being. Our hero, as we know, could never be called a happy man. That is not to say he could be called definitely wretched or pathetic. As a do-nothing with no sympathy for those who found life's coherence in any creed, however trivial, he could believe neither in himself nor in anyone else. He was a fretful loner who stared into every nook and corner of his own feelings, and yet the will to do something stirred him not a whit. Life had become like a dream in a state of half sleep. . . . So he had fallen into that flowing river, he thought. In his dreams a man pushes on steadily in the direction of the flow. . . . It was a common dream, but that dream-filled existence weighed heavily on him. A life of letting things slide, with no will of his own, crept sluggishly over him. With such uneasy, unpleasant apparitions, what would come next? Let that time of despair come when he understands nothing, and, while he endures that condition, a person troubled by dreams tries his best to bury the past quickly for the sake of the momentary present. So he tried to think no longer of things like Emori Shozan. The news that Sho-

zan was seriously ill and had gone to the hospital came to him
unexpectedly from the boy in the secondhand bookstore, the boy
who used to visit him often at his old home on Ghost Hill to tell
him the latest bluster on matters of the arts and ideas.

Punctilious Shozan. Whenever any little thing happened to him
like moving or going on a short trip, Shozan always sent him a
postcard. When his illness became serious enough that he had to
enter a certain Christian hospital, he sent word from the hospital
in a card addressed to his home on Ghost Hill. He, however,
expected neither mail nor visitors but rather avoided them, and
when he moved from Ghost Hill, he left no forwarding address
with anyone in the neighborhood. Shozan's postcard was therefore
returned as undelivered. The bookstore boy brought the returned
card. Shozan had crossed out the original address on the card and
had written in the address of Ozawa Mineo's wife's family. Shozan
had then asked the bookstore boy to go there at his convenience
and find out his present address. "I got a letter from Shozan enclos-
ing the postcard," the boy said.

The boy—he was really a young man—talked of Shozan as if he
were a good friend. In this way Ozawa Mineo learned about Shozan's recent situation. Through the boy Shozan had turned in for a
cash advance the partial draft of a cheap, sensational pirate story.
A friend of the boy, a bookstore clerk who acted on the side as
publisher of dime novels, had advanced twenty yen, but since then
Shozan had written and sent in no more of the story.

"How many pages of that cheap manuscript did Shozan write in
all?"

"Fewer than fifty pages," the boy said. "He told me he needed it
so much that I pushed my friend to lend twenty yen for less than
fifty pages. But Shozan hasn't delivered a thing since then. My
friend who loaned the money, at about my age he's saved as much
as four or five hundred yen, and with that as capital he plans to
make money publishing dime novels. He's the kind of man who
doesn't understand the feelings of a writer at all. He fusses over
that twenty yen. Because I was the middleman, I was troubled, and
now and then I went to see Shozan to urge him on. Shozan regretted it very much, but that's all it was—regret. He made no move to

write more. That wasn't because he was busy with anything else. Whenever I went to see him he was always snuggled into his bedding, his pen and paper laid out by the bed. Spread out before him were what looked like drafts he had already written or printed clippings from his works that he was now reading. The room was dark. I felt sorry for him. . . . Yep, that man has a letter from Natsume Sōseki.[6] It seems he once took a manuscript to Mr. Natsume."

"A long time ago. I knew about that." He spoke out on impulse, oddly befuddled between anger and sorrow at the thought that Shozan had shown the boy that letter, a letter he found it hard to think was any of the boy's business. Intimidated at the sound of his own voice, he added quickly in a calmer tone, half to himself, "Who helped Shozan get to the hospital? Was it really that bad?"

In responding to his question, the boy showed that he knew everything in surprising detail. The young man spoke with his normal, natural eloquence as if he felt pleasure in the knowing. It seemed that in the last three months, he and Shozan had become companions, and their relationship had become quite friendly. That was because Shozan's few friends, although they did not dislike him by any means, were all busy with their own lives. Not one had the time to visit him in his lodgings. Shozan could no longer walk well enough to go out freely. Anyhow, the bookstore boy became a kind of creditor for visiting Shozan. Instead of trumpeting high-sounding news in his cocky way, the boy, not unkindly, when asked, managed to help change Shozan's dirty nightgown. For Shozan in this condition it may have been a relief to trouble this new acquaintance rather than beg further care from friends whom he had already troubled enough.

Since Shozan had stopped showing his face at Ozawa Mineo's place, he had been continuously confined to his sickbed, it seemed. Then one morning he lost the use of his legs and could not go to the toilet alone. Either the landlady or the arsenal worker who roomed next door carried the groaning Shozan on their back to the toilet. He didn't seem to have been in such great pain, but he was annoyed that he could not move his body as he wanted. He talked self-indulgently like a child. All this the landlord reported with a bitter smile of annoyance as he collared the bookstore boy—all this in a tone that without saying so indicated that he wanted Shozan taken away quickly. Shozan, too, thought it couldn't go on like this. It was decided to ask an acquaintance of Shozan's—the intimacy of their acquaintance was not known, but at any rate he was a minister—to arrange for his admission to the S. L. Hospital in Tsukiji.[7] The boy learned this by chance when he happened by the house at that time. He went to the hospital to visit Shozan just as Shozan was being transported there. When Shozan's jinrikisha arrived, the boy saw there was another person, a man of about forty, with him. It was the minister who had introduced Shozan to the hospital.

"That minister," the boy said, "thinking I might be a close, new friend of Shozan, consulted me on many personal things. I got very confused and thought for a time I was getting too involved in what was none of my business. The doctor called us, the minister and me, into a separate room. 'In this hospital we can't accommodate charity patients for more than two months. This patient can't be expected to recover fully in two months. However, he's not expected to die within two months, either. In any event, the long illness has progressed until it has attacked the spinal cord. As of now there is no hope for recovery. Please start considering from now what you want to do after two months.' Shozan has no relatives at all, you know. When the minister reported that, the doctor and a staff person with him agreed. 'In that case we'll keep him here two months. After that we'll arrange from here, as convenient, to place him in a poorhouse. . . . There are cases like that.' . . ."

"A poorhouse?" he broke in on impulse. He scratched a meaningless line across the paper on the desk where he was leaning and then put down his hand and looked up at the face of the speaker. The word *poorhouse* made a harsh impression on him. The impression originated not at all in sympathy. It was like wonder at a story that is totally unexpected but unfolds naturally, or like the impression of a small, wide-eyed child staring at something curious. The other continued speaking, however, without noting his demeanor.

"By the way, how old do you think Shozan is?"

"Thirty-five or thirty-six."

"Seems like. I said I thought he was thirty-six. But really he's thirty-eight. Two years over the price. That man . . . when he was asked by the doctor, he moaned weakly 'thirty-eight, thirty-eight' in his confusion."

It was indeed an interesting discovery that Shozan had concealed two years. When he heard that, though, he could not laugh in innocence. He was struck with a strangely wearied feeling that grew somewhat oppressive while, in a blank space on his doodling paper, he drew English letters in a very elaborate Spencerian script. . . .

*   *   *

Around the time of his move he took comfort in going now and then to see his dogs, who were kept at his wife's family home. The dogs were so attached to him. But soon he stopped going to see them so often. True, his feelings of tranquil love for his dogs had gradually weakened since his move to the city, especially in his present situation, but there were other reasons for not going. These stemmed from his very love for them. . . . Recently when he went to see them, his wife's mother would get hysterical over the weather. She would grab him and grumble. Only half listening, he would start for home, and the two dogs were sure to follow happily. When he was more lighthearted, he was in the mood for a short walk with them just because of their innocence. When he was pressed down by an invisible, overlying weight, he no more than glanced back at his two beloved dogs. They escorted him to his lodgings. They watched with a puzzled look as he opened the glass door. He felt they were saying without actually speaking how sad they were to live apart from their master. When they saw him enter the house, the dogs would not go home at once. They sat down and refused to leave the doorway to his lodgings. He was uneasy at seeing their black shadows through the frosted glass. When he reopened the glass door and waved his hands at them, meaning, "Go home," the dogs jumped up and wagged their tails. When they saw he was not coming out the door, even while standing as if to go, the dogs squatted again on their haunches, watching his face continuously. He gave up the attempt to send them home, closed the door, and made himself invisible so that they would go home on their own when they could no longer see him. No matter, the two black shadows could still be seen through the glass, standing undeterred at the threshold. He felt constrained to think how suspiciously the lodging house people might look on his standing there like that, so he returned decisively to his room. He worried about how long the dogs would wait at the door, and in less than five minutes he went halfway down the stairs again to look out through the door. The shadows were there all right, waiting unmoved. The third time he went to look, it appeared at last they had gone home.

The dogs always followed and awaited him like this. Then, disappointed, they would go home in dejection. What a wonderful instinct dogs have to love their master so much. . . . As he thought about this, he was attacked by an odd kind of distress. To receive such trust from them without himself putting so much value on it was simply inexcusable. He didn't like having them follow and wait. He was troubled, too, by the grumbling of his wife's mother. All these factors engendered feelings that were hard to endure. No longer could he go and pat the dogs casually on the head as he was wont to do.

One night, his wife came unexpectedly to his lodgings, relatively early—that is, it was after eleven. As she came into the room she spoke abruptly.

"About Fratty, a messenger came from the Fukagawa people yesterday, so we gave him to them."

"What?"

His wife's words came out of the blue.

"You say Fukagawa? . . . When did you promise to give them a dog?"

According to his wife's answer, he had recently not been as enthusiastic about the dogs as he used to be. They thought he was tired of them. Her mother was busy and could not take care of two troublesome dogs. If there was someone good to receive them, it would be good to give away one dog. Hadn't he said that himself? . . . Oh, yes, he thought he had said something about the dogs being too much to handle.

"Still," he said, "I spoke vaguely. Why didn't you consult me once you found a home? Why did you give away my dog of your own accord?"

"Oh, you're bad," she replied. "Because you don't come by the house at all. I said we would consult you if you came. You don't come at all. You say I should have come to consult you, but I'm too busy to come. In the meantime they came to get him yesterday with a crate and a car. So we turned him over to them."

"But why didn't you consult me at the time?"

"It was early in the morning and I knew you were still asleep. Isn't that so? . . . It was wrong to give him away."

"Whether it was right or wrong is a different matter. I say why did you give away someone else's property without permission, property that was in your charge, that you pretended was your own? Two dogs are a trouble. I knew that from the beginning. I understood as much when I left them in your care. To say they are a troublesome nuisance and then to give one away without consulting me—is that a good thing? If you're going to give him away, give him. When you did, though, I would have liked to feed him a meal with my own hands. Hah, yes I would." He noticed his laugh resounded with a strange tone, like the voice of something being stifled within him.

His wife asked whether he realized he was laughing hysterically. "What kind of sad laugh is that?"

"Stupid," he shouted, feeling threatened. At this rude outburst of theatrics he looked quickly back at his wife, her eyes riveted on him, and he saw there were tears in her eyes. Seeing them he had no mind to continue screaming at her. Still, his irritation continued unabated, and he said nothing further, nor did he even think of trying for another subject of conversation. For someone who used to chatter on intensely it had recently become unpleasant to say a word to anyone. He looked ominously at his wife, who was crying for some reason he did not understand, and he was suddenly reminded of that scene in the country. He thought of Fratty walking with him through the rural landscape.

"It's all right," he blurted out unexpectedly and rather gently, but as if to himself. "I don't know but that I'll be moving around in my life from now on. Nice as a dog is, it's a hindrance. If we're going to do it someday, it's better that you gave him away early. . . . Meantime, I can go see Fratty if he's at Fukagawa."

The effect of such gentle words may have reached him. That may be why a rare feeling of tenderness welled up in his heart. He felt it within, but still he kept his silence.

The second morning after that evening, he awoke when someone intruded into his room. "Mineo, Mineo." The intruder calling him was his wife's mother. She was very excited. "Get up quick and come see. Fratty's home. Came home alone, he did." He listened and learned that Fratty had unexpectedly come home only thirty minutes earlier that morning. My, how surprised they were when he came alone and impassive through the gate, dragging half a bitten-off chain from his neck. The chain and his whole body were covered with mud. He looked so pathetic she gave him rice. He ate up the usual one-dog portion in one gulp, and, when she gave him another dishful, he ate that in a hurry. Then he walked around her for a bit and jumped up onto the wooden floor of the kitchen. He was lying fast asleep now in his usual place in the entryway. Leo, after greeting Fratty, was asleep beside him. When she went out, the dogs made no move to follow as they usually did. They were so sweet she came to wake him so he could see them, she said. This hysterical woman who was his wife's mother not only liked a very plain and not-at-all-graceful animal; She was as naively happy as a little girl that her dog, yearning for home, had returned on its own like that. She had come to rouse him and urge him to go and see.

Fratty was all muddy, she had said, and when he went out to look, he found the road was terribly muddy. The rain had lifted at about 10 A.M., and the muddy places glistened in the sunlight. He recalled that it had rained like anything yesterday, and last night a gale of strong winds had blown up, characteristic of the cherry-blossom season. Fratty: during that time and through the drenching rains from Fukagawa here—that is, from one end of this big city to the other. Fratty: searching his way, this way and that over a long and unknown route, dragging from his neck a troublesome chain of unknown kind. Fratty: raised in the country and with a tendency to be very frightened by bustling crowds, threatened by people, by vehicles, by stronger dogs. Fratty: when he escaped from Fukagawa was not known, but he may have been wandering around lost for a day and a night, his pointed nose following the ground as he prowled bewildered through unknown places. The figure of that dog Fratty. The feelings of that dog . . . He thought these things to himself as he came out of his lodgings and looked at the muddy street. He thought them as he walked. At the sound of voices nearing the house Leo came bounding out to meet them, but Fratty was not to be seen. When they reached the gate, the sturdy figure of Fratty lay asleep as if dead in the sun at the entryway. Near him were two large empty plates with not a grain of rice remaining. Stopping his wife's mother from calling to wake the dog, he squatted and gazed intently at Fratty. He laid his hand softly on the dog's shoulder. With the slyness of a wild animal Fratty opened his eyes a slit. When the dog saw that he was the person touching his body, he opened his eyes wide. The dog turned his head and licked his hand repeatedly. The half-upright posture looked so cramped that he pushed Fratty down sideways into his former lying position and laid his hand by the dog's mouth to be licked. Fratty lay there on his side, thumping his tail and flicking dust up from the ground.

"He's a sly one. He's tuckered out. Let's not get him up." That's what his wife's mother said—ever so sweetly. He stared endlessly, silently at Fratty, who was so tired that soon the tail stopped wagging and the dog was asleep.

*　　*　　*

That evening he felt like trying to write something after an interval of some ten days. It was a sketch titled "The Dog." . . .

*　　*　　*

A certain pessimist said, "Of course it's not that I don't remember my wife, too, from whom I've parted, but I have not once thought I wanted to see her. Only the dog that we raised together, how is he now? What shape is he in? I want to see him so much; the hopelessness is now my constant condition." . . .

*   *   *

After writing this much he could write no more. "Of course it's not that I don't remember the wife from whom I've parted." There was no exaggeration, was there, in these words he had tossed off so idly. Wasn't that the truth for him? As he began to think about feelings he had never before experienced, he could see various objections to these words. He could write no further on the sketch. . . . He who was so moved just by the act of giving someone a dog, who was so sentimental he could no longer scream at his wife when he saw a few tears welling in her eyes—even if he were to say he did it from free and rational will, how could he know how he would feel when he reached the point that he had to leave his wife? Even when he had left her, he was not one who could guarantee just because he had left that he was no longer fond of his wife. It was a commonplace of life for separated couples to make up. . . . The words that he had written offhandedly now reverberated complexly in his heart.

He wouldn't understand anything if he didn't consider that eventuality. . . . He concluded that he should reject these fussy thoughts of his, but then he wondered what the power of memory was for. How long does it last without fading? Because Fratty had been fed for only a year, he would for that long have to return to his original home. Why and how long must I remember things no longer suitable to my life? So long as I remember, there is no help for the pain. . . . A dog's memory is like that. A person's is, too.

*   *   *

"My acquaintance at the newspaper came back at last after traveling for a month in Kyushu on company business. He spoke about your case. Anyhow, he wants to meet you, but before that we should make preliminary arrangements at my place. Because I'm always here, come by sometime, say in the evening. The sooner the better." He received a postcard saying that, and that very evening he went to visit Kuno. The latter asked when he could go to meet the man. Anytime was fine, he said. Kuno took out from his desk drawer a letter of introduction he must have prepared in advance. It was addressed to Mr. Hata Ryūtaro. There were no other special arrangements to be made, and Kuno served him a delicious piece of cake. He said he had decided to do his graduation thesis on Meredith and that should not be too difficult. After they talked a little of literary things Kuno invited him to go for a walk.

They strolled down the dark, sloping street in the direction of Ikenohata. They had grown tired of talking, and they walked in silence. It seemed to be the date for a night fair, and, as he walked, he looked up at the bright, smoky sky over the buildings.

Kuno said to him suddenly, "Look. This is a little thing, but, when you go to the newspaper, you ought to wear your best clothes. If you like, how about wearing one of my kimonos?"

Kuno spoke rapidly in a tone like someone broaching a subject with great reservation or as if he were rather ashamed to do so. He suddenly realized that Kuno had been reluctant to put these preliminary arrangements into a letter and that this evening he had hesitated to speak about it right away.

"Thank you."

Although he was grateful for his friend's delicate manner of speaking, it suddenly reminded him of Shozan's summer coat. He hadn't thought of that since then, but now he realized that from all appearances his clothing was rather shabby. He was suddenly conscious of his appearance.

"Thank you. But I can probably get something to wear by redeeming it from the pawnshop. . . ." As he spoke, he felt that his answer sounded rather defiant in the face of his friend's kindness.

". . . Still, whether I can actually redeem it or not is questionable. If I can't, I'd like to borrow yours."

"Oh?" Kuno answered nonchalantly, setting at rest his concern that his words had hurt his friend's feelings. He stared more keenly through the darkness at the friend who had understood these frank but delicate feelings. Then unexpectedly he burst into noisy laughter. Kuno did not know what to make of the sudden laughter. With a blank look he said, "What's that? What are you suddenly laughing about so happily?"

"Just think about it . . ." He kept on laughing. The reason Kuno had the nickname of Saigō Takamori was not only his manly temperament; his stocky build of some one hundred and eighty pounds was a factor, too. To *him*, lanky and hardly one hundred pounds, Kuno had said he would lend his own kimono. "Just think about it. With your build! Can I wear Saigō Takamori's kimono?"

Kuno laughed as if he had just thought of it for the first time.

"You're very kind, but you've got no imagination." His words, spoken as in criticism, seemed to him to express the deep affection of the moment for Kuno. In response Kuno gave only a deep, resounding laugh.

This friend with a vast understanding for serious but tender feelings—supposing *he* said something further to this friend, wouldn't the friend offer unstinting consolation, not by saying anything meaningful but just by his unaffected attitude? As they walked along shoulder to shoulder, he feeling scruffy next to his big, stout friend, he was stirred by an impulse to confide to that friend his recent feelings about his wife. For his type of personality the thing that seemed moral and correct would be to hide one's own bitter feelings. Tonight, though, he felt himself on the point of throwing away any posing or morality toward Kuno. The narrow sloping road they walked was dark. He thought the darkness tempted his desire to reveal his feelings. Wanting to get out of that dark street in a hurry, he stepped ahead, speeding up his pace.

He said to Kuno, "Hey, let's go to the lights at the fair."

*   *   *

It was only a moment, but his attitude seemed so conspicuous that even someone as stolid as Kuno wondered at it. Kuno looked at him, standing there amid a crush of people in the glaring light, and said, "What's up? What is it?"

"No. Nothing." Recovering his senses at last, he started walking again. "I thought I saw someone I know slightly. . . . I was about to call him, but he slipped away somewhere." He half swallowed the words in a mutter. Actually he *had* seen someone he knew slightly! . . . A woman—not just any woman, but his wife . . . There was a man, about thirty, of towering height, so tall that he glanced casually in that direction. At that moment his eyes lit on the face of a woman behind the man, looking up at the man's face.

"Oh, my!" he thought, and in the next moment the woman's face was gone behind the man. Both disappeared into the crowd, and from a distance only the man's hat stood out above the throng. The man's features were not far from thirty. It was only a glimpse, but it was surely his wife's face. There wasn't time to confirm it, but there was no mistaking the momentary impression. Even if it were not she, he could not help but see a vision of her in the crowd under the artificial lights brighter than day. Without leave from the Asakusa theater wouldn't she still have to be there? . . .

"Kuno, what time is it?"

"Oh, the time?" As Kuno spoke he looked down at his chest as if he had a pocket watch. "A little before ten. Ten or fifteen minutes before. . . . My watch isn't very reliable, but the fair runs until ten at night."

"Not yet ten. Well, excuse me. If it's that time, there's a place I want to stop by."

So saying, he slipped away from Kuno in the direction where the crowd was thinning. Coming out onto the streetcar street at the foot of the hill, he jumped onto a streetcar just starting to move. He had heard from his wife that she had to be at the theater until eleven. If the theater was not closed today, she should still be there. He thought the best way to learn whether the woman he had seen was really his wife was to go to the theater and see. He had jumped on a streetcar bound for Asakusa, but, when he reached Asakusa he had lost the courage to look for his wife at the stage door. He walked back and forth three or four times in front of the stage door. He went around to the front and looked up vacantly at the gaudy, painted signboard and then went back to the stage door. Thinking that the manager Yoshizawa would be sitting at the entrance, he pulled his felt hat down over his eyes. He entered deliberately, briskly, without glancing aside, as if he knew the place. When he saw an elderly man plumped in what appeared to be the watchman's seat at the door, he thought, yes, that certainly is Yoshizawa from the boarding house in Nezu.

He asked with an air of unconcern, "Is Segawa Ruriko still here?"

As he spoke he kept his head down so the other could not see his face.

"What? . . . Segawa Ruriko? . . ."

Whether he was thinking it over, whether he found the question annoying, or whether he felt somewhat suspicious, the man cut short his words. *He* felt he was being stared at. His face flushed suddenly with a burning feeling. He felt the man must think of him as an admirer or something of that actress. That gave him a titillating feeling of shame or even disgrace.

"Miss Segawa, is it?" He asked again as if he had just remembered and then added, "Miss Segawa has already gone home."

"Gone home? . . . When?"

"Quite a while ago."

"About an hour? . . ."

"More than an hour. Her last curtain was about nine."

He wanted to confirm that more definitely. He felt, though, that he had already pried too far with his questions, and he could not ask anything further.

"Oh, is that so? Thanks for your trouble. . . ." As he began to speak,

"Hey. Ozawa! Ozawa!"

He was startled to hear his name suddenly called. The voice continued with a second blow, "Come to meet your wife, did you?"

As the owner of the voice came lounging out from backstage, he took off to flee from Yoshizawa, dragging the newcomer with him. When the two were finally outside, he said to the ill-mannered fellow who had flustered him, "Hey, Godoh, it's embarrassing. I pretend not to know Yoshizawa although I've known him for a long time, and you call me like that. It's upsetting."

"Oh, you know Yoshizawa? How was I to know that?" said the man he called Godoh. The two of them walked off in the same direction with no place in mind but as if by prearrangement.

Godoh the man was as strange as the name he was called. He would soon be fifty. Or maybe fifty-five . . . It was difficult to guess his age from his appearance—that of an old student wearing a cap and a lined kimono of a splashed pattern. Because he had never asked his age, he did not know precisely. Age was not all. What the man had done or thought, how he had lived up to now, these facts, too, he did not know. It was rumored, though, that he had received a more advanced education than most men his age, that he was a genius at mathematics, and that he had finished school first in his class. When he was young he had been given the literary name of Godoh (for Chinese parasol tree). He had joined a group of writers and poets but had failed to make a name for himself. He became permanently separated from his companions who had succeeded in the world, and so he came to associate mainly with young people. He took to writing articles expressing his feelings in social commentary, or rather in worldly criticism, essays signed with puns on his pen name of Godoh, meaning "Enlightened Man," "Erring Man," or sometimes "The Man Himself." He lived by taking these articles around to magazine offices that did not at all welcome them. The derision and abuse in his writing had a kind of vulgar sweetness, but, when read naively, no matter how debased the Enlightened Man saw a person's character, or how worthless, there were nuances of slight difference in his portrayal of temperament from that of the morally lowest, vulgar classes. Instead of losing their respect for the man, people were happy to endure some trouble for him with a slight smile and no ill will. At first they called him correctly Enlightened Man, but gradually the sound was cut short to Godoh. People seemed to feel the queer and slightly humorous name was appropriate to the man. Everyone called him Godoh now. *He* had known this Godoh since he was in school. Godoh often dropped in without notice at meetings of students aspiring to literature. At these his tone of harmless rejection for the lions of the literary world did not particularly trouble the young people. Often Godoh would solicit pocket money from them with a look as if it were his legitimate right. Saying, "Streetcar fare," he would stick out his hand and nod his massive head with the same expression whether they gave or not. *He* was often visited at his lodgings by Godoh who had thus collected his fare. But whether Godoh became tired of literary young people or they became tired of him, about that time for amusement he gained entrance to the actors' rooms at small theater troupes with pretensions at new artistic drama. He became a frequenter of these places.

He sometimes heard gossip about him through his wife. Godoh had become infatuated with an actress in an Asakusa theater and had become like a manservant to her. Godoh had remained a bachelor until that year.

Godoh had struck him earlier with the words, "Come to meet your wife, did you?" Now that there were only the two of them, Godoh spoke in a normal straightforward manner. "How are you doing? I haven't seen you in quite a while. Let's have a drink somewhere."

"Oh," he answered halfheartedly. However, if he spent a little more time with this fellow, he thought he might naturally learn some news about her—his wife. "Going somewhere is fine, but I haven't any money."

"I've got money. I just snitched some from Yumesuke." He giggled in a voice like a strange bird. Yumesuke or "Floater in a Dream" was a pun on the name of the actress Yumeko for whom he was said to be manservant.

"You've treated me lots of times." *He* spoke as they were entering a squalid little bar.

Godoh stammered out loudly, "Kuh, kuh, crazy!"

He was so loud that a group of people at a table all turned around to look. Godoh wasn't angry. The volley, "Kuh, kuh, crazy" was a sign of his good humor.

*   *   *

He became very drunk. For someone who never liked sake, he must have had twenty cups. Godoh's face took on the look of a heavy drinker, too, and his cheeks quivered from the alcohol. Godoh seemed to have a very low capacity for liquor. After four small bottles between the two of them their speech had become slurred. Godoh reeled and tottered and tediously kept repeating something that sounded like, "Ah cahn't unnerstan wimmen." He said the same to himself. "I just don't understand women, either. . . . Such a good housewife and before I know it she's gone fickle. She's so strange after the change, I just don't understand." . . . He mused on that. He thought about the words that Godoh had said to him before getting so drunk, and about the set of that mouth that mumbled through dirty, yellow teeth. "To begin with, I don't like you. You, Ozawa Mineo, you don't even understand that in making your wife an actress you make yourself an idler. . . . You're not the husband of a lady hairdresser. I wanted to warn you when I saw you. Stop making your wife be an actress. . . . What's an actress? What's the cherry-blossom dance? Women showing off their red loincloths, is that the new popular dance? . . ." When he argued in reply that he certainly was not living off his wife, and that she had become an actress for her own amusement, Godoh had nothing further to say. Maybe what Godoh wanted to warn him was not, "Stop making your wife be an actress," but instead was, "Leave that woman." If he had understood Godoh's meaning right away, maybe Godoh had something concrete he wanted to say as his reason behind those words—maybe something about his wife's reputation in the greenroom. No doubt about it. This fellow knew something or other. . . . What if he suddenly called out, "Godoh"—he fancied through the drunken confusion in his head —what if he suddenly called to Godoh, if he suddenly grabbed the hand of that old friend, as old as his own father, and begged him, "Tell me. Let me know clearly. You must know everything about my wife. Tell me all." Godoh was quite an eccentric; yet basically he was just a kind of romantic. This elderly drunk, what would he do, what would he say?

"Hah, hah, hah." Recalling the sound of Kuno's laughter in his ears, he laughed in the same way. "Hah, hah, hah."

He felt his own laughing voice echoing down the street of movie houses where the shows had closed and the traffic had ceased. Discarded paper flyers lay strewn white underfoot. No one remained in the once-crowded street, and only the lights glaring brighter than the dawn were left to make the emptiness even lonelier. Not intending to do so—but unconsciously he may have sensed as much—he looked up and saw by chance the venomous red signboard of the Asakusa theater. As if the venom had pierced his eyes, the tears started to flow. Without letting his ears take in something Godoh shouted from behind, he strode away briskly, escaping alone.

"Wait in the second-floor reception room, please."

The old man at the reception desk spoke coldly without taking the pipe from his mouth or even looking at him. Then returning the desktop telephone to its cradle, the man looked over his glasses at a clock on the far wall and yawned in deference to no one. Acceding to the yawn, he stared with the old man at the clock, which said twenty to four. He was not late for the designated appointment between three and four, he knew. He climbed the muddy stairs, yielding way to someone, apparently a staff member, who was clattering breezily down the stairway. Reaching the top, he spotted the reception room immediately to his left. The door was closed. Attempting to open it, he put his hand on the door-knob and pushed about two inches, when the words *in use* resounded from a loud voice within. At a loss about what to do, he hesitated in the hall. Then, noticing a second reception room next door, he opened that door fearfully and peeked in. There was no one there, and in he went.

A small, unpainted table was surrounded by three unpainted chairs. It was more a stand than what you might call a table. On the stand and trailing down onto the floor was a stain of jet-black ink from a spill two or three days before. On the stand, too, was a small iron tray set for lighting cigarettes, but there were no live coals or matches. The floor of the room quivered from the reverberations of a rotary press running in a nearby room. A spider web hanging in a corner of the high ceiling was shaking. After staring around the room he sat down in one of the chairs and peered idly at his own face and collar in the dark glass of a closed window, dark because it looked on the wall of a neighboring building. He recalled vividly the shabby, comical figure of himself that he had earlier seen reflected in the mirror of a street-corner shop window. He got the Western-style suit from a pawnshop, but his wife's mother, after a tactful look, was annoyed by it. . . . Just then the door was flung open with vigor, as if it were kicked. He leapt to his feet almost by reflex and made a proper bow.

"Are you Ozawa? I'm Hata Ryūtaro of this paper." The man who had just come in sat down on a chair facing him and spoke deliberately. He puffed incessantly on a cigar that he had clenched in his mouth when he entered. He looked to be in the range of thirty-three to thirty-eight, of evident good health, and of a plumpness denoting that nothing whatever was lacking in life. Because he was plump, he was probably hot. He was wearing an unlined *haori* jacket, although it might be thought more than two weeks early for that. The attire was unimaginable to someone like him; it was impeccably made, and the man had the weight to show it at its best. How much did the man make in a month? . . . As he thought these worldly things, he stared at the cord on the man's jacket. He did not know what he ought to say. Although he thought the other man would say something, the man said nothing and just kept puffing out that sweet-smelling smoke. *He* was in no mood to be stared at like that. He wanted to say, "Do you see how I've come dressed heavily in a funny-looking, wrinkled morning coat? I didn't wear it to be pompous. It was made four years ago, and I pawned it. I've got other things to wear but they're all pawned. All the other things are pawned together in one lot, and they said it would be expensive to take a single one out. I'll say it again for your information, but I didn't wear this to put on airs. I feel cheap about it. For that reason I looked hard at myself just now in the mirror at the corner store. It would have been better to wear a kimono borrowed from Kuno. No, I should have calmly worn that shabby silk one with cotton padding. I say this because you seem to have a real taste in kimonos." He truly wanted to speak like that. . . . At least the characters in Dostoyevsky might talk calmly like that. That's interesting, but . . . It was a time for him to think of such useless things.

"Oh, I had a phone call from Kuno, so I was expecting you today." The man skillfully mended his too-long silence. "What was it Kuno said?"

". . . " By no means could he say that Kuno told him not to go in a very dirty kimono, nor that, if he was hired, he'd probably start at about eighty yen a month. Instead he replied in a daze. "Kuno said he was going to recommend me instead of himself."

"Oh yes, I heard that from Kuno. . . ."

"Kuno said I should meet you."

"Oh. Yes? Indeed." Mr. Hata drew deeply on the last smoke in his cigar and then tossed the small stub nonchalantly onto the floor. "Well," he said, rising and stamping out the smoking cigar butt on the floor with his felt sandal and then returning to his seat. "Well, you must have heard from Kuno, that actually the person we're looking for is someone to work directly under me. If he can learn the business in only two or three months, I'm looking for someone I can turn all the real authority over to as soon as he can do it. . . . That is to say, a reporter who can become one of the chiefs on the city desk. For the first two or three months we'd pay eighty or ninety yen. Later this might rise to one hundred and twenty or one hundred and thirty. We're looking for someone who can be promoted into the most important posts anywhere. You probably don't know about other papers, but here we give absolute preference to our own staff members. On the other hand, there are a great many applicants, and, when someone does enter the company, we examine him carefully. For the two positions we are recruiting for now, there must be about thirty applicants. Of course, I can make the selection, but it's not all that easy. Anyhow, when you consider just this company, there are so many mothers-in-law and sisters-in-law, and when they have recommendations, so long as their choices are not seriously unqualified, it's in fact very hard to ignore the nominees of such influential people just because I want to choose someone else I like. Then it's been a consideration of recent company policy to take college graduates as much as possible. That qualification on a name card may be an advantage in interviews, for example . . . but of course I don't put absolute importance on that factor. I have a wholehearted regard for ability. I'd really like to get someone with a taste for literature, someone who can write human interest stories in a fresh, high-toned style. Do you think you have the interest and the self-confidence for the life of a reporter? How about yourself?"

"The interest? The self-confidence? Well, because I haven't tried it, I can't say." Dismayed, *he* felt his face suddenly redden. "But, I, now I don't have money to live on. If I weren't so pressed, probably

I wouldn't be a reporter. I don't really think I'm all that competent. But others do it and so can I. Because I'm hard up, I'll do my best at any job I can get. . . ."

"Yes, of course," the man said with a senseless laugh. Then thinking he was being too brusque, he added these words that might or might not have meaning: "No, on the contrary, somebody like that would do." He took a watch out of his sash and glanced at it. "Well, all I can say now is, I don't know whether I should really have troubled you to come. In any case, because I need it to make a recommendation to the company president, although it's just a formality, can you give me your résumé? Well, I'll do my best. I've got Kuno's recommendation." As Mr. Hata tidied up his clothes, the import of his statement remained unclear. His manner of talking, though, confirmed that he was a person of influence within the company.

Suddenly changing his mood, he said lightly, "Your wife's in the theater, I understand. Sure enough. How about you? Do you like it? . . . Actually I'm obliged to go to a show today." Mr. Hata then leisurely stood up and said, changing his tone again, "Well, let me leave it at that."

He stood up almost simultaneously and bowed silently. Following the stout, handsome gentleman, he staggered out of the room.

Emerging onto the street, he felt newly freed from the senseless pressure. At last he could breathe deeply without the taste of tobacco on the tip of his tongue. When he thought back on himself ten minutes before, he had to see himself as such an awkward job applicant. When he should have answered, he had been thinking vacantly of other things. He had spoken frankly of things he need not have mentioned. He had blushed. To show how completely unsuited he was to be a newspaper reporter, just for that purpose, he had worn an old-style, wrinkled, ill-made morning coat that presented a wistful appearance. "If I had been doing the hiring," he thought, "I wouldn't have taken on a man who looked like the me of ten minutes earlier. Two years ago I would have been able to face another person more boldly. Why am I so stupid now? To be smart and to be bold. I don't know whether that's good or bad, but it's essential in order to live in this society. I've lost that powerful weapon. As stupid as I was, how skillful the other was in rejecting me. . . ." *He* was convinced, of course, that he had been rejected, and yet he felt there might be a possibility of being hired. After all, though, he had been rejected so diplomatically. In that nervous situation and facing someone who had succeeded so casually in life, why didn't he have the self-confidence to offer to write a single line about anything? When he pictured himself at his first interview with such an eminent man, it was best by far that he not be hired. A résumé—he didn't know what all you should list in a résumé anyway. No doubt it would be better not to send a résumé. No, because he was expressly asked, he should send one. For that matter, either way would do. On top of that, within the next ten days at least he would be interrupted by the need to start the process of getting a loan on his country place. His wife's suspicious behavior—that had become his despair before he knew it, that had to come out quickly but preferably in a way that brought neither shame nor publicity on himself. Absorbed in these thoughts one after another, he walked as was his usual custom staring at the toes of his worn-down shoes. He looked up at the sky. How low the depressing clouds hung down today, he thought. . . . Suddenly he recalled how a week ago he had heard the report about Shozan from the bookstore boy. He thought of an expression that Shozan was a little "to be pitied, like he was in a novel." He didn't know where the S. L. Hospital was, but he thought it wasn't far from there anyway. He felt like going to the hospital to see Shozan, who was like a novel. You had to say it. If Shozan was not "to be pitied, like he was in a novel," he probably wouldn't care to visit him. *He* was that kind of person.

"O.K., I'll go see Shozan."

He was pleased with his idea. With that thought and because he understood Shozan's character, he felt strangely happy about the coincidence of his bogus morning-coat appearance. . . . "Anyhow, this is gentleman's dress without a doubt. That guy Shozan who hid two years off his age may feel honored above others to be visited by a gentleman."

*   *   *

He walked quietly between lines of beds on both sides with the nurse leading the way. They passed thirty beds where patients stared at him, their eyes shining with curiosity. When they reached the farthest bed, and thus the one nearest the window, the nurse spoke to the patient, who turned in bed to look at them. The voice did not suit her appearance.

"Mr. Emori. Someone to see you."

"Emori. It's me."

"Well, well." Shozan's voice had not weakened at all. He rolled over with more agility than might have been expected. But when he looked into his friend's face, he saw it was the color of clay. The nurse had been holding a Bible in her hand with a finger inserted in the pages. Now she slipped the book into the pocket of her white nurse's uniform and used her free hands to pick up things from a small chair next to the bed—a small notebook, other books, and a medicine bottle—in order to make a place for him to sit down. Shozan stopped her with a slight gesture.

"No, that's not necessary. Ozawa, sit anywhere on the bed. As you can see, that chair's not comfortable."

He saw there was no suitable place on the side of the narrow bed, but, moving down three paces, he sat on the foot of the bed.

"This is totally unexpected. Thank you for coming." Shozan looked at him very happily and added, "Hey," in his usual voice.

"Hey, you're really in full dress, aren't you?"

"Oh, this?" Holding the lapels of his coat in his fingers, he smiled in spite of himself. "Because I was coming on a sick visit, I thought I'd doll up in my best." He saw Shozan laugh dubiously at his joke, so he continued. "No, that's not true. There's deep significance in this. Actually, I thought of you in passing and came here right away."

"In passing, or whatever it was, thank you. What is the deep significance?"

"No, rather than that, how's your health been since I saw you last? How's your condition?"

"Thank you. I was a lot of trouble to my friends for a time, but as soon as I came here, I got better quickly. Medicine is very effective for us poor people. Can I walk? No, not really, and most likely it's hopeless in the long run. I've become a splendid cripple." Even as Shozan used mocking words about himself his expression was serene and unmoved by the words. When *he* asked about life in the hospital, he learned that Shozan was completely satisfied here so long as the pain was not severe. Shozan intimated first that the hospital was in a nice quiet neighborhood, then that the structure was well built, just as if he were discussing a newly acquired residence. Then he was pleased to have his bed in a comparatively bright and independent corner of the room by a window, perhaps through the attention of his sponsor. "Look. There's a good view from this window. From here between the roofs you can see the sails of ships spotted about on the river or the sea or wherever they are. I discovered that accidentally after I'd been here a week or so and could finally sit up a little in bed. After that if I paid attention and faced the window as I lay in bed, even if I couldn't see anything else I knew on a clear day that the sails were passing by. . . . Whether it's a reflection or whatever, something like the shadow of a bird flits by. Night is completely quiet. It's rather dark, but I can read. I don't know who it is, but at night in one bed there's someone having the Bible read aloud by a nurse. She has a nice voice. The mood of the evening is not all that bad with the limpid sound of that low voice like flowing water. Even old men like us are a little sentimental. Everyone else strains his ears. That nurse—she seems assigned only to this room. —Say," he said, pointing at his own face, "there she is. She's kind. And when she has time she reads the Bible tenderly. She looks twenty-three or twenty-four, but maybe she's about twenty. Oh, there is a beautiful nurse, too. She comes around occasionally on medical checkup. . . ."

Shozan had always liked to talk, and, having at long last obtained a conversation partner, he opened up happily and rambled on and on. Before he knew it he was sitting up in bed. Whenever *he* cautioned Shozan, Shozan said sitting was fine. There were signs of a door opening and someone entering. They seemed to be coming in Shozan's direction. It was someone bringing his evening meal. The nurse came, too. The short, dark-complexioned woman moved things from the chair that she had earlier been clearing to make a place for him to sit. Putting the things on a corner of the bed, she had the woman who brought the tray of food set it down on the chair. There it was easy for Shozan to eat from, sitting up as he was.

"When you finish eating, it would be good to lie down again."

Leaving Shozan with this admonition, the nurse departed. *He* took the occasion to say he should be going. Shozan said he hoped he would stay. *He* felt then that it would be good to talk further with Shozan.

"It's all right. Please stay a little longer. Oh, how about eating half of this?" Shozan said. He indicated the tray that had been put before him. "How about it? Before I start, please eat half. There's always too much for me."

"No. I'm not hungry," he said, discomfited and taken aback at Shozan's words.

"It's just that I thought it was bad for a sick person if a visitor stayed too long. If you don't mind, I'll stay as long as you want. As far as I'm concerned, please eat what you want."

Here and there in the sickroom, patients murmured prayers to God before their meal. Shozan did not. Instead he merely said to his friend, "Excuse me for eating." He filled the bowl with very soft, boiled rice. Then suddenly in a low voice he added, "See. The food's not so bad. For a 'chare,' that is." *He* didn't know what Shozan meant by *chare*, but probably it stood for "charity patient." Shozan seemed to be fully satisfied with his meal of miso bean paste and egg scrambled like plain tofu bean curd. Earlier *he* had noticed a potted plant not yet in bloom sitting next to the window. He wondered whether it belonged to Shozan, or to another patient, or to the nurse, but he did not make a point of asking. He did stand and go to the window where sometimes the sails of boats could be seen nearby. The view was nothing but rooftops under a leaden sky not yet dusk. Among them were the walls and windows of two or three Western-style buildings and the high roof of something he thought must be a temple. In the foreground within the hospital grounds stood a Chinese parasol tree, its large leaves budded out. Although they were high on a second floor, there was really no view. But if you looked out this window on a clear day, the sky seemed so expansive it surely gave some solace to the ill. No, by some chance Shozan may have found the serenity he was recently lacking, just through being able to eat without anxiety this "charity food that wasn't bad." "Actually, if it were I"—he thought—"lying here might be more suitable to me than working on a newspaper." As he mused on that, he looked without intending at Shozan's books that the nurse had piled up on the side of his bed. One of them was a hymnal. When he picked it up, he saw a red book underneath—*The Pilgrim's Progress.*

"Oh, the nurse lent me that," Shozan said unexpectedly when he noticed that *he* had seen it. "I tried reading the hymnal first. It's very interesting—as literature."

He did not reply. He thought Shozan might have said that because he was secretly worried that he might be laughed at for reading such stuff. Shozan seemed to have finished eating; he had polished off the food that he said he always left uneaten. You saw that by a glance at the coverless casserole. *He* sat down, perching on a corner of the bed where Shozan had lain flat again following the nurse's orders. He opened the hymnal without intending to, and it naturally fell open of its own to a page where it had been repeatedly opened. He didn't know whether the person who had gotten the book into this habit was Shozan or someone else who had borrowed the book. He glanced at the page that opened of itself. The song began with the line, "The setting sun is hidden." As he looked at it in silence, Shozan spoke, as if seeking a topic. "Can't you tell me the reason for your full dress?"

With an indifferent look he told Shozan about the events at the newspaper office. For some reason Shozan wanted to know all the details about what paper it was and what salary it paid. When *he* refused politely, Shozan asked who had interviewed him. Learning that the man's name was Hata, Shozan spoke in a tone of consolation. "If you were hired by that man, how would you become fit for a job in one month?"

"How's that?" He was curious. "Do you know him?"

"I sure do. It was a long time ago, though. . . . If you do what I have done for twenty years, you get to know everybody. He's famous, but he rose from office boy. Of course that has no relation to his character. Look, in my *People of the Ravine* there's a man

named Suzuki, head of a factory for Western-style musical instruments. The older sister of the hero, Ryōta, becomes this man's mistress. Suzuki's companion is a newspaperman. In the episode about
that man—"

"Yes, I remember. It's about a man who coerces a dowry out of a
newly ennobled father to marry the daughter who has become
pregnant illegitimately." He took over the conversation because he
feared Shozan would start relating the outline of his yet-unwritten
masterpiece, *People of the Ravine*. His precaution had no effect. Shozan could not be stopped from retelling the episode from *People of
the Ravine* in a general way. . . .

"That's the way it is in my story, but in fact there is no daughter
of the nobility. . . . She's a geisha made pregnant by a newly rich
man. This man got the woman, of whom he had grown tired, along
with a dowry and the child, but then he took another mistress.
Because he wanted the new mistress, people slander him for having
taken the first woman as his wife. Anyway, he abuses the wife cru-
elly. When she asks for a divorce, Hata reportedly apologizes to her
on his knees. The story is said to come from the wife. Everyone said
Hata should send the wife back and return the dowry, but he was
criticized more for having lost his influence with the wealthy busi-
nessman who had close connections to the newspaper company. In
my different interpretation in *People of the Ravine*, however, Hata
really loves his wife. . . ."

As he listened to the story, he of course felt no interest in it.
Actually, because he paid no attention, he missed hearing what
parts were Shozan's story and what was fact. He wondered why
Shozan had begun to tell the story of his novel, but then he was
struck by a feeling that Shozan wanted to advertise to the people in
beds near his that he was a person with the talent to write novels.
The invalids in nearby beds did seem to be all ears when Shozan
raised his voice. Seeing that he had spontaneously become so
enthused, the nurse came by his bed and said, laughing and scolding gently, "If you get too excited over that story, the fever will
come on again." Taking advantage of the opportunity, he stood up
and prepared to leave. The nurse, thinking he was leaving because
of her words, said there were still thirty minutes before the end of

visiting hours at six. Shozan looked up at him with a sudden lonely look, but he did not sit down again.

"Please come again. And please write down your new address." As Shozan spoke he pulled out the smallest notebook from his bed. He looked down casually as he stood there and saw that Shozan's notebook contained a list of names and addresses of his friends so carefully written they made one wonder whether they hadn't been recently recalled and rewritten in the tedium of the sickbed.

"My lodgings, is it? . . . It's a boarding house, you know. I may be moving again soon. No, I haven't decided where."

"Well, then, if I write to Madam's family home, that should do. Please give Madam my best. Yes, yes. I've neglected Madam. I didn't speak of her at all. Please do give her my best."

"Yeah," he said in a choked voice.

He left the sickroom quickly. When he was halfway down the stairs, he turned on his heels and returned purposefully to Shozan's bedside. He seemed to have forgotten to say something. Avoiding Shozan's questioning face, he said, "A letter—if you need to write, send it somewhere else—I'm possibly, probably soon, that is to say I don't know when, but I'm thinking of getting a divorce."

"Oh! Why so?" Needless to say, Shozan looked intensely surprised.

"Well, sooner or later—and then," he whispered quickly and then continued speaking rapidly. "Do you need any money? Of course I don't have any now. . . . In the near future I'll have a mortgage loan on my country place, I think. If you need any, I'll bring some."

"Thank you. . . . Here where I am there's no need for money. Actually I got some money from a man for that Natsume Sōseki letter."

The two whispered together briefly and then fell silent. During the silence he felt for a moment, for the first time, he touched Shozan's heart in perfect harmony.

After leaving Shozan, for some reason his body was dead tired.

As he went out the gate, he looked back in the darkness of the overcast evening sky at the large, brick building that Shozan had said was a good building and was like a home to him. He gazed at the differing patterns of the dark ivy vines covering the walls. To all appearances Shozan's condition didn't seem so serious, but the nurse's troubling warnings were not a good sign at all. He may be in a good place for his condition. It would be simple sentimentality to say that I don't want to see him die. It's better that he die. For anyone like that, death would be better! "If you do what I have done for twenty years, you get to know everybody," Shozan had said casually, but the words lingered sadly and strangely in his heart. . . . If Shozan died, he'd remember those words forever. . . . Shozan seemed most serene in the hospital, but did he know he would move to a poorhouse in two months? He walked like someone who had walked a long road; he walked thinking these things disconnectedly in his head. A malicious smile played involuntarily at the corners of his mouth—because he saw in simultaneous confusion before him the case of Mr. Hata, that brisk man of affairs with his commanding appearance pleading prostrate before his wife, and the absurd kindness of Shozan offering him half his hospital dinner. The smile quickly disappeared, to be replaced by a scowl. The scowl then turned into a vacant, sad, unpleasant expression. He stood there, continuing to wait at the streetcar stop without the energy to push his way onto the continuously crowded streetcars, one after another at rush hour in the darkening city. Without thinking, he pulled an empty pack of cigarettes out of his pocket, crumpled it up in his hands, and tossed it to the ground at his feet. He started walking again, trudging toward a nearby streetcar transfer point. He wasn't thinking anything in particular. The lights came on brightly shining along the street. . . . He was conscious of wondering absentmindedly whether it was spring or fall, when he was forced to the side of the road in confusion by the screeching roar of an automobile. He was startled by the overpowering, disappearing car.

"Hey! Watch out. People get hit and killed like that," he muttered slowly, covered with dust.

Notes

1. From the *Analects* of Confucius, book 4, chap. 9, trans. James Legge (Oxford University Press; reprint, University of Hong Kong Press, 1960), p. 42.

2. Evidently her stage name. Later her real personal name appears as Yumiko.

3. This room is described in one place in Satō's text as six mat in size and in another place as eight mat. For consistency, the translator has chosen six.

4. Saigō Takamori, 1827–1877, a much admired and daring statesman, general, and leader of an unsuccessful rebellion.

5. Mori Ōgai, 1862–1922, a major modern writer and physician, educated in Germany.

6. Natsume Sōseki, 1867–1916, a very famous writer.

7. Saint Luke's Hospital.

About the Translator

FRANCIS B. TENNY, the first executive director of the Japan–United States Friendship Commission, has served as counselor at the American Embassy in Tokyo and as State Department director of cultural affairs for East Asia during the Nixon years. The third generation of his family to reside in Japan since 1877, Tenny was a career Foreign Service Officer of the Department of State and the United States Information Agency. He is currently an associate in research of the Reischauer Institute of Harvard University. He has been decorated by the Government of Japan with the Order of the Rising Sun and recognized by the Association for Asian Studies with its Distinguished Service Award.

Production Notes

Composition and paging were done on the
Quadex Composing System and typesetting
on the Compugraphic 8400 by the design
and production staff of University of
Hawaii Press.

The text typeface is Goudy Old Style and
the display typeface is Schneidler.

Offset presswork and binding were done by
The Maple-Vail Book Manufacturing Group.
Text paper is Glatfelter Offset Vellum,
basis 50.